提问序列
与学习空间拓展
行动研究

Questioning Sequences
and Extension of Learning Space:
An Action Research Study

刘传江 著

图书在版编目(CIP)数据

提问序列与学习空间拓展行动研究＝Questioning Sequences and Extension of Learning Space：An Action Research Study/刘传江著. 一厦门：厦门大学出版社，2021.6
ISBN 978-7-5615-7177-4

Ⅰ.①提⋯ Ⅱ.①刘⋯ Ⅲ.①外语教学—课堂教学—教学研究 Ⅳ.①H09

中国版本图书馆 CIP 数据核字(2020)第 253658 号

出 版 人	郑文礼
责任编辑	高奕欢

出版发行	厦门大学出版社
社　　址	厦门市软件园二期望海路 39 号
邮政编码	361008
总　　机	0592-2181111　0592-2181406(传真)
营销中心	0592-2184458　0592-2181365
网　　址	http://www.xmupress.com
邮　　箱	xmup@xmupress.com
印　　刷	厦门集大印刷有限公司

开本	720 mm×1 000 mm　1/16
印张	22
插页	1
字数	436 千字
版次	2021 年 6 月第 1 版
印次	2021 年 6 月第 1 次印刷
定价	85.00 元

本书如有印装质量问题请直接寄承印厂调换

厦门大学出版社
微信二维码

厦门大学出版社
微博二维码

前　言

教师提问是启发学生思考的重要手段（Elder & Paul, 1998；Paul & Elder, 2008），是最普遍的教学行为（Sadker, Sadker, & Zittleman, 2010），是观测或检视课堂教学效果的一面镜子（Walsh & Sattes, 2005；Good & Brophy, 2008）。然而，国内专家在讨论我国高校英语课堂教学现状时却指出，教师提问存在"思辨缺席"（黄源深，1998；2010）、"娱乐化倾向"（秦秀白，2012）、"目标失衡"（束定芳，2013）或"目标缺失"（曲卫国，2016）等问题。换言之，教师提问应紧扣教学目标，方能保证其有效性。

综观国内外的外语课堂教学研究，关注教师提问的学者主要致力于对教师提问进行分类描述，进而分析和解读特定类型的教师提问在具体的课堂互动情境中发挥的功能或作用；至于教师如何设计和实施提问以实现超越课堂互动局部目标之外的教学目标，比如课堂、单元、课程甚至专业的教学目标，则鲜有涉足。

研究者梳理相关文献时发现，教育学界的学者尤为关注教师提问与教学目标的关联，新近提出的两个理论概念对外语教师如何设计和实施提问以实现教学目标颇具启示意义。其一是Marzano和Simms（2014）提出的"提问序列"概念，指教师宜根据教学目标设计和实施针对不同认知水平的序列性提问；其二是Marton和Tsui（2004）提出的"学习空间"概念，指教师提问应为学生体验教学目标所涉及的学习行为（act）和学习内容（content）两个方面的"变异"创设必要条件。

同理，外语教师的提问同样需要推动学习者参与不同水平的认知活动，只有让学习者体验到学习行为和学习内容的变异，学习才可能发生。基于此，本书尝试建立以拓展学习空间为目标的提问序列模型，作为英语教师设计和实施提问的指导框架。该框架由内容和认知两个变异维度构成。教师提问的内容可在课文理解、语言学习和个人表达三个方面变异；不同内容导向的教师提问又可在认知维度的三个层级之间变异。如此，则理解类提问（Comprehension Questions）可分为字面理解（literal understanding）、解读（interpreting）和评价（evaluating）三个层级，语言类提问（Language Questions）可分为识别（recognizing）、归类（categorizing）和鉴赏（appreciating）三个层级，表达类提问（Response Questions）则可分为道出（articulating）、详述（elaborating）和论证（justifying）三个层级。

为探究如何在教师提问实践中应用上述框架，提高其可操作性，研究者以英语专业精读课教学为例，在前期调研的基础上，开展了一个学期的行动研究，旨在回答如下三个研究问题：

（1）如何设计和实施教师提问以提高教学有效性？
（2）学生对教师设计和实施的提问有何反响？
（3）影响教师提问有效性的主要因素有哪些？

在三轮行动研究中，研究者通过同行课堂观察、基于课堂录像的刺激性反思、学生的学习日志、课后小组讨论等手段对教学干预效果进行评估，并据此对行动方案做出调整。研究者在第一轮行动研究中尝试应用提问序列开展课堂互动，首先与同事合作确定单元教学目标，尔后根据教学目标设计提问，并在课堂教学过程中以序列性提问的方式加以实施。数据分析结果表明，在教学中应用提问序列有助于促进课堂互动，落实教学目标的要求，转变学生对课程教学目标的认识。

在第二轮行动中，研究者针对学生在前一轮行动中反映的答问准备时间不足的问题，对行动方案做出了调整，将研究者备课设计好的提问清单提前发给学生，并要求他们依此预习课文，做足准备，应对课堂提问。数据分析表明，第二轮行动进一步提升了提问序列的教学效果，主要体现在学生报告的收获更多、参与课堂互动的积极性更高。

在第三轮行动中，研究者针对学生普遍不愿意在课堂上提问而研究者本人又无法预测学生的所有问题，特别是涉及语言知识的问题，再次调整了行动方案。研究者要求学生课前预习课文，并提出自己的问题，然后发给研究者汇总；研究者再将汇总的学生提问融合到教案和课件中，并在课堂上以提问序列的形式加以实施。所得结果显示，与教师独自设计的序列性提问相比，融合了学生提问的提问序列，能在更大程度上满足学生的学习需求，且能进一步激发学习自主性。

行动研究接近尾声之际，研究者组织学生开展了焦点小组访谈，并收集了学生对课程教学的学习总结。学生普遍反映，经过一个学期的教学，学习自主性、课文理解的深度、思辨能力和参与课堂互动的积极性均有提高，而且对课程的教学目标有了新的认识。此外，研究者在教学行动前后，对学生进行了阅读、口语和概要写作测试，并且对他们的阅读策略做了问卷调查。比较行动前后的测试结果和阅读策略使用情况，发现学生在阅读、口语和概要写作以及阅读策略使用方面的提高均有统计学意义。由此，研究者以学习空间为依据，在课堂教学中实施的提问序列行动研究取得了预期的教学效果，落实了课程教学目标。亦即，本研究制定的提问序列模型具有可行性，可用于指导教师设计和实施课堂提问。

对行动研究过程中以及结束后所得反馈作进一步分析，发现在课堂教学中使用提问序列创设学习空间，主要受到以下因素的影响：所提问题的难易度、学生需求的差异性、学生课前准备的充分度、教师对课堂互动的管理方式以及师生关系的亲疏程度等。

因此，教师在设计和实施提问序列时，不仅要紧密联系教学目标，创设体验内容导向和认知层级变异的机会，而且要充分考虑上述因素，以求学习空间的最大化。

最后，研究者在总结主要发现的基础上，探讨了本研究对课堂教学研究、教师提问实践以及教材提问设计等方面的启示，同时指出了本研究的缺憾与不足，展望了进一步研究的课题方向。由于学识和能力所限，书中所述，恐多错谬，敬请方家批评指正。

Contents

List of Abbreviations ... vii
List of Tables ... viii
List of Figures ... x

Chapter 1   Introduction

1.1 Motivation for the study ... 1
    1.1.1 Importance of teacher questions in classroom instruction ... 1
    1.1.2 Ineffective teacher questions due to lack of explicit goals ... 3
    1.1.3 Neglect of instructional objectives in research on teacher questions ... 4

1.2 Rationale for the study ... 6
    1.2.1 Questioning sequences ... 6
    1.2.2 Learning space ... 8

1.3 Overview of the action research ... 10

1.4 Structure of the dissertation ... 12

Chapter 2   Literature Review

2.1 Taxonomies of teacher questions ... 14
    2.1.1 Taxonomies based on forms ... 15
    2.1.2 Taxonomies based on functions ... 16
    2.1.3 Taxonomies based on multiple dimensions ... 18

2.2 Research on language teacher questions ··· 23
    2.2.1 Interaction analysis ·· 23
    2.2.2 Discourse analysis ·· 25
    2.2.3 Conversation analysis ·· 31

2.3 Questioning sequences as units of planning and analysis ················ 36
    2.3.1 Questioning sequences as sequences of questions ························· 36
    2.3.2 Questioning sequences as a series of core and processing questions
    ·· 37
    2.3.3 Questioning sequences as the framework for a unit ······················· 40

2.4 Learning space as the measure of questioning sequences ················ 43
    2.4.1 Learning as the experience of variation ··· 44
    2.4.2 The object of learning ·· 46
    2.4.3 The critical aspects of the object of learning ··································· 48
    2.4.4 Ways to create the space of learning ·· 50

2.5 Questioning sequences for the extension of L2 learning space ······ 53
    2.5.1 The objects of learning of a language course ··································· 53
    2.5.2 Questioning sequences in the light of L2 learning space ················ 59

2.6 Summary ··· 63

Chapter 3   Methodology

3.1 Preliminary work ·· 64
    3.1.1 Context ·· 64
    3.1.2 Procedures ··· 66
    3.1.3 Findings ··· 72
    3.1.4 Summary ·· 80

3.2 Action research ·· 81
    3.2.1 Action research in language teaching ··· 81
    3.2.2 A proactive/structured action research design ································· 84
    3.2.3 Interactional organizations as a tool for reflection ·························· 86

3.3 Research design······89
   3.3.1 Research questions······89
   3.3.2 Participants······90
   3.3.3 Procedures······91

3.4 Data collection and analysis······93
   3.4.1 Data collection and analysis during AR······94
   3.4.2 Data collection and analysis after AR······98

3.5 Validity concerns and ethical issues······102

3.6 Summary······103

Chapter 4   First Cycle of Action Research

4.1 Focusing······104

4.2 Planning······105

4.3 Implementing······108
   4.3.1 Identifying the objects of learning······108
   4.3.2 Designing questions······109
   4.3.3 Enacting questions······112

4.4 Evaluating······133
   4.4.1 Students' learning logs······133
   4.4.2 Peer observation feedback······137
   4.4.3 Group discussion notes······139
   4.4.4 Stimulated reflection journals······139
   4.4.5 Implications······140

Chapter 5   Second Cycle of Action Research

5.1 Focusing······142

5.2 Planning······142

- 5.3 Implementing ············144
  - 5.3.1 Identifying the objects of learning ············144
  - 5.3.2 Designing questions ············145
  - 5.3.3 Handing out the questions as a guide for preview ············147
  - 5.3.4 Enacting questions ············148
- 5.4 Evaluating ············173
  - 5.4.1 Students' learning logs ············174
  - 5.4.2 Peer observation feedback ············183
  - 5.4.3 Group discussion notes ············183
  - 5.4.4 Stimulated reflection journals ············185
  - 5.4.5 Implications ············186

Chapter 6   Third Cycle of Action Research

- 6.1 Focusing ············188
- 6.2 Planning ············188
- 6.3 Implementing ············190
  - 6.3.1 Identifying the objects of learning ············191
  - 6.3.2 Designing questions ············192
  - 6.3.3 Incorporating student questions ············193
  - 6.3.4 Enacting questions ············195
- 6.4 Evaluating ············227
  - 6.4.1 Students' learning logs ············227
  - 6.4.2 Peer observation feedback ············236
  - 6.4.3 Group discussion notes ············237
  - 6.4.4 Stimulated reflection journals ············239
  - 6.4.5 Implications ············240

Chapter 7 Further Discussion

7.1 Design and implementation of teacher questions ······242
    7.1.1 Identifying appropriate instructional objectives ······242
    7.1.2 Sequencing questions by varying acts and contents ······244
    7.1.3 Adapting design and implementation based on reflections ······245

7.2 Contributions to student learning ······246
    7.2.1 Development of autonomous learning ······247
    7.2.2 Improvement of text comprehension ······254
    7.2.3 Increased willingness to participate in classroom interaction ······260
    7.2.4 Cultivation of critical thinking ······266
    7.2.5 Renovated recognition of course objectives ······271
    7.2.6 Further evidence ······275

7.3 Major factors affecting instructional effectiveness ······280
    7.3.1 Difficulty of questions ······281
    7.3.2 Students' varied needs ······282
    7.3.3 Sufficiency of preparation before class ······286
    7.3.4 Management of classroom interaction ······289
    7.3.5 Teacher-student rapport ······290

7.5 Summary ······292

Chapter 8 Conclusion

8.1 Major findings ······294

8.2 Implications ······296

8.3 Limitations ······300

8.4 Suggestions for future research ······302

Bibliography ······305

Appendices

Appendix A: Questionnaire on students' attitude towards teacher questioning and the intensive reading course······318

Appendix B: Questionnaire on reading strategies······322

Appendix C: Summary writing rating scale······325

Appendix D: Peer classroom observation sheet······327

Appendix E: Questions for the after-class group discussions······328

Appendix F: Questions for the focus group interviews······329

Appendix G: Transcription system······331

Acknowledgments······332

List of Abbreviations

AR: action research

CA: conversation analysis

CLT: communicative language teaching

CQ: comprehension question

DA: discourse analysis

DIU: designedly incomplete utterance

EFL: English as a foreign language

ESL: English as a second language

GPS: gains, problems and suggestions

IA: interaction analysis

IRF: initiation, response, feedback/follow-up

L2: second language

LQ: language question

PWP: Pre-reading, While-reading, and Post-reading

RQ: response question

SFL: systemic functional linguistics

TQ: teacher question

List of Tables

Table 2-1　Seven forms of language teacher questions ··················16
Table 2-2　Long and Sato's (1983) taxonomy of teacher questions ··············17
Table 2-3　McCormick's (1997) classification of questions based on their scaffolding functions ··················19
Table 2-4　Thompson's (1997) classification of teacher questions ··············20
Table 2-5　Diana Freeman's (2014) taxonomy of reading comprehension questions ··················22
Table 2-6　Overview of three perspectives of DA studies ··············26
Table 2-7　Summary of IA, DA and CA studies on teacher questions ··············35
Table 2-8　Core questions and processing questions (Dantonio & Beisenherz, 2001) ··················39
Table 2-9　A questioning sequence on the use of end punctuation (Marzano & Simms, 2014) ··················42
Table 2-10　Formulating educational objectives by combining acts and contents ··················47
Table 2-11　An alternative taxonomy of L2 teacher questions ··············61
Table 3-1　Correlation between the raters' scoring of the speaking test before AR ··················69
Table 3-2　Correlation between the raters' scoring of the writing test before AR ··················70
Table 3-3　Routine of classroom instruction ··················71
Table 3-4　Students' puzzlement about the intensive reading course ··············74
Table 3-5　Students' suggestions on teaching the intensive reading course ··················76

List of Tables

Table 3-6	Result of reading strategies survey	77
Table 3-7	Three cycles of AR	92
Table 3-8	Data collected during the three phases of the AR	94
Table 3-9	Correlation between the raters' scoring of the speaking test after AR	99
Table 3-10	Correlation between the raters' scoring of the writing test after AR	99
Table 3-11	Participants of the focus group interview	100
Table 4-1	Solutions planned for the problems identified in AR1	107
Table 4-2	Most impressive questions reported in students' logs of Unit 3	134
Table 5-1	Solutions planned for the problems identified in AR2	143
Table 5-2	Most impressive questions reported in students' logs of Unit 5	174
Table 6-1	Solutions planned for the problems identified in AR3	190
Table 6-2	Words the students thought of to describe the characters of the story	207
Table 7-1	Comparison of the students' use of reading strategies before and after AR	275

List of Figures

Figure 2-1	Marzano and Simms' model of questioning sequences	42
Figure 2-2	The outcome space of learning	45
Figure 2-3	Venn diagram of L2 objects of learning	55
Figure 2-4	The outcome space of L2 learning	56
Figure 2-5	A model of questioning sequences in L2 classes	62
Figure 3-1	Descriptive statistics of the result of reading test	78
Figure 3-2	Descriptive statistics of the result of speaking test	78
Figure 3-3	Descriptive statistics of the result of summary writing test	79
Figure 3-4	Burns' cyclical AR model	82
Figure 3-5	Wen Qiufang's model of AR	83
Figure 3-6	The theoretical departure and overall procedure of the AR	91
Figure 4-1	The general procedure for the teaching of a unit	106
Figure 4-2	Pre-reading Questions for Unit 3	110
Figure 4-3	Questions designed for Para. 1 of Unit 3	110
Figure 4-4	The first group discussion activity for Unit 3	111
Figure 4-5	The second group discussion activity for Unit 3	111
Figure 4-6	Summary writing task for Unit 3	112
Figure 5-1	Pre-reading Questions for Unit 5	146
Figure 5-2	Global Reading Questions for Unit 5	146
Figure 5-3	Detailed Reading Questions for Para. 3 of Unit 5	146
Figure 5-4	Discussion activity for Unit 5	147
Figure 5-5	Summary writing task for Unit 5	147
Figure 6-1	Pre-reading Questions for Unit 7	192

List of Figures

Figure 6-2	Questions designed for Para. 1 of Unit 7	193
Figure 6-3	Discussion activity for Unit 7	193
Figure 6-4	Summary writing task for Unit 7	193
Figure 6-5	Students' questions for Para. 1 of Unit 7	195
Figure 7-1	A cyclical procedure of reflective practice	245
Figure 7-2	Paired samples statistics of the reading strategies surveys	276
Figure 7-3	Paired samples correlations of the reading strategies surveys	276
Figure 7-4	Paired samples test of the reading strategies surveys	276
Figure 7-5	Paired samples statistics of reading tests	278
Figure 7-6	Paired samples correlations of reading tests	278
Figure 7-7	Paired samples test of reading tests	278
Figure 7-8	Paired samples statistics of speaking tests	278
Figure 7-9	Paired samples correlations of speaking tests	278
Figure 7-10	Paired samples T-test of speaking tests	279
Figure 7-11	Descriptive statistics of writing tests	279
Figure 7-12	Paired samples correlations of writing tests	279
Figure 7-13	Paired samples test of writing tests	280

Chapter 1   Introduction

This introductory chapter begins with the motivation for the study and proceeds to review two theoretical constructs, i.e., questioning sequences and learning space, to serve as the rationale for the current study. It then presents the overview of an action research (henceforth AR) on how teacher questions can be designed and implemented as questioning sequences to extend learning space. The chapter ends with the structure of the dissertation.

1.1 Motivation for the study

The motivation for the current study consists in the importance of teacher questions, the major problem in Chinese EFL teachers' use of questions, and the neglect of instructional objectives in existing research on ESL/EFL teacher questions.

1.1.1 Importance of teacher questions in classroom instruction

It has long been understood that questioning is the core or essence of teaching. Socratic questioning has been advocated throughout the history of formal education due to its crucial role in thinking, teaching and learning (Elder & Paul, 1998; Paul & Elder, 2008). John Dewey, hailed as the major education reformer for the 20th century, pointed out that thinking is questioning and characterized the art of teaching as the asking of questions:

> Thinking is inquiry, investigation, turning over, probing or delving into, so as to find something new or to see what is already known in a different light. In short, it is *questioning*. A well-established feature of traditional recitation is the asking

of questions by the teacher.

(Dewey, 1933, p. 266; as cited in Turnbull, 2004, p. 3)

Questioning has been found to be the commonest act of teaching as researchers have reported that a typical teacher asks around one and a half million questions throughout his/her teaching career and estimated that teachers ask an average of 30 to 120 questions per hour (Sadker, Sadker, & Zittleman, 2010). Questioning is so ubiquitous that "such things as a teacher's praising and blaming students, assigning materials for study, and drilling students [are] all 'peripheral acts' of teaching" (MacMillan & Garrison, 1988, p. 21).

When it comes to language education, many researchers and educators have reiterated the significant role of teacher questions as well. Richards and Lockhart (1996, p. 187), for example, listed six ways in which teacher questions can be used to assist L2 classroom teaching:

- They stimulate and maintain students' interest.
- They encourage students to think and focus on the content of the lesson.
- They enable a teacher to clarify what a student has said.
- They enable a teacher to elicit particular structures or vocabulary items.
- They enable teachers to check students' understanding.
- They encourage student participation in a lesson.

H. D. Brown (2001) stated that teacher questions provide "necessary stepping stones to communication" (p.169), and highlighted four prominent functions of teacher questions in second language classrooms, each followed by suggestions on how to effectuate them:

1. Teacher questions give students the impetus and opportunity to produce language comfortably without having to risk initiating language themselves. It's very scary for students to have to initiate conversation or topics for discussion. Appropriately pitched questions can give more reticent students an affective "green light" and a structured opportunity to communicate in their second language.

2. Teacher questions can serve to initiate a chain reaction of student interaction among themselves. One question may be all that is needed to start a discussion; without the initial question, however, students will be reluctant to initiate the process.
3. Teacher questions give the instructor immediate feedback about student comprehension. After posing a question, a teacher can use the student response to diagnose linguistic or content difficulties. Grammatical or phonological problem areas, for example, may be exposed through the student's response and give the teacher some specific information about what to treat.
4. Teacher questions provide students with opportunities to find out what they think by hearing what they say. As they are nudged into responding to questions about, say, a reading or a film, they can discover what their own opinions and reactions are. This self-discovery can be especially useful for a prewriting activity.

(H. D. Brown, 2001, pp. 169-171)

In a word, teacher questions play significant roles in classroom instruction. From a point of view of general education, teachers use questions as a major means to involve students in thinking. From a point of view of language education, teachers use questions not only to involve students in thinking, but to engage them in using the target language; teacher questions typically constitute the first move of the initiation-response-feedback (IRF) sequence of classroom interaction. Nonetheless, despite the increasing research interest in classroom interaction in recent decades, far less attention has been paid to teacher questions than to student responses and teacher feedback.

1.1.2 Ineffective teacher questions due to lack of explicit goals

Despite the crucial roles teacher questions play in language teaching, Chinese EFL teaching scholars have reiterated that the major problem in Chinese EFL classroom discourse is the dis-alignment or disorientation of teacher questions with specified instructional objectives.

Huang Yuanshen (2010) and Qin Xiubai (2012), in their articles reporting their official visits to classrooms as program evaluation experts, both voiced concerns over some key problems in classroom instruction, and called attention to ineffective teacher questions. Huang (2010) wrote that many teacher questions were mostly oriented to lexical items or grammatical structures instead of the messages conveyed in texts and hence classroom instruction was devoid of critical thinking. Qin (2012) observed that a number of teachers were inclined to ask questions that were more entertaining than educating and that in spite of a seemingly joyful classroom atmosphere, the students could hardly learn anything meaningful.

Such concerns were recently echoed by Shu Dingfang and Qu Weiguo, who had served as judges in the SFLEP-sponsored national-level college EFL teaching contests. Both Shu (2013) and Qu (2016) wrote commentary articles on the contestants' performances and drew attention to the lack of explicit goals in teacher questions. Shu (2013) observed that a majority of contestants failed to strike a balance between questions oriented to the learning of language items and questions aimed at the comprehension of content messages, and labeled such acts as manifestations of "catching one and losing the other" or "going extremes" in the setting of teaching objectives (p. 45). Qu (2016) noted that the candidate teachers tended to ignore the 'meta-textual messages' and that their questions failed to lead the students to read between the lines closely and critically.

In sum, teacher questions, if dis-aligned with instructional objectives, are ineffective as they cannot contribute to learning. Quality teacher questions should be designed and implemented to create the space for students to learn what is intended to be learned, rather than simply lighting up the classroom atmosphere.

1.1.3 Neglect of instructional objectives in research on teacher questions

A review of relevant literature shows that insufficient attention has been cast to how language teacher questions are designed and implemented in correspondence with instructional objectives.

The underlying assumption of numerous taxonomies of teacher questions, as will be discussed in Chapter Two, is that all teacher questions can be assigned into preset categories. Some categories, such as referential versus display questions, are idiosyncratic or biased because they are based on some readily-accepted assumptions or hypotheses like communicative language teaching (CLT). Though researchers have recently endeavored to establish multidimensional taxonomies in order to render more comprehensive descriptions and interpretations, their focus is still on the roles of teacher questions in very specific or micro contexts of classroom interaction and the matter of instructional objectives remains untapped.

ESL/EFL teacher questions have been empirically researched via three approaches: interaction analysis (IA), discourse analysis (DA) and conversation analysis (CA). What is of primary concern to IA researchers is the eliciting function of teacher questions, i.e., the quantity and quality of student utterances elicited by a teacher question of a certain type, particularly a display/closed or a referential/open question. What is of greatest interest to DA researchers is the interactional and/or pedagogical functions of teacher questions in specific contexts of classroom interaction. What is of central importance to CA researchers is the institutional organization of Q-A interaction, particularly the teacher's and the students' intersubjective understanding of a question on a turn-by-turn basis, i.e., the teacher's intention of asking a question and the students' understanding of the teacher's intention as manifested in their responses to it.

Despite the insightful findings of the existing studies, it is observed that few of them have put central emphasis on how teacher questions are applied to serve the instructional objectives of a lesson, a unit, a course, or a curriculum in general. Their focus, however, is on what roles individual teacher questions play in specific or micro contexts of classroom interaction rather than how they are sequentially deployed to serve broader instructional objectives.

It is thus considered advisable to draw upon the theoretical constructs of 'questioning sequences' and 'learning space', both underscoring the alignment of teacher questions to instructional objectives, to establish a guiding framework to help improve the instructional effectiveness of language teacher questions.

1.2 Rationale for the study

The rationale for the current study consists in two theoretical constructs: 'questioning sequences' and 'learning space'.

1.2.1 Questioning sequences

Educational researchers have focused their attention on the extent to which teacher questions serve to meet educational objectives, such as the different levels of cognitive processing as elaborated by Bloom and followers (Bloom et al., 1956). Ever since the establishment of Bloom's taxonomy, numerous studies have been conducted to examine the cognitive levels of teacher questions, as demonstrated by some synthetic and meta-analytic studies (e.g., Gall, 1970; Redfield & Rousseau, 1981; Dillon, 1982). These studies, however, suggest that, despite some scholars' call for the use of higher-order questions, there is actually no one-to-one correspondence between the cognitive levels intended by teacher questions and the levels manifested in student answers. Therefore, researchers have steered their course and widened their scope of focus from individual questions to series or sequences of questions in relation to educational objectives.

Good and Brophy (2000/2003/2008) proposed that "sequences of questions [be] designed to help students develop connected understandings" (2008, p. 316) and demonstrated that a sequence can either begin with higher-order questions followed by lower-order questions or otherwise depending on the goals being pursued. They stressed that the central concern should be how sequences of questions are deployed for particular instructional objectives rather than what cognitive levels individual questions belong to.

Dantonio and Beisenherz (2001), as did Good and Brophy, also advocated that combinations of questions of different cognitive levels be used to serve pedagogical purposes. Unlike Good and Brophy (2008), who advocated the avoidance of questions leading to unproductive responses, such as yes-no questions, tagging questions, guessing questions and leading questions (p. 317), Dantonio and Beisenherz (2001) labeled such questions as "processing questions" or "supporting questions" in that they can facilitate the procedures of thought in conversation and help realize the goals intended with the "core questions" focusing on thinking (Dantonio & Beisenherz, 2001, p. 42). They thus coined the term "questioning sequences" and defined it as "a sequential series of cognitively focused questions combined with questions that assist students in clarifying, verifying, supporting, and redirecting their responses" (p. 37).

The above two views on teacher questions, advantageous as they appear, are in accordance with Bloom's taxonomy of educational objectives and only concerned with the cognitive domain. What is missing in them is the content domain, without which cognitive processes would be disoriented as well. Such was noted by Marzano and Simms (2014), who criticized the segregation of content and cognition in previous research on teacher questions and put forth a new concept of 'questioning sequences' by combining both the cognitive and the content domains. They suggested that educational objectives should be realized through questions designed and implemented sequentially at different phases of instruction and defined questioning sequences as follows:

> We regard a questioning sequence as a series of questions or prompts that ask students to articulate details about the content, identify characteristics of content-related categories, generate elaborations about the content, and provide evidence and support for those elaborations.
>
> (Marzano & Simms, 2014, p. 12)

As indicated in the definition, a questioning sequence can be comprised of any two and more of the four types of questions, i.e., detail questions, category questions, elaboration questions and evidence questions.

What needs to be clarified here is that, though in the dissertation such terms as questioning, teacher questioning and classroom questioning are used to refer to the act of asking questions in a general sense, 'questioning' in Marzano and Simms' (2014) notion of 'questioning sequences' is not the general act of asking questions in classroom instruction. Additionally, 'sequence' in 'questioning sequences' is not equivalent to the sequence of initiation-response-feedback (IRF) as usually perceived by classroom discourse researchers. Rather, a questioning sequence is a sequence or series of questions designed and applied for the realization of a certain instructional objective.

The current study draws on Marzano and Simms' (2014) concept of questioning sequences and defines it as sequences of questions designed and enacted around particular instructional objectives, of a lesson, a unit, a course, or a curriculum. What follows naturally would then be how to evaluate or measure the extent to which such questioning sequences serve to meet specific instructional objectives.

1.2.2 Learning space

What is of special interest to the current study is the concept of "the space of learning" brought forth by Marton and associates (Marton & Booth, 1997; Marton, Runesson, & Tsui, 2004; Tsui, Marton, Mok, & Ng, 2004; Tsui, 2004; Marton, 2015). According to Marton, learning always involves the acquisition of knowledge about a certain object of learning which consists of a general aspect, i.e., the act of learning or the indirect object of learning, such as remembering, interpreting, grasping, and a specific aspect, i.e., the subject or content of learning or the direct object of learning, such as formulas, equations, literary works, historical events (Marton, Runesson, & Tsui, 2004, p. 4).

Marton (2015, p. 22) put it simply in a formula: **act + content = educational objective**. To make learning happen, opportunities must be provided for learners to experience 'variation' of the act or the content of what is intended to be learned (Marton & Booth, 1997; Ko & Marton, 2004; Marton & Pang, 2006; Marton, 2015, Chapter 3). Thus, learning, in essence, is the qualitative change in the way of experiencing something and the key for learning is the awareness of variation in the indirect and direct objects of learning (Marton & Booth, 1997; Marton & Pang, 2006).

There are three types of object of learning in line with three different perspectives according to Marton, Runesson and Tsui (2004, pp. 22-24):

(1) the intended object of learning from the teacher's perspective or the perspective of the curriculum;

(2) the enacted object of learning from the researcher's perspective or the perspective of one who observes the extent to which the necessary conditions have been created by the teacher; and

(3) the lived object of learning from the students' perspective.

Simply put, the three types of object of learning relate to three questions: (1) What should be learned? (2) What can be possibly learned? (3) What is actually learned?

Marton et al. (2004) indicated that the space of learning is identical with the enacted object of learning, or what can be possibly learned, and pointed out that in the classroom setting, the students can only possibly learn what they encounter in the classroom. It implies that the teacher's major concern should be creating the necessary conditions for the students to focus their attention on the critical aspect(s) of an object of learning and to experience variation in the critical aspect(s).

'The space of learning' in Marton and associates' view is similar to 'the space for learning' and 'learning space' used by language teaching researchers, such as Walsh (2011) and Waring (2009). According to Marton and Tsui (2004), the space of learning is linguistically constituted in classroom interaction, and similarly, Walsh (2011) maintains that the space for learning is opened up when the learner is offered the opportunity to participate in classroom interaction. Despite their different theoretical backgrounds, both the space of learning and the space for learning point to classroom interaction. What lies in the core of these notions is that learning takes place in interaction and the key for learning to take place is variation in the acts and contents in which students are engaged. Hence, the three terms are used interchangeably in the current study to refer to what is possible to learn in the process of classroom interaction.

In regard to the evaluation of questioning sequences, quality questioning sequences, as indicated by the concept of learning space, are those that can open up the space for learners to experience variation of the critical aspects of an object of learning. In other words, teachers can draw on the variation perspective of learning space to design and implement questioning sequences so as to maximally meet the instructional objectives as specified for a lesson, a unit, a course or a curriculum.

Marton and Booth (1997) found that learners experience a certain object of learning in qualitatively different but hierarchically related ways, which would form a hierarchical structure if pooled together. It is thus advisable for teachers to cater to the needs of different learners by providing the necessary conditions for them to experience the hierarchical variation so as to learn what is intended to be learned.

In view of the two theoretical constructs mentioned above and the multiple objectives of language courses, the researcher endeavored to establish a model of questioning sequences aiming at the extension of learning space as a guiding framework for the design and implementation of L2 teacher questions. The framework, as will be elaborated in Section 2.5 of Chapter Two, is comprised of two dimensions of variation: content focus and cognitive demand. The dimension of content focus can vary between three strands: text comprehension, language learning and personal responses. Each of the three strands can vary between three levels in the dimension of cognitive demand. The comprehension questions can vary between the three levels of literal understanding, interpreting and evaluating; the language questions between recognizing, categorizing and appreciating; and the response questions between articulating, elaborating and justifying.

1.3 Overview of the action research

It is in the light of previous educational research on questioning sequences and learning space that the researcher attempted to conduct an AR study to explore and testify whether it is plausible for the teacher to enrich students' experience of a course by designing and implementing questioning sequences in correspondence with specified instructional objectives. The AR study was conducted to address the following questions:

1) How can teacher questions be designed and implemented to maximize instructional effectiveness?
2) How do students respond to such teacher questions?
3) What are the major factors that may influence the effectiveness of such teacher questions?

The AR was situated in an English majors' intensive reading class at a provincial medical university. The students were in their third semester in college and they had previously had two different intensive reading teachers. The preliminary research, including a set of language proficiency tests and a survey on classroom questioning, revealed that the students were mostly of intermediate level of proficiency and expected the course to be focused on the teaching and learning of vocabulary and grammar as they had mostly been involved in answering questions relating to language points during classroom interaction. The researcher then made the attempt to extend their learning space through interventions in the design and implementation of questions for classroom instruction.

Three cycles of AR were then carried out, with each cycle lending implications for the next. The use of questioning sequences constituted the major pedagogical intervention throughout the AR. Each AR cycle covered the instruction of two units. During the process, qualitative data were collected through peer classroom observation, videotape-based reflection, students' learning logs, and group discussion, and then analyzed to inform improvements or adaptations in the follow-up pedagogical interventions.

By the end of the AR, another set of tests covering reading, speaking and summary writing, and a survey of the students' use of reading strategies were administered. In addition, focus group interviews with three groups of focal students were conducted, and end-of-term reflection essays were collected. All these data were analyzed to evaluate the effects of the pedagogical treatments introduced in the three cycles and to discover the factors that might have influenced the realization of the instructional objectives through questioning sequences.

The study reveals that learning space is a viable construct to guide the design and implementation of questioning sequences for classroom instruction. First of all, as regards the design and implementation of teacher questions to meet course objectives, the AR demonstrates that the teacher should first identify or specify the instructional objectives or the objects of learning and then accordingly design and implement series of questions that vary in content focus and cognitive demand. In addition, it is necessary to allow the students to prepare for answering teacher questions before class and incorporate questions raised by the students themselves while they preview the texts.

Analysis of the qualitative data shows that the pedagogical interventions of the AR were effective in multiple aspects, including the deepening of text comprehension, the improvement of the use of reading strategies, the development of autonomous learning, the cultivation of critical thinking, the building up of classroom atmosphere or the increased willingness to participate in classroom interaction. Such findings were further confirmed by the results of the tests and surveys conducted before and after the AR, as statistically significant improvements were detected in the students' language proficiency and their use of reading strategies.

1.4 Structure of the dissertation

The dissertation consists of eight chapters. The first chapter introduces the motivation and rationale for the study, and outlines the structure of the dissertation.

The second chapter first reviews taxonomies of teacher questions established by language teaching researchers and then proceeds to review relevant literature on teacher questions in L2 classrooms. It points out that language teaching researchers have been primarily concerned with classifying individual questions and interpreting their functions in specific contexts of classroom interaction and have not given sufficient attention to how teacher questions can serve to meet the instructional objectives of a lesson, a course, a unit or a curriculum. Drawing upon educational researchers' recent work on teacher questions, the chapter then introduces the theoretical construct of questioning sequences which takes into account instructional objectives as well as individual questions, and then the concept of learning space which can be capitalized on to guide the design and implementation of quality questioning sequences to serve specified instructional objectives. It ends by integrating the two theoretical constructs into a framework of L2 questioning sequences.

The third chapter details the methodology of the current study. It first gives a detailed account of the preliminary work, including the context of the study, the student participants' language proficiency levels and their attitudes towards classroom interaction and the teaching and learning of the intensive reading course. Based on the findings of the preliminary research, it raises the research questions, draws out the AR design, outlines the plan and procedure of the AR, presents the methods of data collection and analysis, and clarifies the ethical issues and validity concerns.

The full account of the AR, consisting of three cycles, is provided in Chapters Four to Six, following the pattern of focusing, planning, implementing and evaluating. Chapter Four identifies the major problems encountered at the beginning of the course instruction, sketches the plan to solve them, demonstrates the implementation and evaluates the effectiveness of the pedagogical treatment. Each of the next two chapters reports the adaptations based on the findings of the preceding cycle of AR.

Further discussion is provided in Chapter Seven in reference to qualitative and quantitative data collected by the end of the AR. It first recapitulates how teacher questions can be designed and implemented to maximally meet specified instructional objectives as manifested by the pedagogical interventions adopted in the three AR cycles. It then evaluates the effects of such teacher questions on student learning before tapping into the major factors that may influence the opening up and closing down of learning space through teacher questions.

Chapter Eight brings the whole study to its conclusion, summarizing the major findings, pointing out the limitations inherent in the design and methods of the AR, and offering implications for future research and pedagogical practice.

Chapter 2   Literature Review

This chapter consists of five sections. The first section gives an overview of some well-established taxonomies of teacher questions. The second section provides a review of previous studies on ESL/EFL teacher questions, revealing the neglect of the instructional goals in existing research. The next two sections are devoted to the introduction of two theoretical constructs originating in educational research, questioning sequences and learning space. The last section incorporates these two constructs into a preliminary framework of questioning sequences for the extension of learning space.

2.1 Taxonomies of teacher questions

As the classification scheme of teacher questions adopted by a researcher largely determines his/her description and interpretation of teacher questions, it is hence necessary to take a review of the taxonomies of teacher questions ever established.

The burst of interest in teacher questions was inflamed in the 1950's thanks to Bloom's work on the taxonomy of educational objectives (Bloom et al., 1956). The major contribution by educational researchers following Bloom's taxonomy is the multitude of taxonomies of teacher questions based on the levels of cognitive processing: knowledge, comprehension, application, analysis, synthesis, and evaluation. Whereas some borrowed Bloom's taxonomy in their classification of teacher questions, others either expanded Bloom's taxonomy by adding new types of questions or condensed it into more inclusive categories (Gall, 1970; Dillon, 1982; Walsh & Sattes,

2005; Marzano & Simms, 2014). There exists a bulk of research examining the types of questions used by teachers and the instructional effects of the questions as demonstrated in a host of meta-analytic and synthetic studies (e.g., Redfield & Rousseau, 1981; Dillon, 1982; Marzano & Simms, 2014).

Despite the sweeping influence of Bloom's taxonomy in research on subject matter teacher questions, language teaching researchers have chosen to classify language teacher questions alternatively. By and large, the taxonomies of teacher questions could be divided into three types according to the basis on which the taxonomies are established: 1) taxonomies based on forms, 2) taxonomies based on functions, and 3) taxonomies based on multiple dimensions.

2.1.1 Taxonomies based on forms

Grammarians' taxonomies of questions could be the earliest ever adopted by researchers to describe teacher questions, i.e., to classify them into yes/no questions, wh-questions, and alternative questions (Tsui, 1992; Collins COBUILD, 1990). According to Quirk, Greenbaum, Leech and Svartvik (1972), wh-questions are asked for specific information about a particular person, thing, place, reason, method, or amount and cannot be answered by 'yes' or 'no'; yes/no questions are asked for the confirmation or disconfirmation of certain information and hence usually answered by 'yes' or 'no', and tag questions and alternative (either/or) questions are special cases of such. Thus, ESL researchers have referred to the forms of teacher questions as wh-questions, yes/no questions, tag questions and alternative questions.

Besides the four types of questions mentioned above, Koshik (2002a) identified a particular type of questions used by ESL teachers called 'designedly incomplete utterances' (DIUs) which are incomplete statements made by teachers to be completed by students. Additionally, in China's EFL context, another two types of questions, though grammatically not in question forms, are used by teachers to elicit student responses, one called paraphrase questions, the other translation questions (Zhao Xiaohong, 1998; He Anping, 2003). Paraphrase questions are those used by teachers to have students rephrase certain messages in their own words in the target language; and translation questions are those used by teachers to have students translate words, expressions or sentences from a foreign language to one's mother tongue or otherwise. Paraphrase and translation questions, though grammatically not in question forms, are usually initiated by teachers in either interrogative or imperative mood (Zhao Xiaohong, 1998). In all, language teachers can use seven forms of questions to elicit student responses as illustrated in Table 2-1 below.

Table 2-1 Seven forms of language teacher questions

Forms	Definitions and examples
Wh-question	a question containing a WH-word, typically in initial position, and calling for an item of information to be supplied, as *What's your question?*
Yes-no question	a question calling for an answer of yes or no, as *Do you think so?*
Tag question	a question used after a statement when seeking or expecting confirmation of that statement, as *You agree with him, don't you?*
Alternative question	a question that offers a choice of two or more alternatives, as *Which do you think is correct, A, B, or C?*
DIU	an incomplete statement to elicit student response to complete the turn, as *You think the correct answer is _____?*
Paraphrase question	a question that calls for rephrasing of certain information in one's own words, as *Can you tell us what the author means in your own words?*
Translation question	a question that asks the student to translate, as *How to say '炸药'?*

2.1.2 Taxonomies based on functions

As a certain form of teacher questions can be used to serve different purposes or functions in classroom interaction, it is suggested that they be classified according to their functions, or more specifically, the responses elicited by the questions (Tsui, 1992).

Barnes' (1969) classification of teacher questions is reportedly the earliest ever constructed with a functional orientation. In an attempt to describe language used in British secondary classrooms, Barnes (1969) set up

a framework of teacher questions comprised of four categories:
- factual questions that pertain to the seeking of factual information;
- reasoning questions that involve the listener in reasoning to give an answer;
- social questions that are aimed at establishing or maintaining communication; and
- open questions that seek information that is unknown to the teacher.

Language teaching researchers, somehow, have reduced Barnes' framework to a binary distinction between closed-ended and open-ended questions, or simply closed and open questions, with the former referring to questions requesting only one acceptable answer, and the latter to questions inviting a number of acceptable responses (Chaudron, 1988; Ellis, 2012).

Another taxonomy of teacher questions, similar to Barnes' to some degree, was established by Long and Sato (1983) who looked into different types of teacher questions in ESL classrooms and the quality of student utterances elicited by them. Long and Sato divided teacher questions into two broad categories of echoic and epistemic questions and both were respectively further divided into several sub-categories (see Table 2-2). Comprehensive as the taxonomy was intended to be, only two sub-types of epistemic questions—referential and display—have been of greatest concern to language teaching researchers. Referential questions are those that the teacher does not know the answer in advance and display questions those that the teacher already knows the answer. It is widely advocated that teachers ask more referential questions out of the assumption that referential questions are more effective than display ones in eliciting longer and syntactically more complex responses from students.

Table 2-2 Long and Sato's (1983) taxonomy of teacher questions

Types	Sub-types	Examples
Echoic questions	Comprehension checks	*Alright?; OK?; Does everyone understand "polite"?*
	Clarification requests	*What do you mean? I don't understand; What?*
	Confirmation checks	*Did you say "he"?*

Continued

Types	Sub-types	Examples
Epistemic questions	Referential questions	*Why didn't you do your homework?*
	Display questions	*What's the opposite of "up" in English?*
	Expressive questions	*It's interesting, isn't it?*
	Rhetorical questions	*Why did I do that? Because I ...*

Due to the similarity between the two pairs of distinction, one between closed VS open questions and other display VS referential questions, they are often used interchangeably as researchers, such as Wu (1993) and Ellis (2012), usually refer to teacher questions as either display/closed and referential/open.

Some researchers are more interested in the pedagogical functions served than the responses elicited by teacher questions. McCormick (1997; McCormick and Donato, 2002), for example, drawing upon the six tutoring roles identified by Wood, Bruner, and Ross (1976) from a Vygotskyan sociocultural perspective, established a framework of teacher questions according to their scaffolding functions. The framework, as displayed in Table 2-3, makes it possible to describe how teacher questions scaffold student learning in classroom interaction as each question can be identified with a specific scaffolding function. It has spawned a number of studies in different L2 contexts, like Chang (2009) and McNeil (2012). Nevertheless, it seems that there is difficulty in assigning questions to the categories of functions consistently, as the inter-rater reliability reported in McCormick's (1997) study was merely 60% across all the six functions.

2.1.3 Taxonomies based on multiple dimensions

Noting that it is insufficient to describe a teacher question in terms of one single dimension, Thompson (1997) proposed that form, content and function should all be taken into consideration in classifying teacher questions. Accordingly, there are yes/no and *wh-* questions in the dimension of grammatical form; questions about outside facts (facts not specifically

Table 2-3 McCormick's (1997) classification of questions based on their scaffolding functions

Types of Questions	Functions	Examples
Recruitment (R)	Drawing the novice's attention to the task and its requirements	*Why don't you guys give one of your questions?* (R) *Does anybody have any questions about the papers I gave you, returned to you?* (R)
Reduction in degrees of freedom (RDF)	Simplifying the task into subtasks that still allow the novice to reach a solution	*Well, how is the word global being used here?* (RDF) *What part of speech is it?* (RDF)
Direction maintenance (DM)	Helping to keep the novice motivated, calling attention to the goal, and working towards the overall task goal	*In other words, I guess what Sally is trying to ask is what were some of the flaws with the studies?* (DM)
Direction maintenance clarification request questions (DM-CR)	Encouraging students to clarify, expand, elaborate, or reiterate some aspect of their discourse	*Could you explain what you said in another way?* (DM-CR)
Direction maintenance comprehension check questions (DM-CC)	Promoting "on-line" pursuit of the course goal, namely comprehension of the target language that emerges during class	*Do you know what I mean?* (DM-CC)
Marking critical features (MCF)	Calling the novice's attention to important aspects of the overall task, in particular when a mismatch between the novice's work and the expert's preferred solution exists	*Castle, special place, very nice. Who usually lives in palaces?* (MCF)
Frustration control (FC)	Decreasing the stress on the novice without encouraging the novice's dependency on the expert	*Do you want some help, Gemma?* (FC) *Do you want the question to be repeated?* (FC)
Demonstrating (D)	Modelling the ideal procedures to achieve the goal of the task	*What does pontoons mean?* (D) *Repeat.*

related to the learner), personal facts (facts related to the learner's own lives), and opinions relating to the content; and display and communicative questions regarding the purpose or function. Thus, Thompson (1997) set up a multidimensional framework, as demonstrated in Table 2-4.

Table 2-4 Thompson's (1997) classification of teacher questions

#	Form	Content	Purpose	Examples
1	yes/no	outside fact	display	*Are cats cheaper to own than dogs?*
2	wh-	outside fact	display	*How much do dog owners spend on pet food each week?*
3	yes/no	personal fact	display	*Do you have a dog at home?*
4	wh-	personal fact	display	*Which of the pets mentioned in the text do you have?*
5	yes/no	opinion	display	*Do you like dogs?*
6	wh-	opinion	display	*Which kind of dog do you prefer?*
7	yes/no	outside fact	communicative	*Do dogs usually live longer than cats?*
8	wh-	outside fact	communicative	*Why do dogs need insurance?*
9	yes/no	personal fact	communicative	*Do you have any pets at home?*
10	wh-	personal fact	communicative	*How much a year, roughly, do you spend on your pets?*
11	yes/no	opinion	communicative	*Do you find the information in the text surprising?*
12	wh-	opinion	communicative	*Why do you think people spend so much on their pets?*

As mentioned at the very beginning of this section, what is of primary concern to educational researchers with an interest in teacher questions is the cognitive processes in which students are engaged while answering the questions. Despite the prevalence of cognitive taxonomies in educational research on teacher questions, it seems that language teaching researchers have not shown much interest in that area. Although some cognitive taxonomies of teacher questions have been introduced into the field of language teaching (e.g., Brown, 2001; Mei Deming, 1986; Tollefson & Zhuang Zhixiang, 1989), such taxonomies have rarely been applied to empirical studies on EFL/ESL teacher questions. Nevertheless, it is maintained that a complementary or combined approach to L2 teacher questions can be more effective in respect of descriptive adequacy and more insightful in terms of interpretive quality.

Diana Freeman (2014), however, established a taxonomy of ESL reading textbook questions, by taking account of both content orientations and cognitive levels of questions. Freeman's (2014) taxonomy is comprised of three categories of questions, namely content questions, language questions and affect questions, which are respectively divided into subcategories. As can be seen in Table 2-5, the three types of content questions are cognitively hierarchical, i.e., answering a textually implicit question requires an explicit understanding of the text, and answering an inferential comprehension question requires an implicit understanding of the text. The two types of affect questions, though not necessarily hierarchical, or one preconditioned by the other, do involve different levels of cognitive effort as well. The three types of language questions, however, are intended to cover three different aspects of language learning and are not differentiated according to the degree of cognitive demand. Despite the incoherence in the division of the subtypes of questions, Freeman's (2014) framework constitutes an alternative to existing taxonomies of questions and has been proved valid in evaluating reading comprehension questions in ESL textbooks.

What the above-mentioned taxonomies have in common is the assumption that individual teacher questions can be precisely assigned to certain categories according to some preset criteria. Though some recent taxonomies, such as Thompson's (1997) and Diana Freeman's (2014), consist of more than one dimension and appear to be more comprehensive, the focus remains yet unchanged, that is, on individual questions.

Table 2-5 Diana Freeman's (2014) taxonomy of reading comprehension questions

Categories	Subcategories	Description	Examples
Content questions	Textually explicit	The answer can be found stated directly in the text. There is word-matching between the question and the text.	Question: *When did Harry meet Sally?* Text: Harry met Sally in 1995 or Harry met Sally 15 years ago.
	Textually implicit	The answer is stated directly in the text but is not expressed in the same language as the questions.	Question: *When did Harry meet Sally?* Text: Sally and Harry first *came across each other* in 1995.
	Inferential comprehension	The answer is not stated explicitly in the text but rather alluded to. The reader has to connect the information in the text with their background knowledge to arrive at the answer.	Question: *How old was Harry when he met Sally?* or *How long ago did Harry meet Sally?* Text: Harry was a final year undergraduate working part time in a local bar when Sally came in with all her friends to celebrate her birthday.
	Reorganization	The reader is required to reorder, rearrange or transfer information in the text.	• put sequences in chronological order • transfer data into parallel forms (e.g., label pictures/maps, complete a table, translate)
Language questions	Lexical	The reader is required to focus specifically on *vocabulary*, not information.	• guess the meaning of a word or phrase from the context • match definition A with word/phrase B • use a dictionary
	Form	The reader is required to focus specifically on *grammar* or *form*, not information.	• change a sentence from the affirmative to the negative • form the question that goes with a given answer • explain the use of one tense rather than another
Affect questions	Personal response	The reader is required to offer their personal reaction to the text in terms of likes/dislikes, what they found funny, surprising etc.	Question: *What do you think? Which facts in Pizza Trivia do you find most interesting? Do you like Pizza? What are your favorite toppings?*
	Evaluation	The reader is required to make a judgement or assessment of the text/information according to some understood criteria with a reasoned justification.	Question: *In the context of the 20th century and its two world wars, what message is the writer trying to make about nature and the importance of individual human beings?*

2.2 Research on language teacher questions

The multitudinous question taxonomies have spawned a plethora of empirical studies on language teacher questions. As teacher questions are one stream of classroom discourse, and classroom discourse is usually approached through interaction analysis, discourse analysis or conversation analysis (Walsh, 2011; Cazden, 2001), previous research on ESL/EFL teacher questions can be reviewed in accordance with these three approaches.

2.2.1 Interaction analysis

Interaction analysis (IA) is rooted in the sociological analysis of 'group processes' with the assistance of well-developed observation systems (Chaudron, 1988; Walsh, 2006, 2011). According to Chaudron (1988), researchers opting for this approach bear two assumptions. One is that student behaviors are dependent on the atmosphere and interaction intended and brought by the teacher. The other is that the frequency of specific behaviors can be a measure of classroom interaction.

As regards classroom questioning, the matters of interest to researchers have been the frequency of specific forms of questions (e.g., yes/no- and wh-questions), the occurrence of specific types of questions (particularly referential and display questions), the length of wait time before and after allocating a question, and the types of feedback provided by the teacher to student responses, and occasionally the effect of any or all of the above mentioned factors on students' learning outcome or their target language output. In other words, IA studies of teacher questions can be subsumed under the process-product paradigm (Carlsen, 1991) as teacher questions are considered a process variable relating to the ultimate goal of classroom-based SLA (Long & Sato, 1983).

The key concern of IA studies of teacher questions, against the backdrop of communicative language teaching (CLT), is to determine whether certain types of teacher questions are more effective than others as judged by the length and syntactic complexity of student responses elicited by the questions. A review of relevant research shows that what is most disputable is whether referential/open questions are more effective than display/closed questions.

In ESL contexts, there appears the trend that the dichotomous distinction between the two types of questions is getting less applied. In the 1980's, research findings seemed to support that referential/open questions are more effective than display/closed questions as regards the length and syntactic complexity of student responses and hence researchers made the call that teachers use more referential questions/open questions to make classroom interaction more communicative (e.g., Long & Sato, 1983; Brock, 1986; Long and Crookes, 1986; Nunan, 1987). Nunan (1990) even suggested that teachers conduct AR to testify the instructional effects of asking more referential questions and less display questions.

Later on, the postulated advantage of referential/open questions over display/closed questions, however, was questioned by researchers as they found that the two types of questions have different roles to play in the process of classroom interaction. Consequently, some researchers advocated that neither type of questions should be favored over the other (e.g., Banbrook & Skehan, 1990; Wu, 1993; Ho, 2005; Lee, 2006). Meanwhile, other researchers even cast doubt on the validity of the dichotomous distinction between the two as they found it hard to assign a teacher question to any of the two types without doubt or dispute (e.g., van Lier, 1988; Nunan, 1990; Waring, 2012a).

In spite of the trend in ESL contexts as demonstrated above, Chinese TEFL scholars seem to have been steadfastly attracted to the referential/open VS display/closed dichotomy. A host of existing studies, almost entirely situated in higher education contexts, have investigated the instructional effects of the two types of teacher questions following Long and Sato's (1983) design and lent support to the preference of the former over the latter (e.g., Zhao Xiaohong, 1998; Zhou Xing & Zhou Yun, 2002; Xu Feng, 2003; Hu Qingqiu, 2007a, 2007b; Lu Yanfang & Lv Daoli, 2011; Wang Xiaoyan, 2013).

A noteworthy point that might have been neglected in TEFL research in China is the difference between the objectives of ESL courses and the objectives of Chinese EFL courses. As mentioned earlier, the call for the use of more referential/open questions than display/closed questions in ESL classrooms was driven by the CLT movement where students' participation in genuine communication was regarded as the key to the development of communicative competence. Chinese EFL courses, especially those offered at tertiary institutions, however, are loaded with multiple objectives, i.e., not only aimed at the development of communicative competence but also the development of other capabilities, such as the accumulation of metalinguistic and cultural knowledge and the development of critical thinking. Hence, it is not reasonable to judge the instructional effectiveness of teacher questions simply by the quantity and quality of student responses elicited by them, not to mention that the distinction between referential/open and display/closed questions has been found to be a controversial, if not invalid, construct.

2.2.2 Discourse analysis

Discourse analysis (DA) originated in the structural-functional linguistics and the central concern of DA studies of classroom discourse is the structure or sequence of moves of classroom interaction in association with the functions realized by each move in the immediate pedagogical context (Chaudron, 1988; Carlsen, 1991; Walsh, 2006, 2011).

One of the earliest examples of this approach is the study of Bellack et al. (1966), who identified four moves of classroom interaction: structure, solicit, respond, and react. The most influential work, however, is that of Sinclair and Coulthard (1975), who established a hierarchically structured system consisting of five ranks: lesson, transaction, exchange, move, and act, with each constituted by elements of the hierarchically lower rank. Forty years since its inception, the initiation, response, and feedback/follow-up (IRF) structure has served as a model for quantitatively describing the structural units and pedagogical functions of classroom discourse. When it comes to teacher questions, three major perspectives can be identified in existing research: 1) the classroom-context perspective, 2) the sociocultural perspective, and 3) the systemic functional linguistic (SFL) perspective. An overview of the major arguments and examples of the three perspectives is demonstrated in Table 2-6.

Table 2-6 Overview of three perspectives of DA studies

Perspectives	Major arguments	Examples
Classroom-context	TQs play different roles on different levels of classroom context.	Cullen (1998); Nunn (1999)
Sociocultural	Different TQs play different scaffolding roles.	McCormick (1997); Chang (2009)
SFL	TQs have ideational, interpersonal and textual meaning potentials.	Wallace (2003); Yang Xueyan (2007)

2.2.2.1 The classroom-context perspective

The classroom-context perspective is represented by Cullen (1998) and Nunn (1999), who attempted to establish fine-grained frameworks of question types in order to better capture the dynamic nature of the classroom context. Cullen (1998) brought into question the unidimensional view of classroom context and put forward a two-dimensional view of the classroom context, one being outside the classroom and the other inside the classroom, which makes it possible to give a more comprehensive description of classroom interaction.

Nunn (1999) made an attempt similar to Cullen's but narrowed his focus on the functions of display questions and proposed that the functions of teacher questions be analyzed on three levels of classroom context. The first or "primary" level refers to the most immediate context of classroom communication where the teacher and students play their typical classroom roles. The second level refers to the "displaced" context where the teacher and students play roles in a non-classroom setting, i.e., simulating discourse situated in a "displaced" world beyond the classroom. The third or "code-focus" level refers to the context where the topic is the discourse of the subject being studied, i.e., the language itself.

Kirckhoff and Klippel (2014) applied Nunn's three-level model to the analysis of teacher-student IRF exchanges in German EFL classrooms and verified that the distinction between the three levels of context is "helpful in highlighting the multifunctional layers of classroom discourse, referring to the content area of the lesson as well as the language focus" (p. 95) instead of reducing teacher questions to either display or referential ones. Meanwhile, they pointed out the need to fine-tune Nunn's framework in order to examine how teacher questions scaffold the development of learner fluency.

There is no denying that such endeavors made by Cullen (1998), Nunn (1999), and Kirckhoff and Klippel (2014) to establish fine-grained frameworks of the classroom context are conducive to describing and interpreting language teacher's questions more comprehensively and accurately. The models of classroom context reviewed above are driven by the urge to argue against the assumption that what happens in classroom interaction is not genuine communication. However fine-grained these models seem to be, it would be over-ambitious to set up a model that can fully capture the dynamics of classroom interaction. As with IA researchers, who have established numerous coding schemes to categorize teacher questions, it seems that DA researchers can frame the classroom context in as many ways as possible.

2.2.2.2 The sociocultural perspective

In DA studies from a sociocultural perspective (e.g., McCormick, 1997; McCormick & Donato, 2000; Chin, 2007; Chang, 2009; McNeil, 2012), each individual question is assigned to a specific function specified in Wood, Bruner, and Ross' (1976) framework and the scaffolding patterns of questions in different instructional stages are analyzed and interpreted in relation to the instructional objectives reported by the teachers.

McCormick (1997, McCormick & Donato, 2000) conducted an ethnographic case study using discourse analysis to investigate the scaffolding functions of a teacher's questions during teacher-fronted activities in an adult ESL class for integrated skills. Altogether 829 questions emerged in teacher-fronted activities throughout the course and all the questions were individually assigned to six categories of scaffolding functions established by Wood et al. (1976), as presented in Table 2-3. It was found that the teacher's effective use of questions assisted the students to achieve tasks beyond their current level of ability, and that the teacher's questioning patterns were closely related to the teacher's intended pedagogical goals.

McCormick's study is informative to researchers in that it has attested the applicability of scaffolding as a framework in investigating teacher questions. A number of studies have been conducted in light of the scaffolding framework in different contexts in recent years (e.g., Chang, 2009; McNeil, 2012; Zhao Nisha, 2012; Kayi-Aydar, 2013; Verplaetse, 2014). However, as acknowledged by McCormick herself, the research is not free of limitations, such as the lack of sufficient 'external generalizability', which is deemed to be inherent in case studies (McCormick, 1997, pp. 148-149). Another noteworthy issue is the consistency of coding questions with specific functions, as McCormick reported that the inter-coder reliability was merely 60 per cent and confessed that a question could serve more than one scaffolding function.

Sociocultural DA studies of teacher questions have rendered insightful implications for language teaching and research as they have provided new interpretations of the pedagogical roles of teacher questions, whether they are categorized as referential or display, cognitively lower-order or higher-order. Nevertheless, they are not free of limitations and the biggest challenge is the matter of validity and reliability, as a question or a type of question can be interpreted to play more than one scaffolding role. Another issue is that the scaffolding functions are examined in reference to the accomplishment of pedagogical goals at specific or immediate contexts of classroom interaction rather than to the accomplishment of instructional objectives of a lesson, unit, course or curriculum.

2.2.2.3 The SFL perspective

In DA studies from the SFL perspective, the Hallidayn framework of register is used to describe the classroom context, i.e., the three aspects of field, mode and tenor in relation to the ideational, textual and interpersonal meaning potentials. In such a framework, teacher questions are seen as goal-directed actions employed to realize meaning potentials relating to the field, mode and tenor of the situation and thus the educational effectiveness of teacher questions can be evaluated in terms of the overarching goals (Wells, 1993, p. 7).

The Hallidayan framework was adopted in Wallace's (2003) analysis of classroom interaction in a critical reading lessons, where the ideational, textual and interpersonal functions of IRF moves of segments of teacher-student interaction were interpreted in correspondence to the field, mode and tenor of talk around texts. Wallace concluded that even within the restriction of conventional classroom talk, teacher questions can involve students in classroom interaction as critical readers and "authors rather just animators" of classroom discourse, as long as teachers shift their footing and assert authorship of their materials, views of teaching and views of the world (Wallace, 2003, p. 155). In other words, teacher questions are more than a means of initiating classroom interaction, but have the potential to involve the students as critical readers, authors of materials, and contributors of values and views.

Yang Xueyan, a Chinese EFL teaching researcher, contributed two pieces of research on teacher questions from the SFL perspective. Yang Xueyan (2007) set up a discourse analytic model to address the lexico-grammatical, semantic, and situational features of EFL teacher questions. The model consists of three dimensions—the interpersonal, the logical, and the textual. The interpersonal dimension is realized by the interrogative mood of questions (i.e., the subject and the form of a question), the logical dimension by logical and/or semantic relationships between and/or within clauses (i.e., subordination and collaboration; projection and expansion), and the textual dimension by lexical cohesive devices (i.e., repetition, synonyms, and collocations). Enlightening as the analytical model appears to be, it may not be consistently applied in that researchers strange to SFL can hardly accomplish the analytic task systematically. As Yang herself noted, the categorization of the teacher's questioning strategies was largely based on theoretical inference and further trials were needed to validate the analytical model (Yang, 2007, p. 55). In other words, investigating teacher questions in light of the analytical model is a high-inference task and hence validity and reliability issues remain unresolved.

Yang Xueyan & Xie Min (2012) set up another analytical system to investigate the interactiveness of teacher questions, which consists of three sub-systems, namely, the mood, the subject person, and the interpersonal deicticity. They demonstrated that questioning is an interpersonal phenomenon and that teachers, when asking questions, make choices from three interpersonal systems, i.e., they choose different grammatical resources to realize mood, subject person and interpersonal deicticity. Laudable as their attempt was to offer a tool for describing teacher questions accurately, the analytical system they set up, as with the model reviewed above, would be challenging for researchers as well as practitioners to use consistently and reliably if they lack a specialized training in SFL.

If put in comparison, it can be noted that while IA researchers are concerned with the quantity and quality of student responses elicited by teacher questions, DA researchers are interested in rendering a microscopic account of what roles teacher questions can play in specific contexts of classroom interaction. More specifically, IA researchers are searching for the type(s) of questions that are most effective in involving the students in genuine communication, whereas DA researchers maintain that all types of questions have their roles to play.

However, as with IA studies, DA studies are faced with challenges as well. Firstly, it is nearly impossible to establish a one-to-one correspondence between individual teacher questions and specific roles or functions, as noted by McCormick (1997) and McNeil (2012). Secondly, the interpretation of the functions or roles of teacher questions is high-inference work and subjectivity is unavoidable. Todd and colleagues (2007) replicated the coding procedure in one of his earlier DA studies on teacher questions, and were astounded to find that the interpretation of data is a highly subjective matter. Though in some recent studies, multiple methods have been used for the purpose of data triangulation, most of them have only taken account of the teacher's perception and very few have tapped into how the students perceive the effects of teacher questions on them. Most important of all, as with IA researchers, DA researchers seem to have neglected how teacher questions serve the pedagogical goals of a broader scope, that is, the goals of a lesson, a unit, a course or a curriculum.

2.2.3 Conversation analysis

DA and CA are deemed as approaches to teacher questions that fall in the sociolinguistic paradigm which addresses not only the cognitive processes, content, form and purpose of a question, but also the dynamic context in which a question occurs (Carlsen, 1991). Theoretically rooted in sociolinguistics as they are, DA and CA have distinctive characteristics. According to Levinson (1983), these two approaches apply to quite different analytical procedures and methods. While DA subscribes to the methodology and theoretical principles typical of linguistics, which involves categorizing the units of discourse and formulating the rules for coherent discourse, CA is more of sociological interpretation, which avoids predetermined categories but aims to search for systematic properties of natural interaction.

In contrast to the vulnerabilities in DA, CA is claimed to be advantageous in generating an insider's view of participants (Markee, 2007; Seedhouse, 2004; Walsh, 2011). What is of prime concern to CA researchers of classroom discourse is the mechanism or interactional organization of classroom interaction. Seedhouse (2004) specified four types of interactional organization: adjacency pair, preference, turn taking and repair, which constitute a reference framework for doing conversation analysis of teacher questions.

One strand of CA studies addresses the functions of different forms of teacher questions. Koshik (2002b, 2003, 2005) successively examined the actions performed by teachers' yes/no, wh- and alternative questions and found that there is no one-to-one form-function relationship because the interpretation of questions depends on the knowledge or epistemic status that unfolds in the course of interaction. Waring (2012a) investigated the critical stance embodied in teachers' yes/no questions and students' interpretation of and reaction to that stance and concluded that students would dis-align themselves from the teacher's critical stance otherwise their concerns for learner competence or peer support would be threatened. Lee (2006) adopted the CA approach to investigate the pedagogical functions of display questions, and suggested that any judgment in that regard should be based on the analysis of students' "real-time interpretation" (p. 695). Lee's sequential analysis also showed that display questions are often exploited as a "core resource" for the co-construction and joint-management of classroom interaction (p. 708).

Preference organization of classroom interaction initiated by teacher questions is also of keen concern to CA researchers. Waring (2012b) analyzed students' responses to an ESL teacher's comprehension checks like "Any questions?" and found that despite the designed preference being an affirmative response, students are inclined to produce a negative answer for fear of displaying their lack of understanding or a negative attitude towards the teacher's professional competence (p. 745). Hosoda and Arline (2013) looked into the preference organization of yes/no questions in a Japanese primary English class and concluded that unlike the preference for progressivity in everyday conversation, the preferred response to a yes/no question in the classroom under observation is "the selected student to provide an answer". (p. 83)

Another issue of interest to CA researchers concerning teacher questions is how learning opportunities arise during the course of classroom interaction. Many of the interactional extracts discussed in Walsh (2011) were presented to show how display questions close down the space for learning and how referential questions open up the space for learning. Walsh (2011) also demonstrated how a set of post-expansion strategies contribute to the extension of learning space. Such strategies are employed by teachers after a student response that is not preferred and hence occur in the follow-up moves, but Walsh referred to them as interactional strategies for "shaping learner contributions" and deemed the teacher's ability to use such strategies as an important part of his or her "classroom interactional competence" (CIC) (Walsh, 2011, p. 168).

Yaqubi and Mozaffari (2011) combined CA with sociocultural theory in the examination of the ways in which teacher questions can scaffold learning processes. Their analysis of questions collected from eleven 90-minute EFL lessons revealed that only a small number of teacher questions with specific unfolding patterns are effective in providing learning opportunities. Altogether four scaffolding patterns of teacher questions were identified: 1) simplifying questions where the teacher broke down unanswered or difficult questions into specific ones; 2) marking-critical-features questions where the teacher called students' attention towards important aspects of the task in question; 3) asking-for-agreement questions where the teacher created a space for students to react to conflicting ideas; and 4) prompting questions where the teacher used clarification or elaboration requests to help out the students in expressing themselves.

CA studies conducted by some Chinese scholars have rendered some distinct findings concerning some subtle issues. Xie (2010, 2011), for example, investigated English major students' low level of involvement in teacher-fronted classroom interaction. Xie (2010) looked into the cause of students' reticence in teacher-student interaction through microscopic conversation analysis combined with other qualitative means and revealed that teachers' thematic control as evidenced by the restrictive IRF sequences leads to students' low levels of interaction. In another study, Xie (2011) examined the patterns of turn allocation in three English major classrooms at two Chinese universities and explored how the observed patterns inhibited students' opportunities to participate in classroom interaction. Pointing out the advantages and disadvantages inherent in each pattern, she suggested that teachers employ a variety of ways of turn management to maximize students' involvement (Xie, 2011, p. 249).

Li Qingsheng and Sun Zhiyong (2011) also employed conversation analysis to address the problem of reticence in teacher-student interaction. They identified the patterns of interaction, calculated the proportion of each pattern and found that most students would not volunteer to answer teacher questions even though the question were repeated more than once. Unlike Xie (2010, 2011) who attributed students' low levels of interaction to teachers' dominance of interaction pattern and thematic control, Li and Sun (2011) speculated that the traditional tenet of teacher-student relationship in Chinese culture was to blame, for in the students' eyes, a teacher question was more a challenge to their comprehension and courage than a request for information. They suggested that teacher-student interaction would not be effective unless an egalitarian power relationship is constructed and an equal distribution of information is assured between teachers and students.

Yang Lifang (2015) cast attention to the role of teacher questioning in developing students' critical thinking, one of the key objectives in English majors' reading course. Adopting Bloom's taxonomy of cognitive development, Yang identified four patterns of cognitive development in teacher questions: 1) the parallel pattern, 2) the upward pattern, 3) the downward pattern, and 4) the wavy pattern. The conversation analysis of teacher-student interaction shows that the wavy pattern is most efficient in training students' critical thinking in that such pattern of questioning, especially the use of follow-up questions of varying cognitive levels, enriches the cognitive domain of educational objectives and thus is more heuristic, just like Socratic questioning, than the closed IRE pattern. However, Yang indicated that such pattern of questioning is more demanding for the teacher as he/she has to consider the global situation of classroom interaction and evaluate students' responses instantly so as to proceed the interaction with follow-up questions of varying cognitive levels.

As can be noted, CA studies of ESL teacher questions are concerned with the interactional mechanism of classroom interaction initiated by teacher questions, whereas those of EFL teacher questions mainly deal with the interactional and/or pedagogical effects of certain types of teacher questions. Due to the emic stance or the insider's view taken by CA researchers, such studies seem to be less vulnerable than IA and DA studies in terms of validity and reliability. Nevertheless, the focus of CA studies is on the micro-context of classroom interaction, i.e., even more specific than the other two approaches. Among the CA studies mentioned above, only Yang Lifang (2015) related the patterns of teacher questions to the development of critical thinking, one of the major objectives of the course. To put it in a nutshell, as with IA and DA researchers, CA researchers have scarcely paid attention to how teacher questions serve the overarching objectives of a lesson, a unit, a course or a curriculum.

The three streams of research on teacher questions can be summarized as shown in Table 2-7. All the three approaches focus on the specific roles played by individual questions in specific contexts of classroom interaction. IA researchers are interested in the quantity and quality of student utterances elicited by teacher questions; DA researchers are concerned with the pedagogical and/or interactional functions of teacher questions; and CA researchers are fond of the interactional organization of teacher-fronted Q-A interaction. Rarely have researchers submitting to any of the three approaches paid attention to how teacher questions contribute to the realization of instructional objectives of a broader scope, such as objectives of a lesson, a unit, a course or a curriculum.

Table 2-7 Summary of IA, DA and CA studies on teacher questions

Approaches	Units of analysis	Focuses
IA	Individual questions	Eliciting function
DA	Individual questions	Pedagogical and/or interactional functions
CA	Individual questions	Interactional organization of Q-A interaction

As EFL courses, unlike ESL courses, are loaded with multiple objectives, it is advisable to turn to educational studies on teacher questions for conceptual inspirations and practical solutions. As mentioned at the beginning of Section 2.1, unlike language teaching researchers, educational researchers are keenly interested in the cognitive processes in which teachers involve their students through their questions. For some time, the cognitive levels of individual questions were of primary concern and varieties of taxonomies of teacher questions were established in that respect. More recently, however, educational researchers have reiterated that educational objectives cannot be realized by individual questions of a certain cognitive level but rather by series or sequences of questions of different cognitive levels (Dantonio & Beisenherz, 2001; Good & Brophy, 2008; Marzano & Simms, 2014). These studies indicate that the units of planning and analysis should be extended from individual questions to questioning sequences.

2.3 Questioning sequences as units of planning and analysis

Numerous taxonomies of teacher questions have been established by educational researchers based on the cognitive dimension of Bloom's taxonomy of educational objectives (Marzano & Simms, 2014; Sadker, Sadker, & Zittleman, 2010; Walsh & Sattes, 2005). What is particularly worth noting since the entrance of the 21st century is the theoretical construct of 'questioning sequences' proposed by educational researchers as they have found it tricky to assign individual questions to certain cognitive levels and even more so to measure the correspondence between the cognitive level intended in a teacher question and the cognitive level manifested in a student response (Dantonio & Beisenherz, 2001; Good & Brophy, 2008; Marzano & Simms, 2014).

The term 'questioning sequences' has also been widely used by applied linguists. While questioning sequences in applied linguistic studies are sequences of IRF, i.e., stretches of interaction initiated by questions (Basturkmen, 2001; Lee, 2006; Lefstein, Snell, and Israeli, 2015), questioning sequences in educational research refer to sequences of questions designed and employed by a teacher for the realization of specific pedagogical goals. What follows is an overview of three different definitions of questioning sequences given by educational researchers followed by some implications derived therefrom for language teaching and research.

2.3.1 Questioning sequences as sequences of questions

Good and Brophy (2000/2003/2008), seeing the mixed findings about the effects of teacher questions of different cognitive levels, proposed that teachers "plan *sequences of questions* designed to help students develop connected understanding" (2008, p. 316; emphasis original). They advocated the use of two types of sequences to help students attain the intended understandings.

Sequences that begin with a higher-level question and then proceed through several lower-level follow-up questions are appropriate for purposes such as asking students to suggest possible applications of an idea and then probing for details about how these applications might work. However, sequences featuring a series of lower-level questions followed by a higher-level question would be appropriate for purposes such as calling students' attention to relevant facts and then stimulating them to integrate these facts and draw a conclusion.

(Good & Brophy, 2008, p. 316)

They suggested that teachers plan sequences of questions in advance and integrate them as units of instruction and that by so doing "the cognitive level of questions should take care of themselves" (Ibid., p. 317).

The four patterns of development of the cognitive levels of teacher questions proposed by Yang Lifang (2015), as reviewed in Section 2.2.3, can be deemed as an expansion of the patterns of questioning sequences proposed by Good and Brophy. Yang's study reveals that the wavy pattern, consisting of questions of varying cognitive levels, is most efficient in training students' critical thinking and hence lends support to the argument that questioning sequences are valid units for the planning and analysis of teacher questions.

2.3.2 Questioning sequences as a series of core and processing questions

Dantonio and Beisenherz (2001) used the term 'questioning sequences' to refer to "a series of cognitively focused questions combined with questions that assist students in clarifying, verifying, supporting, and redirecting their responses" (p. 37). They draw a distinction between core questions and processing questions. Core questions are those that "focus and direct the content and cognitive operation for classroom discourse" (p. 39). In other words, the use of core questions is for the purpose of engaging students in thinking about the content in question. Processing questions are those that "ask students to rethink their original responses in order to clarify, to verify, to support, or to personalize what they are saying" (p. 42). By definition, such questions are similar to what Long and Sato (1983) called echoic questions, such as comprehension checks and clarification requests. Whilst echoic questions are used to elicit longer student utterances or help students complete their utterances, processing questions are used to engage students in metacognitive processes (Dantonio & Beisenherz, 2001, p. 43).

As demonstrated in Table 2-8, the core questions and processing questions can be further divided into sub-types based on the specific goals they serve. The use of core questions, according to the authors, is more a matter of planning and they should be designed in accordance with educational objectives as well as students' needs. In respect of the design of core questions, Dantonio and Beisenherz (2001) held that teachers "carefully choose action verbs that connote cognitive operations, such as recalling, comparing, and determining causes and effects" (p. 39) in a way that they bear the following features:

(1) contain words that are easily understood by learners;
(2) are stated simply, without cluttering the question with additional questions or explanations;
(3) help students foucus on the content and
(4) identify the individual thinking operation students are to use in answering the question.
        (Dantonio, 1990, p.14; as cited in Dantonio & Beisenherz, 2001, p. 39)

Dantonio and Beisenherz also suggested that core questions be sequentially developed to scaffold students' thinking from a lower-order operation to higher ones. Below is a sequenced pattern of four core questions:

- Observing: What do you notice about the epic poem (the Shakespearean sonnet)?
- Recalling: What do you recall about the critical characteristics of each?
- Comparing: How are they alike?
- Contrasting: In what ways are they different?
        (Dantonio & Beisenherz, 2001, p. 41)

The use of processing questions, however, seems to be more a matter of teachers' online management in the process of instruction as they are questions mobilized by teachers to assist students' thinking stimulated by core questions based on students' performance in answering them. Dantonio and Beisenherz argued that processing questions can "bring out the beauty in student thinking" as they create opportunities for students to manage their own thinking:

> The more processing questions that are asked during the lesson, the greater the opportunities students have to elaborate on their ideas, rethink and qualify their responses, and trace their thinking.
>
> (Ibid., p. 172)

To summarize, Dantonio and Bersenherz's concept of questioning sequences involves the combination of core questions and processing questions. They suggested that teachers should not only design core questions with clear content focus and well-intended cognitive operation before class, but also have a storage of processing questions ready to be used in class to help bring about the cognitive operation intended in the core questions.

Table 2-8 Core questions and processing questions (Dantonio & Beisenherz, 2001)

Types	Sub-types and Examples
Core questions	Collecting strategies: used to help collect details • Observing questions: *What do you notice about ...?* • Recalling questions: *What do you remember about ...?*
	Bridging strategies: used to help identify relationships • Comparing questions: *What similarities are there between ... and ... ?* • Contrasting questions: *What differences are there between ... and ... ?* • Grouping questions: *In what ways do these items go together?*
	Anchoring strategies: used to help construct concepts • Labeling questions: *What can we call ...?* • Classifying questions: *How can we classify ...?*

Continued

Types	Sub-types and Examples
Processing questions	• Refocusing questions: refocusing off-focus response. *What are you noticing that makes you say the rose is pretty?* • Clarifying questions: defining and using additional or more precise language to clarify a student's response. *What do you mean by ...?* *How can you state that in other words?* • Verifying questions: verifying details for accuracy. *How do you know ...?* *In what way is ... like ...?* • Narrow focusing questions: narrowing the focus of a student's response. *What do you think about ...?* • Supporting questions: providing evidence for one's ideas or reasons for thinking *What makes you think that ...?* *How can you make sure that ... is ...?* • Redirecting questions: attaining more student participation. *What else can you tell me about ...?* *Who else notices something about ...?*

2.3.3 Questioning sequences as the framework for a unit

Noting the deficiencies in classifying questions in view of Bloom's taxonomy of educational objectives, which was intended to guide curriculum design and assessment, Marzano and Simms (2014) put forth a new concept of 'questioning sequences' which they claimed to be "a unique approach" (p. 12). Drawing upon previous studies, especially the work of Good and Brophy (2003) and that of Dantonio and Beisenherz (2001), they established a model of questioning sequences which takes account of both the cognitive level and the content focus of questions. Such an endeavor was intended to guide teachers' design of questions to realize certain educational objectives at different phases of instruction:

> We regard a questioning sequence as a series of questions or prompts that ask students to articulate details about the content, identify characteristics of content-related categories, generate elaborations about the content, and provide evidence and support for those elaborations. The questioning sequence

concept presented here is specifically designed to guide students through the process of making a claim by collecting information, categorizing it, drawing a conclusion, and providing evidence to support it.

(Marzano & Simms, 2014, p. 12)

According to Marzano and Simms, a question taxonomy should center around the content and questions should be designed in sequences with the intention to "guide students through the thinking necessary to generate deep understanding of the content and its implications" (p.24). Thus, the model they built, consisting of four phases as demonstrated in Figure 2-1, is meant to provide "a structure that teachers can use to plan and implement effective questioning sequences in their classrooms", and "embraces all 'levels' of questions, acknowledging that each has its proper place and is very powerful when used in the right way at the right time" (p.31).

Marzano and Simms (2014) suggested that questioning sequences of such be based on a common theme and goal derived from the instructional objectives of a unit, which are in turn derived from a set of standards. They illustrated this point with a questioning sequence designed for the teaching of 'end punctuation' in accordance with the standards set by the Common Core State Standards for English language arts. As can be seen in Table 2-9, the sequence begins with detail questions that ask students about pertinent details about the use of end punctuation. In the second phase, questions are asked about a logical category wherein end punctuation falls, that is, about the similarities and differences between end punctuation and other types of punctuation. After that, elaboration questions are asked to set students thinking about the reason for a certain phenomenon. The final phase of the sequence requires students to support their elaborations with evidence.

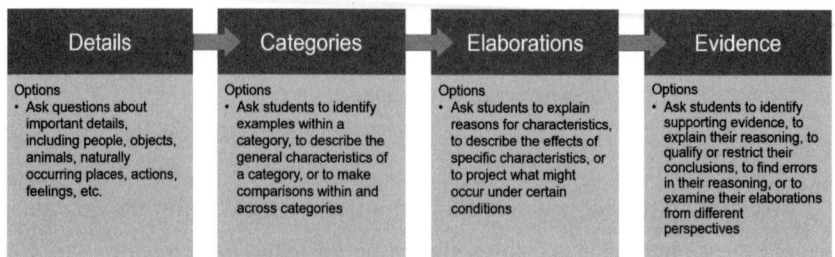

**Figure 2-1 Marzano and Simms' model of questioning sequences
(Adapted from Marzano & Simms, 2014, p. 30)**

Table 2-9   A questioning sequence on the use of end punctuation (Marzano & Simms, 2014)

Phases	Questions
Details	*When is it appropriate to use a question mark?* *When is it appropriate to use a period?* *What type of end punctuation would you use in each of the following sentences?* • I think we can go now • Doesn't anybody want to come with me • Look what I can do • I wonder how old he is
Categories	*What are some other types of punctuation that help us know when a sentence is over?* *How is a semicolon different from a period in terms of what it is telling the reader?*
Elaboration	*Why do you think we tend to see relatively few colons (compared to periods or question marks) used in writing?*
Evidence	*How do you know that your answer is accurate?*

After demonstrating the use of questioning sequences with vignettes of lessons, Marzano and Simms (2014) pointed out that the model can be used flexibly within a phase of a lesson, across phases within a lesson, and even across lessons as well. Within each phase, varieties of forms of questions can be selected. Within a lesson, varieties of questioning sequences can be selected. More than that, a questioning sequence can span within a lesson as well as across multiple lessons.

Marzano and Simms' (2014) model of questioning sequences is to be drawn upon in the current study because it fits well with the research purpose, i.e., to investigate how teacher question can be designed and implemented so as to realize the instructional objectives of a lesson, unit, course or curriculum. More often than not, an instructional objective is realized through the use of a series of questions rather than a single question. It is thus maintained that when planning for classroom instruction, teachers should design their questions as questioning sequences relating to the specified instructional objectives, and when examining or evaluating teacher questions, researchers should identify the sequences of questions relating to the specified objectives and make judgments about the extent to which the objectives have been realized by the sequences of questions.

2.4 Learning space as the measure of questioning sequences

If the units of planning and analysis of teacher questions are questioning sequences rather than individual questions, then what are the criteria to evaluate the quality or efficiency of questioning sequences? A number of criteria for quality teacher questions have been established both for content area or subject matter classrooms (e.g., Walsh & Sattes, 2005) and for language classrooms (e.g., Lockhart and Richards, 1996). However, they are all focused on individual questions.

As a questioning sequence is comprised of a series of questions used for a certain instructional objective within one phase and across different phases of instruction, it is then worthwhile to turn to the concept of 'the space of learning' from the variation theory of learning put forth by the Swedish educational scholar Ference Marton (Marton and Booth, 1997; Marton & Tsui, 2004; Marton, 2015). What is essential in the space of learning is that it lies in the space for learners to experience variation in the object of learning (Marton's term for educational objectives) and that it is constituted linguistically in classroom interaction (Marton & Tsui, 2004, p. ix). Simply put, the space of learning bridges classroom discourse and educational objectives. It is thus maintained that the space of learning can be used as the measure of questioning sequences, i.e., to guide teachers to design and implement sequences of questions that can meet the specified instructional objectives.

Notably, a similar term, 'the space for learning', was invented by Steve Walsh (2006, 2011), from a socio-cognitive perspective of learning, to refer to the affordance of opportunities for learners to participate in classroom interaction. Though rooted in different theories of learning, the two concepts are complementary in nature. Additionally, in research on classroom discourse of both content area and language classrooms, the term 'learning space' has been widely used. Hence, the researcher chooses to use learning space, the space of learning and the space for learning interchangeably. Before tapping into what learning space is, it is necessary to turn to what learning is from a variation perspective.

2.4.1 Learning as the experience of variation

Marton and associates investigated what learning is from an internal perspective, i.e., from the perspective of the learners, and found that learning takes place when the learner appropriates the object of learning in a way that is qualitatively different from his/her previous experience. In correspondence with such observation, they put forward the variation theory of learning and defined learning as the learner's "coming to experience the world, or aspects of the world, in particular ways", and proposed that research on learning be aimed at seeking "the variation in ways people experience situations and phenomena in their worlds" (Marton & Booth, 1997, p. vii). They argued that learning from the variation perspective is not the acquisition of knowledge about the world which proceeds from simpler to more complex and advanced forms, but the change in the ways of experiencing or seeing a situation or phenomenon "from an undifferentiated and poorly integrated understanding of the whole to an increased differentiation and integration of the whole and its parts" (Ibid., p. viii).

Reviewing studies conducted to explore variation in ways of learning, Marton and associates argued that the qualitatively different ways of learning form a hierarchy of variation consisting of two dimensions: a temporal dimension and a dimension of depth. They identified three different phases of overall experience of learning for the dimension of temporal variation: (1) acquiring, (2) knowing, and (3) exploiting or making use of. For the depth dimension, they took account of three intertwined aspects, namely, the agency of learning (i.e., learning initiated by the teacher of the learner him/herself), the act of learning (i.e., memorizing and understanding), and the object of learning (i.e., words, meaning and phenomenon), and hence identified four levels of learning: (1) memorizing (words), (2) memorizing (meaning), (3) understanding (meaning), and (4) understanding (phenomenon). Figure 2-2 visualizes the hierarchical variation in the ways of learning.

Ways of experiencing learning	Temporal facet		
	acquiring	knowing	making use of
committing to memory (words)	memorizing (words)	remembering (words)	reproducing (words)
committing to memory (meaning)	memorizing (meaning)	remembering (meaning)	reproducing (meaning)
understanding (meaning)	gaining understanding (meaning)	having understanding (meaning)	being able to do something being able to do something differently being able to do something different
understanding (phenomenon)	gaining understanding (phenomenon)	having understanding (phenomenon)	relating

Figure 2-2 The outcome space of learning
[Reproduced from Marton & Booth (1997, p. 43)]

Marton and Booth pointed out that from an individual perspective, individual learners' experience of learning is discontinuous, i.e., falling within particular cells in the outcome space, whereas from a collective perspective, the experience of learning is continuous, i.e., forming a continuum from the surface approach to the deep to learning as demonstrated in the three temporal aspects. They elaborated the logical continuum from three different perspectives: in terms of function, in terms of structure, and in terms of mechanism. Functionally, memorization and understanding are in parallel, understanding stemming from memorization on the one hand and understanding replacing memorization on the other. Structurally, learning proceeds from reproducing merely words to 'relating' to or coping with new situations on the basis of what has been learned. In terms of mechanism, transformation of learning takes place in connection with the change in the demands of learning, or the actual tasks in which learners are involved. In view of these observations, they stated that the approach to learning adopted by an individual in a particular situation is "a combination of the ways in which that person experiences learning and the way he or she experiences the situation" (p. 47).

In respect of pedagogy, Marton and Booth suggested that tasks or activities be designed and implemented to enrich learners' 'awareness' of the variation in the ways of learning, or "the totality of all experiences" (p. 108). In the final chapter titled *A Pedagogy of Awareness*, they established two principles of teaching to experience: 1) Building the relevance structure; 2) The architecture of variation. The first principle indicates that the teacher should stage situations for learning, i.e., designing stages of instruction relating to "what is aimed, what it demands, and where it will lead" (p. 180), which echoes Marzano and Simms' (2014) concept of 'questioning sequences' as reviewed in Section 2.3. The second principle indicates that the teacher should bring about hierarchical variation in the ways in which students experience 'the object of learning' (Marton & Booth, 1997, p. 185), a concept to be explicated as follows.

2.4.2 The object of learning

The verb "to learn", as depicted by Marton and associates, has two objects: the direct object and the indirect object (Marton & Booth, 1997, p. 84; Marton, Runesson, & Tsui, 2004, p. 4; Marton, 2015, p. 22). The direct object is the content that is to be learned, and the indirect object is the capability the learner needs to master or the act that is to be carried out on the direct object of learning. Marton et al. (2004) pointed out that whereas learners usually focus on the specific aspect of learning, i.e., the content to be learned, teachers should focus on both what the learners is trying to learn and the way in which they act upon what they are trying to learn (p. 4). Marton (2015, p. 22) suggested that educational objectives (as an equivalent to instructional objectives, learning targets, learning goals, learning outcomes or any other terms of the like) be formulated in accordance with the following formula:

act + content = educational objective

To further illustrate the use of the above formula, Marton (2015) exemplified with a list of acts and another list of contents which could be combined to formulate educational objectives. Table 2-10 below recaptures Marton's discussion to that end. Marton also noted that educational objectives formulated in the aforementioned manner can be qualified by additional expressions, such as 'independently', 'in detail', 'with the aid of', 'in writing', and so on, to specify the way the learners are expected to deal with the object of learning in question.

Table 2-10 Formulating educational objectives by combining acts and contents

Acts	Contents	Educational objectives
recall interpret explain describe in one's own words ...	Newton's laws of motion World War II pricing baroque music narrative ...	Using Newton's laws, when they apply, for solving problems Explaining the relationship between WWI and WWII in writing Distinguishing between different styles of music Describing the same event as a narrative and as a documentary report

Marton's formula of educational objectives or objects of learning has rich implications for the design and evaluation of teacher questions. Likewise, a teacher can design a question by assembling the act and the content intended to be learned, and a researcher can evaluate a question by examining the act and the content demonstrated in the question.

Another noteworthy point brought by Marton and colleagues to the issue under discussion is that there are three different perspectives of the object of learning (Marton et al., 2004, p. 4):

- the *intended* object of learning, i.e., what should be learned from the teacher's perspective,
- the *enacted* object of learning, i.e., what can be possibly learned from the researcher's perspective, and
- the *lived* object of learning, i.e., what is actually learned from the learner's perspective.

The educational or instructional objectives are 'the intended objects of learning' as they are of direct concern to teachers. What is of primary interest to the researcher is what is possible to learn on the part of the learners in an actual setting, because it is the enacted object of learning that constitutes 'the space of learning' (Marton & Tsui, 2004, Preface). From the learner's perspective, however, what is of decisive importance is what they actually learn, or the change in the way in which they experience the object of learning. The distinction between the three has been widely adopted by researchers conducting phenomenographic studies on learning which are characterized by the comparison of the object of learning from the three perspectives to evaluate or testify the effectiveness of certain pedagogical treatments (e.g., Maybee et al., 2016; Lam, 2013; Lam & Tsui, 2013).

2.4.3 The critical aspects of the object of learning

As mentioned earlier, learning consists in the change in the way of experiencing a certain object of learning, and the qualitatively different ways of experiencing an object of learning are hierarchically ordered. Marton and colleagues attributed the qualitatively different ways of learning to the learners' attention being directed to or focused on different aspects of the object of learning (Marton & Booth, 1997, p. 86; Marton et al., 2004, p. 9; Marton, 2015, p. 23). Accordingly, to ensure that learning takes place in an educational setting, the teacher needs to enable the learners to discern the critical or necessary aspects of the object of learning from non-critical or unnecessary aspects.

Critical aspects, in Marton's definition, are those aspects of the object of learning that the learner has to but is not yet able to notice in reference to the educational objectives (Marton, 2015, p. 26). For instance, there are three critical aspects of numbers: the ordinal property, the cardinal property, and being wholes that can be divided into parts. Hence, to successfully learn numbers, the learner has to appropriate all the three aspects. Another example is the learning of words, which consists in the learner's discernment and awareness of the critical aspects of form, meaning and pronunciation. It goes naturally that the primary task for the teacher is to identify the critical aspects of the object of learning and to provide the necessary conditions for appropriating these aspects.

However, as noted by Marton, critical aspects are not easy to discover and "have to be searched for and found" (Ibid.) for the reason that the critical aspects of learning something vary not only from situation to situation but also from individual to individual. A good case in point is Dahlgren's (1979 study, as cited in Pang & Ki, 2016), on how primary school students of different grades perceive price of market economy in qualitatively different ways:

(A) Price is determined by the relationship between the supply of and demand for a commodity.
(B) Price is determined by the value of a commodity or the accumulated value of its constituents.
(C) Price is determined by other properties of the commodity, such as its taste, shape, and size.

(Pang & Ki, 2016, p. 325)

The three conceptualizations of price identified by the participant students can be distinguished in terms of the critical aspects they attended to. Conception C foregrounds only the features of the product and disregards the market system. Whilst Conception B presumes the supply of the market system as the critical feature, Conception A attends to both supply and demand.

The discernment of critical aspects is a matter of relativity, as put in

Marton's (2015, p. 27) words: "What is critical is relative to the object of learning, and relative to the learners as well." In other words, the primary task for the teacher is not simply identify the critical aspects in their own eyes but the critical aspects in the eyes of particular learners. However, the concept of critical aspects, as Pang and Ki (2016) revisited, has been understood in a variety of problematic ways amongst researchers and practitioners. Many teachers have taken it as what is *intended* to be learned as prescribed in a curriculum, or simply as perceived by teachers themselves. They reiterated that critical aspects are relational in nature and should be defined "in relation to the phenomenon in question as experienced by learners rather than in relation to what is deemed critical in the curriculum or subject line" (Pang & Ki, 2016, p. 328). That means, to identify what are the critical aspects of an object of learning, teachers should connect the particular critical aspects available from a disciplinary perspective to the possible ways in which the object of learning could be experienced by learners.

In all, the essence of learning lies in the discernment of the critical aspects and the necessary conditions for the discernment rests with learners' awareness of variation of the critical aspects with the non-critical aspects held invariant.

2.4.4 Ways to create the space of learning

In light of the figure-ground and part-whole relationships that are external and internal to the object of learning (Marton & Booth, 1997, pp. 86-87), Marton, Runesson and Tsui (2004, p. 21) points out that creating a space means "opening up a dimension of variation (as compared to the taken-for-granted nature of the absence of variation)", indicating that the object of learning has to be separated from its context or environment and that certain necessary aspects have to be discerned from others.

Marton and colleaguges (Ibid., pp. 16-17) identified four patterns of variation—contrast, generalization, separation and fusion—that can be generally applied to understanding what is possible to learn in a certain learning situation.

- *Contrast* refers to comparing the object of learning with something else, i.e., something that is not the object of learning. For instance, a person cannot understand poetry academic essays without knowing other styles of writing.
- *Generalization* indicates abstracting the same aspect from various instances. For example, a person can only identify what color means by experiencing different colors of different colored objects.
- *Separation* means to discern a certain aspect of the object of learning, and one has to separate this aspect that varies from other aspects that remain invariant. In other words, the critical aspect must be focally attended to while other aspects sink to the background. The learning of Chinese characters is a good case in point as demonstrated in Lam and Tsui's (2013) study which indicated that the learning of constituent components results from varying the semantic radicals while keeping other aspects invariant.
- *Fusion* refers to the simultaneous experience of several critical aspects of a certain object of learning. For example, though the three critical aspects (form, meaning and pronunciation) are separated analytically, one cannot successfully learn the word if he or she cannot experience all the three aspects at the same time.

To oversimplify it, what the four patterns of variation boil down to is the learner's attention being focused on what varies and what is invariant. As stated in Marton et al. (2004, p. 18), the four patterns are identified in relevant empirical studies departing from the variation theory of learning. Hence they can be drawn upon by teachers in pedagogical practice. Marton (2015) drew a clearer picture of what the teacher needs to do to help make learning possible, i.e., to create 'the space of learning':

- through the way instances (examples, problems, illustrations, etc.) are combined,
- through the way the learner's attention is focused on certain aspects of certain instances, but not on others and

- through the way certain aspects of the same instance are changed or remain unchanged.

(Marton, 2015, p. 166)

Marton and associates suggested that lessons be designed and executed, and classroom discourse be adapted and improved, to create the space for learners to discern such critical aspects and experience the variation of them. Marton and colleagues underscored the role of classroom discourse in creating the necessary conditions for learning to happen for the reason that the space of learning is linguistically constituted:

[L]anguage plays a central role in learning, and understanding how the learning experience is being constituted by language is crucial to understanding how different ways of experiencing the object of learning are being brought about in the classroom.

(Marton, Runesson & Tsui, 2004, p. 25)

They gave special weight to teacher questions and demonstrated with an entire chapter on how different teacher questions could draw students' focal attention to different aspects of the object of learning. That is to say, it is essential for teachers to design questions and organize Q-A interaction in a way to focus students' attention on certain critical aspects of the object of learning. Tsui et al. (2004), in the chapter devoted to teacher questions and the space of learning, resorted to conversation analysis to evaluate the extent to which teacher questions opened up or reduced the space of learning in two learning studies where physics lessons and English lessons were examined.

In sum, according to the variation theory of learning, learning lies in the change in the way one experiences something, the qualitatively different ways of learning are hierarchically ordered, and the qualitative differences result from the different aspects being attended to, which are either critical or not so. These three statements, indicating the necessary conditions for the experience of variation of critical aspects of the object of learning, are the theoretical departure point of the space of learning. To create the space of learning for a certain object of learning, the teacher needs to be aware of the different ways of learning it, and strive to enrich his or her students' experience of learning it through classroom discourse, especially the use of questions, to draw their focal attention to the critical aspects in question.

Returning to the issue of questioning sequences, the quality of a sequence of questions lies in whether it offers the necessary conditions for the students to experience the variation of the critical aspect of either the indirect act or the direct content of the object of learning. In other words, learning space can be exploited by researchers, and practitioners as well, to measure the effectiveness or efficiency of questioning sequences. It is in view of such that a conceptual framework is established for the current study.

2.5 Questioning sequences for the extension of L2 learning space

The two theoretical constructs reviewed above, questioning sequences and learning space, constitute the theoretical departure point of the AR study. The construct of questioning sequences indicates that teacher questions should be designed, applied and examined as sequences of questions relating to the specified instructional objectives, or the objects of learning as referred to by Marton and followers; and the construct of learning space implicates that the efficiency or effectiveness of questioning sequences rests with whether they open up the space for the experience of variation of the critical aspects of the objects of learning. As the current study involves language teacher questions, what follows naturally then is the delineation of the objects of learning of a language course.

2.5.1 The objects of learning of a language course

Paul Nation (1996; 2007; 2010; Nation & Macalister, 2010, Chapter 4) put forward a framework consisting of four strands to describe instructed L2 learning: meaning-focused input, language-focused learning, meaning-focused output, and fluency development, which can be represented as follows:

- Meaning-focused input:
  Learning through listening and reading where the learner' attention is on the ideas and messages conveyed by the language.
- Language-focused learning:
  Learning through deliberate attention to language items and language features, including attention to the sounds and spelling of the language, direct vocabulary study, grammar exercises and explanation, and discourse features.
- Meaning-focused output:
  Learning through speaking and writing where the learners' attention is on conveying ideas and messages to another person.
- Fluency development:
  Developing fluent use of known language items and features over the four skills of listening, speaking, reading and writing.

As noted by Macalister (2016), the four strands in Nation's framework should not be confused with the skills of reading, listening, speaking and writing, for the development of fluency occurs across all the four skills. In light of the caveat made by Macalister, fluency development could be understood as the ultimate goal of the other three strands of learning, though both Nation (1996) and Macalister (2016) suggested that fluency development activities be distinct from activities of the other three strands.

As mentioned earlier, in Marton and Tsui's (2004) view, an object of learning comprises two aspects: the general and the specific. The general aspect is the capability of doing something, or the acts of learning, such as remembering, interpreting, or evaluating; the specific aspect of an object of learning is the thing or subject on which an act of learning is carried out; messages conveyed in a text, the language items used to convey those messages, and the learner's own ideas and messages to be conveyed, would be instances of the specific aspect of learning object in the case of language learning.

Seeing this light, each of the three strands of language learning can be delineated as comprising a specific aspect of what is to be acted upon and a general aspect of what act is to be carried out on the specific aspect. For the moment, suffice it to call the general aspects involved in the three strands of language learning *comprehending*, *learning* and *producing*, and the specific aspects *input*, *language* and *output*. What is worthy of note at this point is that the three strands of language learning do not stand alone but rather they could overlap. Accordingly, the objects of language learning can be visualized by the Venn diagram in Figure 2-3.

As noted by Nation (1996), the different strands of a language course should be balanced even though different approaches could be employed to help with the development of the different strands. Nevertheless, in actual practice, teachers often go to extremes. Those who have a communicative focus usually discourage form-focused learning; and those who elect to focus on formal features tend to ignore the use of language features to comprehend and produce authentic messages. From a variation point of view, opportunities should be afforded in classroom instruction for students to experience all the three strands of language learning.

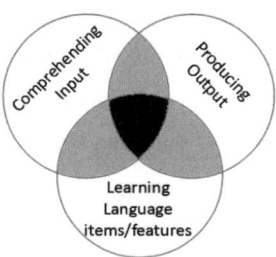

Figure 2-3 Venn diagram of L2 objects of learning

Nation (2007) referred to teaching that balances the four strands as a 'commonsense approach' and justified it with the time-on-task principle which, as Nation argued, takes account of the ways in which language learning is distinct from other kinds of learning. There are two factors underlying the time-on-task principle: the quality of the activity and the quantity of the activity, indicating that an activity should be specifically focused and only quantities of such activities can lead to the development of fluency. The time-on-task principle can be rephrased from the perspective of the variation theory of learning, especially in terms of the three key concepts of discernment, awareness and simultaneity: a quality language learning activity must be one that helps the learner discern the critical aspect of the object of learning, be it the comprehension of a textual message, the learning of a language feature, or the production of a personal message; and the learner's engagement in quantities of such activities where different instances are afforded enables him or her to be simultaneously aware of the aspect(s) critical for the development of fluency.

Input comprehension, output production and form- or language-focused learning are far from capturing the variation in the ways of language learning. As mentioned earlier, according to Marton and Booth (1997), though we may not have exhaustively explored all the possible ways of learning, the number of qualitatively different ways is limited and they are hierarchically ordered (See Figure 2-2 in Section 2.4.1.1). The hierarchical variation of language learning experiences can be illuminated by Manzo and Manzo's (1993; as cited in Truscott, 1994, p. 708) definition of reading as the act of 1) reading the lines, 2) reading between the lines, and 3) reading beyond the lines simultaneously. These three levels of reading are placed in a hierarchical order as much as are the different ways of learning in Marton and Booth's (1997, p. 43) presentation of the outcome space of learning in the temporal dimension of variation: acquiring (words or meaning), knowing (words or meaning), and relating to one's previous experience. On top of this, successful reading is the simultaneous experience of the three levels which corroborates Marton and colleagues' concept of simultaneous awareness. It is suggested that this three-tiered hierarchical framework of reading could be expanded to describe all the three strands of a language course.

Content		Act	
Textual message	Literal understanding	Interpreting	Evaluating
Language features	Recognizing	Categorizing	Appreciating
Personal response	Articulating	Elaborating	Justifying

Figure 2-4　The outcome space of L2 learning

Accordingly, a temporary framework of the outcome space of L2 learning can be devised as shown in Figure 2-4. The framework is inspired by several scholars' work on language curriculum, especially studies by Qin Xiubai (2010), Qu Weiguo (2016) and Diana Freeman (2014) on teacher questions. All the aforementioned scholars have voiced their views on the hierarchical variation in a language curriculum, which lends support to dividing the strand of input comprehension into literal understanding, interpreting and evaluating. It can be considered as an expansion of Manzo and Manzo's (1993) definition of reading. What follows is the exposition of the division of the other two strands.

In an article on the teaching of Integrated College English in terms of 'reading critically', Qin Xiubai and colleagues (2010) wrote:

> Critical thinking is a mental process of integrating, discerning, analyzing, evaluating and reconstructing information. For instance, when explaining words used in the text, the teacher should go beyond having students grasp the meaning of words, but rather elicit them to think about such questions as "Why does the author select this word instead of others?", "What particular meaning does this word convey in the context?", "Can it be replaced by another expression?", and "What effect would the replacement bring about?". When it comes to the instruction of a paragraph, the teacher should not merely induce students to grasp its content, but have them think about such questions as "What question(s) has this paragraph answered?", "What function does it play in the whole text?", "Is it semantically coherent?", "Why does the author write it in this way instead of others?", "Could it be written alternatively?" and "How can it be improved?"
>
> (Qin et al., 2010, p. 85; translated by the researcher)

Qu Weiguo (2016) voiced the view that instruction on the language used in a text should be aimed at grasping the meta-textual knowledge:

> Instruction of the text should not be aimed at understanding or acquiring the messages conveyed in the text but rather at grasping the meta-textual knowledge about how the author successfully conveyed his messages.
>
> (Qu Weiguo, 2016, p. 3; translated by the researcher)

What Qu Weiguo (2016) suggested for the instruction of meta-textual knowledge is inducing students' thoughts into the in-depth and minute details of the text by asking such questions as: Why a particular word is used instead of any of its synonyms?

The two scholars' views are congruent on the ultimate goal of language-focused learning, i.e., appreciation of the language features or items. However, appreciation would not be possible without the precondition of basic language knowledge. To appreciate the use of a particular word instead of other expressions, for example, one has to, first of all, know the particular word, including its pronunciation, form and meaning, and next to it, know how it is associated with other expressions, that is how they are similar to and different from each other. The three-tiered hierarchical variation of language-focused learning is derived from such reasoning.

As mentioned earlier, it is hard to separate the three strands of learning objects from each other because they are virtually intertwined or overlapping. To display one's understanding of the content or learning of language features, of whatever level, one has to produce output. However, for the sake of analytical convenience, the third strand is restricted to the production of personal feelings and/or thoughts stimulated by or related to the content of the input. That is why it is labeled as 'personal response'. In Diana Freeman's (2014) framework of ESL textbook questions, as referred to earlier in Section 2.1.3, there is a type of affect questions divided into two sub-types: personal response and evaluation. Personal response questions are those that require the reader to offer their personal reaction to the text in terms of likes/dislikes, what they found funny, surprising, etc. Evaluation questions are those that require the reader to make a judgement or assessment of the text/information according to some understood criteria with a reasoned justification. Freeman suggested that these two sub-types are not hierarchical. However, it could be argued that whatever response one makes, it falls within any of the following three hierarchical levels:

- Articulation: the mere act of speaking out or writing down a feeling or thought

- Elaboration: the act of developing or expanding the response with specific details
- Justification: the act of justifying or qualifying the response with sound reasoning

In the case of teacher-student Q-A interaction aimed to elicit personal response to a certain topic or issue, if the teacher is not satisfied with a certain student's simply articulating a feeling or thought, he/she could probe the student to elaborate or expand the response, and yet if the teacher is not contented with the reasoning or logic in the further elaborated response, he/she could opt to challenge the student for further evidence or sound reasoning.

2.5.2 Questioning sequences in the light of L2 learning space

Marton and Booth (1997) emphasized the hierarchical structure of variation in the ways of learning or experiencing something and suggested that in pedagogical practice, the teacher should adhere to two principles: 1) building the relevance structure through staged and interlinked instructional design and 2) bringing about the architecture of variation by making students realize that there are qualitatively different ways of experiencing a certain object of learning. However, in Marton and colleague's definition of the space of learning in *Classroom Discourse and the Space of Learning*, they did not give due weight to these two principles and focused more on instruction that brings about one particular way of experiencing a certain object of learning, that is, the way that draws students' focal attention or awareness to the critical aspect of the object.

Whilst Marton and associates' discussion on variation provides a macro picture of the differentiation between successful and less successful ways of learning, their definition of the space of learning in terms of discernment and simultaneous awareness of what is critical gives a microscopic insight into the essence of experiencing specific leaning objects. In other words, variation in Marton's view of learning can be understood in two senses: the macro sense referring to the qualitatively different ways of learning; and the micro sense referring to the discernment of critical aspects that vary against the background of noncritical ones.

In view of the particularity of language learning, which involves the balance of different strands of learning objects, it is suggested in the current study that both the macro and micro senses of variation be taken into consideration in defining L2 learning space: the opportunities offered by the teacher for students not only to be aware of the different strands of language learning but also to experience what is critical of any object of learning. The first half of the definition indicates that qualitatively different ways arise out of a situation of L2 learning (be it of a lesson, a unit, or a course), and the teacher should design and implement the instruction so that students can be aware of other ways instead of taking their own way of learning for granted. The second half of the definition concerns the learning of a specific object in terms of its critical aspect(s).

Both senses of variation are highlighted in the definition in that in actual instructional settings, one strand of language learning is often skewed over the others and that activities or tasks are often found to be disoriented or ineffective due to the lack of a well defined object of learning or a critical aspect of the object. In other words, the space for learning a specific object, is created by focusing students' attention to the critical aspect, whereas the space for learning in general is extended by making students aware of the different ways to experience learning. The framework of the outcome space of L2 objects of learning can serve as a model for the intended, enacted, or lived objects of learning of an L2 course. As advocated by Marton and colleagues, the focus of classroom instruction should be on the enacted objects of learning, which constitute the space of learning, and the key in the creation of the space of learning lies in the provision of opportunities for the students to experience variation in the critical aspects of the object of learning. Hence the concept of questioning sequences could be modified so that a questioning sequence comprises not only questions of varying levels of cognitive demand relating to a certain content focus but also questions of varying content focus relating to a certain cognitive act.

Drawing upon the hierarchical outcome space of L2 learning as displayed in Figure 2-4, a taxonomy of L2 teacher questions can be established as demonstrated in Table 2-11. The taxonomy comprises two dimensions, one of content focus consisting of three aspects, and the other cognitive demand consisting of three levels.

Table 2-11 An alternative taxonomy of L2 teacher questions

Focus	Level 1	Level 2	Level 3
Comprehension questions	Literal understanding (CQ1)	Interpreting (CQ2)	Evaluating (CQ3)
Language questions	Recognizing (LQ1)	Categorizing (LQ2)	Appreciating (LQ3)
Response questions	Articulating (RQ1)	Elaborating (RQ2)	Justifying (RQ3)

Comprehension questions are aimed at eliciting students' answers to questions concerning the comprehension of certain textual messages. Literal understanding questions (CQ1) concern the understanding or identification of specific details; interpreting questions (CQ2) involve making inferences or interpretations about certain specific details; and evaluating questions (CQ3) require students to evaluate the ideas conveyed in a text against some established criteria.

Language questions deal with the learning of language items or features. Recognizing questions (LQ1) are asked to check whether the students can recognize certain language items or features; categorizing questions (LQ2) involve the students in distinguishing or characterizing a language item or feature from another; and appreciating questions (LQ3) require the students to tell the reason why a certain language item or feature is used in a textual context.

Response questions are intended to involve the students in expressing their own affects and/or thoughts relating to certain issues in a text. Articulating questions (RQ1) engage the students in simply uttering their feelings and/or thoughts without giving any reasons; elaborating questions

(RQ2) involve the students in giving reasons for their feelings and/or thoughts about a certain issue; and justifying questions (RQ3) are asked to challenge the students about their reasoning.

The three levels of questions for each aspect of content focus form a hierarchy. In other words, for instance, the cognitive act involved in a CQ3 preconditions the cognitive act involved in a CQ2 which preconditions the cognitive act involved in CQ1. However, in practice, especially in the instruction of text-based courses, the text is regarded as an integrated whole or a global object of learning, and questions of all the three aspects and all the three levels may be asked depending on the identified objects of learning.

Thus, varieties of questioning sequences can be formulated as demonstrated in Figure 2-5. A questioning sequence can be made of a series of questions of any cognitive level concerning any aspect of content focus and followed by any another question. Additionally, a questioning sequence can be applied across different phases of instruction, and even across different units. Whether a question can be regarded as a component of a questioning sequence relies upon the identified object of learning, comprising the two aspects of content and act. If the question is applied to serve or assist the learning of the identified object, then it counts as one constituent of the sequence.

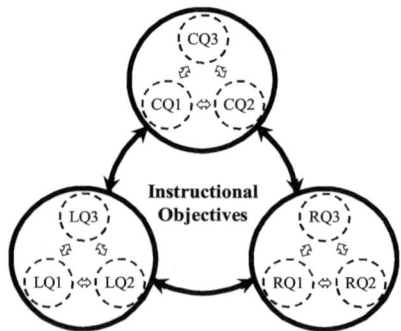

Figure 2-5　A model of questioning sequences in L2 classes

As advised by Paul Nation in his account of the 'four strands' of language curriculum (Nation, 1996; 2007; 2010; Nation & Macalister,

2010), a language course should be balanced in the four strands of meaning-focused input, meaning-focused output, language-focused learning and the development of fluency, so should be teacher questions designed and implemented in consideration of the three content orientations of the three cognitive levels to ensure that the students can have a rich and balanced experience of a course. Nevertheless, as for courses with specifically designated orientations or objectives, such as a course aimed at training students' oral presentation skills or fast reading skills, the intended objects of learning may be skewed towards some particular strand(s) over the others and so will be the questioning sequences. No matter what courses are to be taught and learned, regardless of the composition of their objectives, it is advisable that teacher questions be designed and sequentially implemented in close correspondence with the identified objectives of learning so as to maximize the space of learning.

2.6 Summary

Existing taxonomies of teacher questions are mainly focused on the forms and functions of individual questions in specific contexts of classroom interaction, with little attention paid to instructional objectives beyond the local level. Previous studies on language teacher questions have cast scarce attention to the alignment of teacher questions to instructional objectives of a lesson, unit, course or curriculum. The theoretical constructs of questioning sequences and learning space proposed by educational researchers, however, can be drawn upon to examine how teacher questions can be designed and implemented to serve that purpose. It is maintained that questioning sequences should be designed and applied so as to provide students with the necessary conditions to experience variation in the two dimensions of the objects of learning, i.e., content focus and cognitive demand.

Chapter 3 Methodology

This chapter is comprised of six sections. The first section gives a detailed account of the preliminary work which paved the way for the upcoming AR. The second section explicates the choice of an AR design. The third section sketches the research questions, the participants and the procedures of the AR. The fourth section presents the methods and instruments of data collection and analysis. The last section addresses the validity concerns and ethical issues.

3.1 Preliminary work

The study was conducted with a class of English major sophomores at a provincial medical university where the researcher was assigned to teach the intensive reading course. Upon publication of the teaching assignments, the researcher set out to do some preliminary investigations about the class.

3.1.1 Context

3.1.1.1 The setting

The research was situated in an English majors' intensive reading class offered by the department of foreign languages of a provincial medical university. The department was set up in the year 2006 at the call of the university administration to promote the university's academic status and influence. The English majors' undergraduate program was launched the same year and ever since two classes of undergraduates are recruited each academic year.

3.1.1.2 The students

39 sophomores in one of the two classes recruited in the year 2016 were involved in the study. Among them, 32 were female and 7 male, and their average age was 20. All of them were from the province where the university is located, which means they took the college entrance examination in the same province and their English scores were comparable. Generally speaking, the students did well in the English test of the entrance exam as the average score was nearly 120 (with the total score being 150), and 20 of them scored higher than 120. It seems that the students, upon beginning their college life, had been equipped with the fundamental language knowledge and skills to identify themselves as English major students.

3.1.1.3 The curriculum, the course and the textbook

The courses offered by the program are designed and arranged in accordance with *The National Curriculum for English as a Specialty in Chinese Tertiary Institutions* (henceforth *the National Curriculum*). That is to say, they are broken into three modules: the skills courses, the knowledge courses, and the relevant knowledge courses. Of all the three modules, the skills module is the most weighted with regard to the number of courses offered as well as the class hours prescribed.

Among all the courses listed in the curriculum, the intensive reading course, including fundamental and advanced English, is the most heavily weighted in that it comprises a total of 514 class hours, nearly the summation of the class hours of listening and speaking (272 respectively), spanning from the first semester to the sixth.

The syllabus of the intensive reading course is also drafted in close correspondence with the course description provided in *the National Curriculum*. As discussed in the first chapter, the principal pedagogical objectives of the intensive reading course reside in the students' incremental command of one knowledge domain and three skill domains. The knowledge domain comprises three levels: the lexical, the grammatical, and the discoursal or textual. The three domains of skills are reading comprehension, language production (writing and speaking), and critical thinking.

English majors generally have high expectations of this course because they believe that it is conducive to the learning of language knowledge and skills. The total class hours allocated for the course in the third semester is 96. The schedule for each course at this medical university is not fixed or regular on a weekly basis due to some officially unknown reasons, neither are the sessions held in the same classroom. Averagely, 6 class hours are spent on the intensive reading course every week.

The textbook designated for this course is *An Integrated English Course* (Book 1-6) edited by Prof. He Zhaoxiong of Shanghai International Studies University (SISU), of the New Century Higher Education English Majors' Textbook series, the general-editor of which is Prof. Dai Weidong of SISU. The book used in the third semester is the third volume, chief-edited by Prof. Shi Zhikang of SISU. The textbook consists of 14 units, each made up of two texts and relevant materials designed around or based on the texts.

According to the distinction made by Nuttall (1996) between skills-based and text-based teaching, this course is more text-based than skills-based as it is intended to bring about the development of all skills by exploiting one text in a unit rather than the development of a particular skill by using a number of texts.

3.1.2 Procedures

3.1.2.1 Building up teacher-student rapport

After the publication of the teaching assignments in June 2017, the researcher got the list of the students' names and consulted the teacher about the students' general proficiency levels, their participation and performance in class, and other relevant information. Then the researcher had himself dragged into the QQ group of the class and introduced himself to the whole class. The researcher also created a WeChat group in the name of "Intensive Reading Workshop" (IRW) and shared the QR Code in the QQ group and invited all the class members to join the so-called workshop. To establish a better rapport with the class, the researcher forwarded to the IRW some articles or essays published on WeChat Public Accounts which the researcher read and conceived worthy of reading, for example, the audio-series of short stories and poems published in Prof. Zheng Xinmin's public account. Most of the students were active to respond to his messages. Some even exchanged their own ideas with him after reading the materials shared in the WeChat Group.

3.1.2.2 Questionnaire on attitude towards classroom questions

During the summer vacation, the researcher administered a questionnaire on the students' attitude towards teacher questioning in the intensive reading class. The questionnaire was adapted from Chang (2009) and consisted of 39 items falling within five sections (See Appendix A). The first section was aimed to collect demographic information, the second the factors relating to students' attitudes towards teacher questioning, the third those relating to dynamic classroom interaction, the fourth the students' attitudes towards language use in answering teacher questions, and the last section the students' puzzlement in learning the intensive reading course and their suggestions for teaching the course. Except for the first and the last sections, all the remaining sections are made up of Likert-scale questions to be answered by ticking 1 (strongly disagree), 2 (disagree), 3 (agree) and 4 (strongly agree). The last section comprised two open questions, one concerning the students' puzzlement in learning the course and the other their suggestions for the teacher's instruction.

The questionnaire was uploaded to the Tencent Survey online platform (https://wj.qq.com/index.html), and the hyperlink was delivered to both the WeChat and QQ groups. The students were then notified to complete it before the onset of the summer vacation. The return rate of the questionnaire was 100 per cent as all the students completed it in time.

Frequency counts of the students' responses to the Likert-scale questions were automatically generated by the survey platform. The students' answers to the last two questions were analyzed qualitatively by the researcher to identify the emerging themes. The researcher then invited a colleague of his to check his work so as to ensure validity of the analysis. If any point appeared disputable, the researcher and his colleague would discuss over it till they reached an agreement.

3.1.2.3 Questionnaire on reading strategies

In the first week of the semester, the researcher conducted a survey on the students' use of reading strategies to know how the students would cope with the texts given in the intensive reading textbook. The questionnaire used was originally designed by Xia Ganlin (2008), comprising four categories of reading strategies to deal with: 1) textual functions; 2) textual themes; 3) textual structure; and 4) textual meaning (See Appendix B for the full text of the questionnaire). Xia developed the questionnaire on the basis of Nuttall's research on reading and Halliday's work on functional grammar. The questionnaire originally consisted of 29 items and each item was designed to be rated on a Likert scale ranging from 1 to 5, with 1 indicating "strongly disagree" and 5 "strongly agree". It was reported to be reliable as the Cronbach's Alpha was as high as 0.829. Xia reduced the number of items to 23 after three rounds of factorial analysis. Though the original version of the questionnaire was used in the current study, only the results of these 23 items will be reported here.

The day when the survey was conducted, one student was absent for the class and did not make it up later. So altogether 38 students returned their questionnaire and all were valid. The students' responses were manually typed into an MS Excel document and then frequency counts were generated.

3.1.2.4 Tests of reading, speaking and summary writing

To assess the students' language proficiency, three tests were carried out on reading, speaking, and writing respectively. The reading comprehension test was administered in the first week and the test material was taken from one of the sample tests provided by the IELTS official website. The writing test was assigned to the students upon the closure of the previous semester and the task was devised in the form of the TEM4 summary writing. The speaking test was conducted after class in the first two weeks and the tasks were taken from the sample tests provided by the IELTS official website.

The IELTS reading and speaking sample tests were adopted because of their high validity and reliability as proved by many (e.g., Weir, 2005;

Fulcher & Davidson, 2007). The TEM4 summary writing task was adopted since the students had been assigned to write summary essays based on the intensive reading texts in the previous semester, and their essays written as required could manifest their understanding of the texts and their digestion of what they had been taught in class, which thus had been proved to be of high validity and reliability as well (Zeng Binghui, 1989; Chen Ruina, 2013).

38 of the class took part in the reading test as one student (S24) was absent when the reading test was conducted. The reading test papers were rated by the researcher himself in reference to the answers provided by the IELTS official website.

All the students took the speaking test which was administered in the afternoons of the first week when the school was over. In the process, the researcher served as the interviewer and videotaped each student's performance with a digital camera. The videotapes were then rated by two of the researcher's colleagues according to the IELTS Speaking Band Descriptors, consisting of the four dimensions of 1) Fluency and coherence, 2) Lexical resource, 3) Grammatical range and accuracy, and 4) Pronunciation. The two raters reached a high degree of consistency as the scores they gave in all the four dimensions were significantly correlated, as shown in Table 3-1. The score of a student's speaking was the average of the scores given by the two raters.

The summary writing task was assigned by the preceding teacher approaching the end of the previous semester. For some reason, 33 students of the class delivered their essays on to the *pigai.com* platform as required. The six who didn't submit their essays were S1, S3, S20, S25, S30, S35.

Table 3-1 Correlation between the raters' scoring of the speaking test before AR

Indicator	Number	Pearson correlation	Sig. (2-tailed)
Fluency and coherence	39	0.784	0.000
Lexical resource	39	0.867	0.000
Grammatical range and accuracy	39	0.754	0.000
Pronunciation	39	0.815	0.000

As argumentative writing is considered to be an effective instrument to measure students' critical thinking (Wen Qiufang & Liu Runqing, 2006), the researcher intended to look into the students' general level of critical thinking through their performance in the summary writing. Hence, the researcher combined the rating scale developed by Wen Qiufang and Liu Runqing (2006) and the current TEM-4 summary writing rating scale into one. The two scales are compatible and complementary regarding the rubrics and both are comprised of indicators specified into *five bands*. Wen and Liu (2006) noted that the first indicator—'relevance to the demand of the task' (文章切题性)—of their scale is meant for the samples they collected and should be replaced if used otherwise. They also suggested that if used for summary writing, it can be changed into the 'exactitude of summary' (概括准确性), which is one of the indicators of the TEM4 scale. In addition, both scales share the indicator of coherence. Thus, combing the two scales, the researcher came up with a rating scheme consisting of 7 indicators (See Appendix C): 1) exactitude of summary, 2) explicitness of thesis statement, 3) clarity of argumentation, 4) coherence, 5) lexical resource, 6) grammatical range and accuracy, and 7) syntactic complexity. The first four indicators point to critical thinking in light of Wen and Liu's (2006) research and the last four language ability as described in the TEM4 rating scale. According to Wen and Liu (2006), a score of at least 3.5 on a dimension of measurement could be considered as reaching the higher level in that respect.

Table 3-2 Correlation between the raters' scoring of the writing test before AR

Indicator	Number	Pearson correlation	Sig. (2-tailed)
Exactitude of summary	33	0.696	0.000
Explicitness of thesis statement	33	0.702	0.000
Clarity of argumentation	33	0.625	0.000
Coherence	33	0.588	0.000
Lexical resource	33	0.627	0.000
Grammatical range and accuracy	33	0.541	0.000
Syntactic complexity	33	0.660	0.000

The students' summary writing essays were rated by another two of the researcher's colleagues according to the above-mentioned rating scale. The scores they gave were also significantly correlated in all the seven dimensions, as shown in Table 3-2. The average of the scores given by the two raters on each indicator was taken to be the score of the writing test.

3.1.2.5 Mutual adaptation through instruction of the first two units

When the semester began, the researcher devoted three weeks to teaching the first two units, which allowed him and the students to adapt to each other.

The researcher followed **the PWP approach**—pre-reading, while-reading and post-reading (Chen Zehang, 2016) in teaching the first two units and established the routine of instruction for the rest of the semester (See Table 3-3).

Table 3-3 Routine of classroom instruction

Stage	Activities	Allocation of time
Pre-reading	• Pre-reading questions • Words and expressions • Background information	2 class hours
While-reading	• Global reading (main ideas) • Detailed reading (content and language details)	4-6 class hours
Post-reading	• Discussions • Exercises • Writing assignment • Dictations	2 class hours

In the pre-reading stage, pre-reading questions were to be answered, new words and expressions discussed, and background information introduced; in the while-reading stage, the instruction would be focused on both global reading and detailed reading; and in the post-reading stage, discussions were to be held, exercises discussed, writing tasks assigned, and key words and paragraphs of the text dictated. Each unit was planned to consume 8 to 10 class hours (i.e., 4 to 5 sessions).

To collect the students' feedback on classroom instruction, the researcher had the students write a learning log to report their gains, problems and suggestions (GPS) after learning a unit.

3.1.3 Findings

The preliminary work generated rich findings that could be exploited for the design of the AR.

3.1.3.1 Attitude towards teacher questions and the course

A) General attitude

The students had a mixed perception of themselves as English majors. Ten (over 1/4) of them indicated that they disliked to major in English (Q4). Nevertheless, they all acknowledged the importance of the intensive reading course (Q5), and conceived oral English proficiency as a symbol of their major identity (Q6). They believed that participating in classroom interaction actively could help them learn the language better, though one of them reported conversely (Q7). Generally speaking, their responses to Q4-Q7 revealed that most of them had a positive attitude towards majoring in English, taking the intensive reading course and participating in classroom interaction.

B) Attitude towards teacher questioning

As regards teacher questioning, the students indicated that they were generally more willing to answer teacher questions if provided with preparation time (Q8). Though most of them would feel less comfortable if they were the only person answering a question, some few did not take it so seriously (Q9). Two thirds of them preferred not to answer questions in front of the whole class and the remaining deemed it acceptable (Q10), which was grossly in correspondence with their responses to how the degree of familiarity might have an effect on how they would feel when answering a question in front of the class (Q13). As to whether providing an incorrect answer concerns them, their responses were almost half-half (Q11).

Interestingly, most of them did not like being nominated by the teacher to answer questions (Q12). Neither did they show a great interest in volunteering an answer (Q14, Q15) and their unwillingness seemed not to result from their concern over peer perception (Q16, Q17). On the whole, the students' responses to Q8-Q17 indicated that their willingness to participate in teacher-fronted classroom interaction seemed to depend on how well they were prepared for answering teacher questions rather than due to peer pressure or face.

C) Attitude towards dynamic classroom interaction

In respect of dynamic classroom interaction (Section C of the questionnaire), it seemed that there had been a high degree of "receptivity" in terms of classroom atmosphere (Allwright & Bailey, 1991, p.23) as the students indicated that both the teacher and the students had played a positive role in constructing classroom interaction. The teacher encouraged the students to speak (Q18), provided support to them when answering questions (Q21), had a good sense of humor (Q23), respected what students said in class (Q28) and often praised them (Q30), though might interrupt sometimes according to some students (Q25). As for the students, though some of them might feel at ease without answering teacher questions actively (Q20), they did respect and paid attention to their classmates (Q19, Q20), and tended to be supportive (Q22) rather than discouraging (Q26), and most of them professed that they felt confident to speak up in class (Q31) and deemed that participation in classroom interaction had benefited their friendships (Q29).

Despite all their positive responses to the aforementioned questions, what appeared to be a problem was that only a few students had been actively engaged in classroom interaction (Q24) and the reason for this was probably the lack of confidence as evidenced by nearly one third of the class (Q31). Their lack of confidence was in turn due to their insufficient language proficiency and the type of questions asked by the teacher, as will be mentioned below in the discussion of the students' responses to the open questions of the questionnaire.

D) Attitude towards language use

Section D of the questionnaire pointed to the students' attitudes toward the use of language when answering teacher questions. Although an absolute majority of the students believed that answering questions in

English were helpful to their learning (Q32), over half of them attributed their unwillingness to respond in English to their insufficient language proficiency (Q33) and reported that answering in Chinese could relieve their stress (Q34). In addition, there was a landsliding agreement among the students that when meeting a difficult question, they would rather answer it in Chinese (Q37). It seemed that the teacher's language use had an influence on the students' language use when answering the teacher's questions in that most students would choose to answer in the language in which the teacher asked a question (Q35, Q36). Yet what seemed interesting was that nearly a quarter of the class were inclined to answer in the target language even if the interaction were initiated in Chinese (Q36). It could be understood that the students, despite their insufficient language proficiency, were generally highly motivated and had a strong desire to practice English speaking in the classroom.

E) Students' puzzlement and suggestions

The last two questions were intended to know about what was puzzling or perplexing to them in regard of the intensive reading course. The students' reported puzzlement (Q38) centered around two major aspects, one being the pedagogical contents of the course, the other the pedagogical goals. The major points gleaned from their responses relating to these two aspects are demonstrated in Table 3-4.

Table 3-4 Students' puzzlement about the intensive reading course

Themes	Specifications
Pedagogical contents (23)*	• The coverage is broad and complex. (8) • It is difficult to memorize words. (5) • It is difficult to learn grammar. (4) • It is hard to fully comprehend a text, especially the textual structure and the author's intention. (3) • It is hard to deal with the paraphrase and translation tasks. (2) • There is insufficient listening practice. (1)
Pedagogical goals (8)	• The course doesn't afford much specialized knowledge. (4) • The course doesn't have much to do with the TEM test. (2) • The course is not practical. (1) • Not much progress has been sensed as a result of taking the course. (1)

*Note: The bracketed digits indicate the number of students reporting the issue.

The biggest perplexity regarding the pedagogical contents had to do with the wide and complex coverage of the course, which seemed to be a body of fragmentary knowledge or trivial details, so much so that some students indicated that they were at a loss as to "what details to focus on" and "what notes to take". Vocabulary and grammar, though respectively reported by a few to be a challenge, might be a burden to many. The lack of a profound comprehension of the texts was another cause of puzzlement in that focal attention was drawn to the learning of language points rather than content messages.

The students' puzzlement with the pedagogical contents was very likely a result of their biased understanding of the pedagogical goals of the course. Though only eight students' responses pointed to that regard, very few of the class perceived the course as expected in *the National Curriculum*, as will be discussed in Section 3.1.3.4. According to the syllabus of the program, the students were required to sit for the TEM 4 and 8 and obligated to pass the TEM 4, otherwise they would graduate without a degree. Hence, it was normal for the students to expect that the courses be oriented towards the examinations. It was not surprising for them to have such practical expectations that all courses, including the fundamental ones such as intensive reading, offer them specialized and practical knowledge or skills which could be immediately put into use upon graduation. However, the intensive reading course, also called integrated English, is aimed at improving all language skills and expanding the learners' knowledge about the English language.

The second open question related to students' suggestions on the upcoming semester's intensive reading course. As can be seen in Table 3-5, their responses centered around three issues: 1) classroom atmosphere, 2) pedagogical procedures, and 3) pedagogical contents.

Table 3-5 Students' suggestions on teaching the intensive reading course

Themes	Specifications
classroom atmosphere (19)	• create an active, interesting and humorous atmosphere (19) • be more student-centered (1)
pedagogical procedures (10)	• have more interactional activities and discussions (6) • have a clearer line of thought (1) • use Chinese when necessary (1) • ask questions in English (1) • slow down a little and leave more time to digest (1) • be stricter with doing the exercises (1) • use the blackboard when necessary (1) • instruct the text globally before going into details (1) • play the soundtrack of the texts before instructing (1)
pedagogical contents (11)	• focus on details (3) • strengthen grammar and vocabulary (2) • introduce relevant background information (2) • expand relevant knowledge points or extracurricular knowledge (2) • deepen text comprehension (1) • explain key sentence structures (1) • prepare for the TEM (1)

Altogether 19 students put forward their suggestions on classroom atmosphere, and almost all of them hoped that the teacher could create an active, interesting and humorous atmosphere. There was also one student who wrote that the class should be more student-centered. Ten students offered suggestions about the pedagogical procedures in classroom instruction, especially calling for more interactional activities and discussions. Eleven of the class wrote of contents to be covered in classroom instruction, ranging from going into details to preparing for the TEM (Test of English Majors).

In sum, the questionnaire results revealed that the students had a generally positive attitude towards the intensive reading course and classroom questioning. They desired to participate in classroom interaction and wanted to practice English speaking, but were not confident of their language proficiency. They preferred to be nominated to answer teacher questions and the teacher's use of language largely determined the language in which they would use. As indicated in their responses to the open questions, they were expecting that the classroom atmosphere would be more active and that they could be engaged in more interactional activities. Though a few students suggested that classroom instruction helped expand their extracurricular knowledge, most of them were more concerned about the expansion of vocabulary and grammatical knowledge, which could be understood as a manifestation of their narrow perception of the intensive course, i.e., a course which is merely focused on the learning of language points.

3.1.3.2 Use of reading strategies

As can be seen in Table 3-6, all the four categories of reading strategies were underused by the students. Among the four categories, the first was the least used, though the average scores of the other three were barely higher. Among all the 23 strategies, only three of them were reported to be used at a frequency level slightly higher than medium (B7, B3, B21). Of these three strategies, only B3 points to the global understanding of a text, and both of the other two relate to the identification of specific details.

It can be inferred that that the students had not been well-trained, either explicitly or implicitly, to use appropriate strategies to address the four aspects of the intensive reading texts: function, theme, structure and meaning. An absolute majority of them would concentrate on specific language or factual details rather than the global idea and the structural organization of the texts.

Table 3-6 Result of reading strategies survey

Categories of strategies	AVG	SD
Textual function strategies	2.59	0.83
Textual theme strategies	2.76	0.90
Text structure strategies	2.71	0.91
Textual meaning strategies	2.84	0.94

3.1.3.3 Language proficiency and critical thinking

A) Reading

The reading test was comprised of three passages and 40 test items. While rating the papers, the researcher found that very few of the students had finished all the 40 items and many of them had barely finished reading all the three passages, indicating the students' low speed of reading and small size of vocabulary.

As shown in the descriptive statistics (See Figure 3-1), though the maximum score was as high as 31, the minimum was merely 6, and the mean was 14.92, which means that most of the students could not do half of the items correctly. In other words, the students had a low level of reading comprehension.

Descriptive Statistics

	N	Minimum	Maximum	Mean	Std. Deviation
Reading1	38	6	31	14.92	4.750
Valid N (listwise)	38				

Figure 3-1 Descriptive statistics of the result of reading test

B) Speaking

As can be seen in Figure 3-2, the students' speaking was not satisfactory in any of the five dimensions. Their performance in pronunciation was slightly higher than in the other three dimensions though, the average score was 4.365, lower than the medium of the scoring range. Hence, it can be concluded that the students, though having finished one year in college learning as English majors, were still at the intermediate level or even lower in terms of speaking.

Descriptive Statistics

	N	Minimum	Maximum	Mean	Std. Deviation
FC1	39	2.3	6.3	3.782	.8074
LR1	39	2.3	6.3	3.763	.7894
GRA1	39	2.0	6.3	3.776	.7604
Pront	39	2.8	6.3	4.365	.8108
Overall1	39	2.3	6.3	3.921	.7480
Valid N(listwise)	39				

Figure 3-2 Descriptive statistics of the result of speaking test

C) Writing and critical thinking

As can be seen in Figure 3-3, the overall performance of the 33 students' summary writing was weak in all the seven dimensions except for their performance in respect of the exactitude of summary.

Descriptive Statistics

	N	Minimum	Maximum	Mean	Std. Deviation
Summary1	33	2.50	4.00	3.4621	.41983
Thesis1	33	2.00	4.25	3.0682	.55295
Argument1	33	2.00	3.75	2.9773	.52053
Coherence1	33	2.50	4.00	3.1288	.35422
Lexical1	33	2.50	4.00	3.2197	.37374
Grammar1	33	3.00	4.00	3.3788	.33728
Syntactic1	33	2.75	4.00	3.2803	.36847
Valid N (listwise)	33				

Figure 3-3 Descriptive statistics of the result of summary writing test

As mentioned earlier, the first four indicators are signs of students' critical thinking and the last four language abilities. Thus, it can be said that the students' writing hardly reached the intermediate level in either critical thinking and language ability, as evidenced by their performance in the seven dimensions.

3.1.3.4 Feedback on the teaching of the first two units

The students' GPS learning logs provided feedback on the teaching of the first two units. Analysis of the learning logs revealed that the students had a hard time adapting to the researcher's style of teaching as they were expecting that the researcher would 'feed' them with knowledge about language points, such as sentence structures, useful phrases, synonyms and antonyms, etc. However, as time went by, they began to realize the advantages of learning autonomously in dealing with vocabulary and grammar points, the benefits of being more involved in classroom interaction and the value of reading and thinking critically.

By and large, the researcher and the students had mutually adapted to each other by the end of the instruction of the first two units. Due to the researcher's insistence in orienting the instruction to the course objectives and his use of questions accordingly, the students started to renovate their recognition of the objectives of the intensive reading course.

3.1.4 Summary

To summarize, the preliminary investigations revealed that the students held a generally positive view of the intensive reading course and classroom questioning. Their general language proficiency hardly reached the intermediate level, and their use of reading strategies in coping with the intensive reading texts was imbalanced and underdeveloped. Despite their high expectations of the course, they had a narrow perception of what they were supposed to learn from it, i.e., the mere acquisition of knowledge concerning language points. In spite of their desire to speak English in classroom interaction, they lacked the confidence to use it correctly and hence most of them preferred to answer teacher questions in chorus or by nomination. In view of these observations, the researcher endeavored, in the teaching of the first two units, to change the students' attitude towards and perception of the course through varieties of questions oriented to the key objectives of the course, i.e., reading comprehension, language learning, personal response, and critical thinking. As manifested in the students' GPS learning logs, the researcher's endeavor was rewarding as the students were willing to adapt to the researcher's teaching style and began to shift their perception of the course.

While the students' prior experience with the intensive reading course rendered them a narrow perception of the course, i.e., a course offered merely for the acquisition of vocabulary and grammar instead of the development of integrated abilities, the researcher's initial pedagogical attempts as demonstrated by the questions designed and implemented in correspondence with the multilayered course objectives proved effective in enriching their experience of the course.

To further enrich the students' experience of the intensive reading course, and to practically realize the multilayered objectives of the course, the researcher decided to conduct an AR study with a focus on the design and implementation of teacher questions.

3.2 Action research

AR, since its inception in Lewin's work in social psychology and philosophy of science in the mid-1940s, has found its way to all research areas of human practice, and is now regarded as "a family of practices of living inquiry that aims, in a great variety of ways, to link practice with ideas in the service of human flourishing" (Reason & Bradbury, 2007, p. 1). As a collection of practices, AR is characterized as being problem-focused, cyclical and collaborative (Peters & Robinson, 1984; Coghlan & Brydon-Miller, 2014; Kemmis, McTaggart, & Nixon, 2014; Bruce, Shosh, & Riel, 2017). In other words, AR is a cyclical inquiry process in which participants collaborate to make improvements or changes in their practices.

3.2.1 Action research in language teaching

AR has been widely adopted by language teaching practitioners and some typical models have been established by renowned language teaching researchers. Burns (2010) acknowledged that educational AR is part of the teacher-as-researcher movement and pointed out that it involves the practitioners in adopting "a self-reflective, critical and systematic approach" (p. 2) to exploring their own teaching contexts. The key ideas of AR, according to Burns (Ibid.), are "taking a questioning and problematising stance" towards teaching, i.e., seeing the gaps between what is happening and what the teachers ideally want to see happening in the teaching situation, and then deliberately applying interventions to bring about changes and improvements in the problematic situation.

Burns (2010) adapted Kemmis and McTaggart's (1988) framework of AR and sketched a four-phase cyclical model for language teaching practitioners (See Figure 3-4). The four phases involved in each cycle are planning, action, observation and reflection. In the planning phase, the researcher identifies a problem or issue and develops a plan of action aimed at improving a specific aspect of the situation. In the action phase, the researcher implements the plan through some deliberate interventions over a period of time. In the third phase, the researcher collects data concerning effects of the action through systematic observation. In the last phase of the cycle, the researcher reflects and evaluates the effects of the action so as to make decisions about what to do in further cycles.

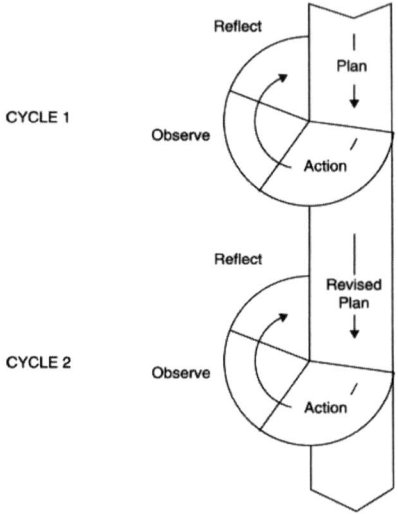

Figure 3-4　Burns' cyclical AR model [Reproduced from Burns (2010, p. 9)]

Burns' work on AR has influenced many studies and her cyclical model has been widely applied by language teaching practitioners. Nevertheless, it does not mean that the model is flawless. In a book review on Burns' monograph, Wen Qiufang (2011) cautioned that Burns' model does not provide a comprehensive description of the dynamic process of AR.

To make up for that disadvantage, Wen Qiufang (2011) proposed an alternative model which consists of an inner circle and an outer circle within each of which a set of iterative and dynamic steps are involved. As demonstrated in Figure 3-5, the four steps in the inner circle are somewhat similar to the four phases in Burns' cyclical model. What distinguishes it from Burns' model and others alike resides in the outer circle which captures three types of conducive action the researcher needs to be engaged in throughout the whole process of AR so as to make appropriate changes or adaptations, namely, reading relevant literature, consulting specialists or associates, and reflecting on the practice.

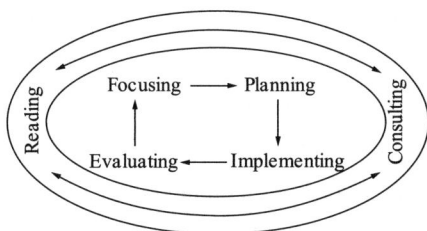

Figure 3-5 Wen Qiufang's model of AR (Wen, 2011, p. 62)

For a clear description of the model, it would be wise to cite Wen's (2011) words as follows:

> [T]he model better describes the whole process of action research. The inner circle consists of four phases of action research: (1) focusing on the issue or problem; (2) working out the (problem-solving) plan; (3) implementing the plan; (4) evaluating the effect. These four phases form a cyclical chain, that is, the end of an action research study leads to a new action research. As the whole process iterates continuously, teaching gets promoted along with research and research gets deepened along with teaching. The outer circle comprises three types of actions: (1) learning from books, i.e., reading relevant literature; (2) consulting others, i.e., learning from associates; (3) the researcher's self-reflection. All these actions are pervasive throughout the whole process of action research. To ensure that the actions within the inner circle are more scientific and effective, the researcher needs to read relevant literature incessantly, to consult experienced associates continuously, to reflect on the ongoing practice in accordance with the external resources, and to make timely and appropriate adjustments to the four phases of action research.
>
> (Wen Qiufang, 2011, p.62; translated by the researcher)

Wen's model fits the current study in that the development of the entire process was a result of the combination of the researcher's reflection on his own teaching practice as well as observation of his colleagues' teaching behaviors, his reading of relevant literature on classroom interaction (especially interaction initiated by teacher questions), and his consulting with his supervisor as well as other specialists and fellow teachers. More than that, in the course of the AR, the researcher is continuously in search of resources and inspirations in order to make appropriate adjustments.

Previous studies on learning space, however, were either approached through learning studies or natural observation. Marton and associates advocated to do learning studies to promote classroom discourse for the extension of learning space (Marton & Booth, 1997; Lo, Marton, Pang, & Pong, 2004). Learning studies are conducted by a group of teachers under the guidance of a researcher departing from the variation theory of learning. A learning study is intended to seek for a set of lesson procedures which can bring about the experience of variation and hence result in learning. It involves cooperative treatment throughout the cyclical process from identifying learning objects, planning activities all the way to evaluating and sharing the lesson. Natural observation, however, is expected to identify merits and/or demerits in teachers' ways of teaching through observing without intervention. Despite the advantages of learning studies in reaching effective methods to address certain learning objects, it may not be an ideal approach for teachers of different courses to collaborate on an instructional design and test it out in a cyclical manner. In spite of the objective insights derived from natural observation, there is still the need for teachers to translate these insights into practice. On account of these observations, AR stands a better chance of filling up the gap. On the one hand, AR, as an approach of practitioner research, can be conducted by the practitioner independent of other teachers or researchers. On the other hand, AR has been proved effective to translate new conceptions or methods into practice.

Due to the restriction of the teaching context, however, the researcher could not find other teachers and classes to do learning studies as a learning study requires a group of teachers teaching the same lesson cyclically under the guidance of a researcher who brings into the group the variation theory of learning. Nevertheless, AR fits well with the research purpose, as Pang and Ki (2016) pointed out that learning study is also akin to AR (p. 323).

3.2.2 A proactive/structured action research design

The design of the current study as inspired by the distinction drawn by Schmuch (2006, 2008; cf. Zhang Wenjuan, 2017) between responsive/reactive and proactive AR. Responsive/reactive AR typically starts with a problem in practice and aims to find solutions to this problem, whereas proactive AR starts with a new method, means or technique and aims at testifying and improving it. Zhang Wenjuan (2017) wrote that the different departing points residing in the two types of AR manifest practitioners' two different attitudes towards "change": the former being passive as pressed by the looming problem to change and the latter being active as motivated by an inner desire to look for change (pp. 48-49).

Wang Qiang (2002; cf. Wang Qiang & Zhang Hong, 2013) pointed out that the process of AR should be decided in line with the specified research questions and the research context. Accordingly, two types of AR could be distinguished: open AR and structured AR. Open AR starts with a problem in practice and proceeds to hypotheses on possible solutions to the problem, followed by surveys or investigations to reaffirm the problem in practice. Once the problem is reaffirmed, plans or measures are to be designed, implemented, and adapted along with the processes of observation, data collection, analysis, reflection and evaluation. The whole process ends with the researchers' writing the AR report.

Structured AR, however, starts not with a specific problem in practice, but with a new conception or a new method which the researcher deems applicable to his/her teaching. The remaining processes of structured AR are the same as those of open AR, that is, the researcher works up a plan according to the new conception or method, and implements the plan in accompaniment of observation, data collection and analysis, reflection and evaluation, till the writing up of the AR report.

The current study belongs to proactive/structured AR in that the researcher had been actively seeking for ways to create the necessary learning space through questioning sequences across different phases of instruction, and ultimately to renovate the students' recognition of the objectives of the intensive reading course.

3.2.3 Interactional organizations as a tool for reflection

Walsh (2006) made a mention of the application of "structured action research" in the investigation of classroom discourse and advocated that a tool for reflection be adopted to ensure systematic procedures in "deriv[ing] outcomes from untranscribed data and partial lesson recordings" (p. 162). The tool that Walsh (2006) proposed for that purpose is the framework of Self-Evaluation of Teacher Talk (SETT) (Walsh, 2003, 2006, 2011), which comprises four classroom micro-contexts, each identified by specific pedagogical goals and relevant interactional features. The framework is based on the observation that classroom discourse evolves in relation to a series of complex and interrelated micro-contexts co-constructed by teachers and learners (Walsh, 2011, p. 110). The four micro-contexts, called modes, are each characterized by the pedagogical goals at certain moments of classroom interaction, which are realized or manifested by teachers' and learners' use of language or interactional features or interactures in Walsh's (2011) terms.

Walsh suggested that teachers involved in reflective practice or structured AR use the framework in a cyclical manner. The practitioner proceeds his reflective practice or AR through the following steps: 1) record classroom interaction of a certain length, 2) identify modes using SETT, 3) identify interactional features using SETT, 4) evaluate the interaction and identify areas for attention or change, 5) discuss with a colleague, 6) make another recording and repeat the previous steps (2011, p. 149). The framework has been validated and attested to be useful in a couple of studies describing and evaluating teacher talk (e.g., Li & Walsh, 2011; Sert & Walsh, 2013; Howard, 2010).

The four classroom contexts and the SETT framework established by Walsh were meant to be used by teachers as a tool to enhance their CIC. The focus is on how teachers can capitalize on a set of post-expansion strategies to sustain students' participation in classroom interaction using the target language. Nonetheless, students' pushed output and access to teacher's shaping assistance has a role to play in language learning, but interactional space may not be the necessary condition for classroom-based language learning. As Tomlinson (2017, conference presentation) said, students who are reticent in class are just not ready for speaking or talking, or filling up the interactional space. Walsh himself also pointed out that a classroom is a multi-party setting (Walsh, 2011, p. 82) where students who are not addressed directly may as well benefit from others' contributions as bystanders (Schwab, 2011, p. 5). Despite Walsh's suggestion that other modes of classroom context be established in correspondence with particular research purposes (Walsh, 2011, p. 129), it is suggested here that it is sufficient to employ conversation analysis as a reflection tool without any pre-established modes. In actuality, the four modes were identified as a result of conversation analysis of transcripts of sample lessons.

Seedhouse (2005), in his state-of-the-art article published in *Language Teaching*, specified four types of interactional organization to be used both as a normative action template for interactants and as a point of reference for interpretation of their actions in language classroom contexts. Seedhouse's account of the four organizations can be summarized as follows:

- **Adjacency pairs**

  Interactional utterances occur in pairs where the second pair part is conditionally relevant to the first pair part. Hence, in a question-answer sequence, the question is the first pair part to which the answer is conditionally relevant. From a CA perspective, teachers' feedback in an IRF sequence is a minimal post-expansion turn of a pair of question and answer.

- **Preference**

  For many adjacency pairs, there are preferred and dispreferred second pair parts, with the former being affiliative and conducive to social solidarity and the latter disaffiliative.

- **Turn taking**

  The organization of turn taking concerns "the distribution of opportunities to talk among parties to interaction and constrain the size of turns, by making the possible completion of a turn 'transition-relevant'" (Schegloff, Koshik, Jakoby, & Olsher, 1992, p. 6). The basis of the turn-taking system is turn-constructional units (TCUs) and transition relevance place (TRP). In teacher-fronted classroom interaction, what is fundamental is teachers' allocation of turns on the speaking floor (Xie, 2011, p. 240).

- **Repair**

Repair occurs in interactive language use when there is trouble impeding communication. In L2 classroom interaction, it is a vital mechanism of intersubjectivity whereby teachers and learners understand where communication breaks down and how misunderstandings are repaired. Distinctions are made between self-initiated repair and other-initiated repair and between self-repair and other-repair.

As Seedhouse (2005) pointed out, these organizations, though omnipresent in all institutional interaction, should not be understood as 'units of analysis' in describing classroom discourse. Rather they are, in essence, context-free mechanisms that participants employ "in a context-sensitive way to display their social actions" (p. 168). The four organizations can also be used as a tool for reflection on teachers' use of language for the institutional goals in a classroom setting. Xie's (2011) investigation on three Chinese EFL teachers' turn allocation patterns and learning opportunities, for example, involved the teachers' **stimulated reflection (SR)** on the reasoning behind their turn allocating behaviors. In the process, the teachers' lessons were audio- and video-taped and transcribed. When the patterns of turn allocation were identified, the teachers were asked to reflect and comment on their techniques of turn allocation management. Xie's study shows that the interactional organizations are not only the norms for social actions and interpretation of actions in foreign language classrooms, but also can be used as a tool of reflection on teachers' use of language in regard of the creation of learning opportunities.

The above discussion boils down to that the interactional organizations can be adopted by teachers as a tool of reflection on the extent to which learning space has been created for a specific object of learning. In the current study, the researcher engaged himself in stimulated reflection on the interactional organizations as carried out in Q-A interaction around certain questioning sequences with a view to observing the enacted object of learning, i.e., the learning space created to that end.

3.3 Research design

In view of the findings of the preliminary research and the applicability of AR to the teaching situation, the researcher designed a proactive/structured AR study in which the notions of learning space and questioning sequences were exploited to improve teacher questions in order to help better realize the multilayered course objectives of intensive reading.

3.3.1 Research questions

The AR was intended to address the following research questions:

1) How can teacher questions be designed and implemented to maximize instructional effectiveness?
2) How do students respond to such teacher questions?
3) What are the major factors that may influence the effectiveness of such teacher questions?

The first research question points to two successive and interrelated actions: the design of teacher questions before classroom instruction and the application of them during classroom instruction. Both actions are closely related to the opening up of learning space. Though teacher questions were to be designed ahead of classroom instruction, i.e., at the stage of instruction planning or design, it was assumed that the questions sequentially implemented across different phases of instruction would constitute the conditions for the experience of variation on the part of the students.

The second research question concerns the pedagogical effect of the learning space as created by the teacher's designed and enacted questioning sequences. Such effect needs to be observed from the learner's perspective and is called by Marton and colleagues 'the outcome space of learning' (Marton & Booth, 1997) or 'the lived object of learning' (Marton & Tsui, 2004). In the current study, the outcome space of learning was investigated by interviewing the students after the learning process (Marton & Booth, 1997,

p. 16), such as reading a text or a chapter or attending a lesson, and then supplemented by more quantitative means like tests or questionnaires (Lo, Marton, Pang, & Pong, 2004).

The third research question concerns the possible factors that may influence the extent to which instructional objectives are realized through questioning sequences. It was assumed that learning space would not only be determined by variation in the content focus and cognitive demand in sequences of questions, but also by such factors as classroom atmosphere, student participation, teacher-student rapport, etc.

3.3.2 Participants

To ensure the consistency and validity of the research, participants other than the teacher-researcher and his students were involved in the design of the study and the planning and observation of classroom instruction. As the teacher-researcher and the students have been introduced in the preliminary research (Section 3.1), what follows here is an introduction to the other participants.

The researcher's supervisor served as the consultant throughout the process of the study, ranging from the drafting of the research proposal, through the preliminary research, the design of the AR, and the adjustment of the pedagogical interventions, to the evaluation of the AR and the writing up of thesis.

During the three cycles of AR, one colleague of the researcher's, Miss Zhou, was invited to collaborate with him in designing an instructional plan for each unit. They worked together to identify the objects of learning for the instruction of the main text of each unit and to find solutions to problems concerning text comprehension, language points or exercises. By the onset of the research, Miss Zhou, with an MA in education, had been teaching intensive reading for nearly ten years and she was assigned to teach the intensive reading course of the other class of the same grade.

Another three colleagues of the researcher's were invited to serve as peer observers of classroom instruction. As the course schedule of the university was not fixed, it was impossible for the researcher to invite the same colleague to observe every session of his teaching. All of the three colleagues, namely Miss Li, Miss Ding, and Miss Zhu, had graduated from MA programs of English language and literature, though their teaching career ranged from months to years. That is to say, they could be regarded as language teaching professionals and qualified peer observers.

3.3.3 Procedures

The AR was carried out in view of the two theoretical constructs of learning space and questioning sequences as reviewed in Chapter Two and on the basis of the preliminary research as described above. In other words, learning space and questioning sequences constituted the conceptual framework for the research; and the pedagogical interventions implemented in the AR were based on the findings of the preliminary research. Therefore, the overall procedure of the AR can be visualized by Figure 3-6.

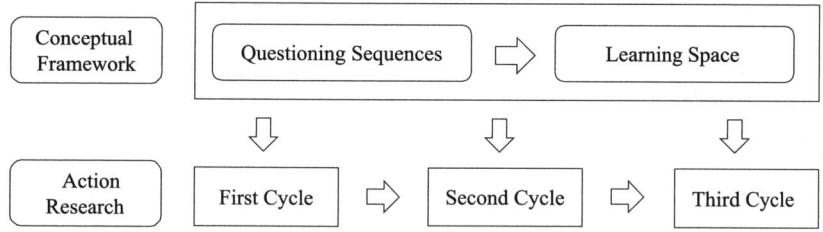

Figure 3-6 The theoretical departure and overall procedure of the AR

As the instruction of all the units ran successively and the feedback on each unit from the students as well as from the peer observers lagged behind the closing of the unit, the researcher decided that each cycle of AR be spread over the instruction of two units. Another consideration for such a scheme was that it would be insufficient to test the efficiency of a treatment through the instruction of one single unit. Therefore, the three AR cycles as a whole covered the instruction of 6 units, as demonstrated in Table 3-7.

As introduced in Section 3.1, the AR was not immediately launched at the very beginning of the semester in that the first few weeks were utilized as a preliminary stage where the researcher attempted to know well of the problems in the situation as well as to bring about teacher-student mutual adaptation through the instruction of the first two units. Based on self-reflection and feedback from students on the preliminary stage as well as suggestions from the consultant of the research, the researcher 'problematised' the students' narrow experience of the intensive reading course. Drawing upon the notions of learning space and questioning sequences, he planned to change the students' perception of the course through questioning sequences designed and enacted in correspondence with the instructional objectives or 'the intended objects of learning'.

Table 3-7　Three cycles of AR

Cycle	Duration of time	Units covered	Major interventions
AR1	Sept. 29-Oct. 16	Unit 3, Unit 4	Trialing questioning sequences
AR2	Nov. 01- Nov. 22	Unit 5, Unit 6	Allowing preparation in advance
AR3	Nov. 27-Dec.21	Unit 7, Unit 10	Incorporating student questions

The first cycle was largely based on the findings of the preliminary research. The researcher found that asking varieties of questions oriented to text comprehension, language learning and personal response could help enrich the students' experience of the intensive reading course as they began to realize that it was not only the learning of discrete language points but also the profound understanding of the text, the sharing of ideas and the training of critical thinking matter. To further improve the efficiency of Q-A interaction, the researcher referred to literature related to questioning sequences and learning space and consulted his supervisor and then decided to apply these two notions in guiding the design and implementation of teacher questions. While trialing the use of questioning sequences, he collaborated with Miss Zhou in identifying the intended objects of learning of a unit in reference to the objectives of the course, designed sequences of questions in accordance with these intended objects of learning, implemented the sequences of questions in classroom interaction, and evaluated the instructional effects through peer classroom observation, students' learning logs, group discussion and stimulated reflection.

The second and third cycles of AR followed suit except that some adaptations were made to the pedagogical interventions based on the findings of the preceding cycle. In the second cycle, the major pedagogical intervention added was the researcher's handing out to the students the questions he had designed for text instruction so that the students could make full preparations to answer the questions in advance. In the third cycle, taking account of the students' reticence when invited to ask their questions during classroom interaction, the researcher adapted the pedagogical interventions by having the students raise their own questions while previewing the text and then incorporating the students' questions into his questions for text instruction. The details of the three cycles of AR will be presented in Chapters Four to Six.

By the end of the third cycle, a questionnaire of the students' use of reading strategies was conducted and a set of tests including reading comprehension, speaking and summary writing were administered. The results of the questionnaire and the tests were then compared with those of the preliminary research to see whether there were signs of improvement in the students' use of reading strategies, reading comprehension, speaking, summary writing and critical thinking. In the meantime, focus group interviews and reflection essays were used to evaluate the effectiveness of the whole AR.

3.4 Data collection and analysis

Both qualitative and quantitative data were collected before and after the AR, with quantitative used as auxiliary evidence of the impact of the AR, that is, to observe whether the AR conducted had any effect on the attainment of the educational objectives of the course, including reading comprehension ability, the use of reading strategies, speaking, writing, and critical thinking. The data collected during the AR were all qualitative and used for the description and interpretation of the learning space opened up by the teacher through the use of questioning sequences. Table 3-8 lists all the data collected.

As data collection and analysis for the preliminary research has been explicated in Section 3.1, what follows is the account of data collection and analysis during and after the three cycles of AR.

Table 3-8 Data collected during the three phases of the AR

Before the three cycles	• Tests: IELTS reading; IELTS speaking; summary writing • Questionnaire on attitudes towards the course and teacher questioning • Questionnaire on students' reading strategies • Students' learning logs • Video-taped lessons
During the three cycles	• Video-taped lessons • Stimulated reflection journals • Post-observation debriefing notes • Students learning logs • Students summary writing essays • After-class group discussion notes
After the three cycles	• Tests: IELTS reading; IELTS speaking; summary writing • Questionnaire on students' use of reading strategies • Focus group interviews • Students' end-of-term reflection essays

3.4.1 Data collection and analysis during AR

In the AR stage, the data collected were all qualitative, for they were intended to observe the learning space created or opened up by the teacher's use of questioning sequences and what the students had actually learned as a result. In other words, both the enacted objects of learning and the lived objects of learning were to be observed or detected in the qualitative evidences.

3.4.1.1 Video-taped lessons

All the lessons were video-taped with a Canon digital camcorder (CANON LEGRIA HF R86 Camcorder). The camcorder was placed on a tripod at a corner beside the platform of the classroom so that almost all the students could be caught by the camera. The video-taped lessons were to be reviewed by the researcher for stimulated reflection which will be introduced in Section 3.4.1.2. Relevant episodes where interaction was initiated by questions relating to the intended objects of learning were transcribed for further analysis. The transcription system (See Appendix G) was adapted from Walsh (2011) with some minor modifications indicating tones of speaking, suprasegmental features and nonverbal communication.

All the transcribing work was done by the researcher himself using an application called Aegisub (Aegisub Advanced Subtitle Editor; See http://docs.aegisub.org/), a free, cross-platform open source tool widely used by video- and audio-producers for creating and modifying subtitles. Aegisub has many of the functions of such specialized transcribing applications as ELAN and Transcriber. In comparison, Aegisub is quicker and easier to time subtitles or transcripts to audio and video, and to add annotations where necessary, though some minute codes need to be added manually. The researcher had tried both ELAN and Aegisub and found that the latter was much more efficient and no less functional for the purpose of the current research.

3.4.1.2 Stimulated reflection journals

The researcher kept a journal to record his stimulated reflection in the form of a diary as suggested by Farrell and Mom (2015) where the teacher could express his thoughts about whatever he wanted to write about the classes observed. The tool for reflection was the four types of interactional organizations as introduced in Section 3.2.3, namely adjacency pairs, preference, turn allocation, and repair. The reflection was focused on the interactional organizations in relation to the opening up or closing down of learning space for the students' experience of the intended objects of learning.

3.4.1.3 Post-observation debriefing notes

Besides video-taping and stimulated reflection, the researcher also invited three of his colleagues, as introduced in Section 3.3.2, to observe his instruction whenever they were available. All together, the three colleagues participated in four lessons, with one of them being present in two lessons. Each time an observer would be given a form of classroom observation sheet (See Appendix D) to make notes; and after observation, they were invited to give their evaluative feedback to the researcher on his instruction. Besides their global impression of the lessons, the researcher would intentionally ask them questions on the effectiveness of his questions.

The conferences between the observers and the researcher mostly took place immediately after the classes. There was no fixed venue for the conferences. One of the conferences was held right outside the classroom, one on the way to the dining hall, and the other two in the office of the foreign language department. Within the day of the observation, the researcher would note down the key messages provided by his colleagues on the merits and demerits of his instruction, especially the effects of the questions from the peer observers' perspective. The notes were then delivered to the observers who would then check if the researcher had missed or misunderstood any significant information.

3.4.1.4 Students' learning logs

Upon the completion of each unit, the students were required to write a GPS learning log, as introduced in Section 3.1.2.5 in the preliminary research, where they could report their gains and unresolved problems as a consequence of the teacher's instruction on the text, and their suggestions for the teacher's future lessons. They were advised to focus their writing particularly on the teacher's use of questions, their classmates' and their own performance in answering the teacher's questions. Such an assignment was intended to detect what the students had learned or failed to learn from the questioning sequences designed and enacted by the researcher, and to collect their suggestions on how to improve the instruction of upcoming units.

While analyzing the learning logs, the researcher would read through each with a view to identifying the themes that emerged relating to what the students had learned in reference to the intended objects of learning of a unit. Should there be any confusing or ambiguous points in a log, the researcher would contact the student for confirmation or reaffirmation.

3.4.1.5 Students' summary writing essays

Summary writing has been widely used in large scale tests in that it is effective in measuring learners' abilities in comprehending, critiquing and summarizing the original text and in expressing their own ideas as well

(Zeng Binghui, 1989; Chen Ruina, 2013). Hence, to further check whether the learning space created by the questioning sequences enacted in classroom instruction led to learning on the part of the students, the researcher devised a summary writing task. The students were required to summarize the text discussed and write their own comments on an issue related to the theme of the text. They could write the composition after class at any time but they were required to submit their compositions to the *pigai.org* ahead of the deadline, usually within 3 days after the completion of a unit.

The tasks were not devised for the purpose of training the students' summary writing skills, though this might be a by-product, neither were them to be rated by the teacher or other raters to check the students' development in that regard. Instead, they were used as evidence of students' learning of a text. There is no doubt that doing such tasks is beneficial to the development of their language proficiency. However, summary writing was employed in the current study mainly for two reasons as follows. The students' summary of the original text must be based on their comprehension, be it literal, interpretive or evaluative. Likewise, their comments on a particular issue were supposed to be related to the theme of the text, be them articulation, elaboration or justification of their responses. In other words, the researcher capitalized on the students' compositions to find whether there were traces of outcomes that resulted from the questioning sequences.

3.4.1.6 After-class group discussions

In order to help the students improve their spoken English, the researcher decided to have the class divided into 10 groups of threes or fours, and offered to work with each group at least once on an after-class oral English activity. At the very beginning, the researcher suggested that each group bring a topic for group discussion. However, they responded that it was hard for the group members to reach agreement and thus requested their teacher to give them a topic. The researcher then came up with the idea of having them exchange their views on their college life and hence streamlined each group discussion into three serial phases: 1) campus life, 2) English major studies, and 3) the intensive reading course. The last phase of the group discussion was intended to collect their ongoing feedback on the researcher's teaching. The questions for the after-class group discussion are demonstrated in Appendix E.

In the process of each discussion, the researcher would take notes of the students' thoughts, feelings, problems and suggestions in regard of the three issues. By the end of the day on which a discussion was held, the researcher would sort out the notes and write a memo of the discussion. The students' feedback on the intensive reading course would be highlighted.

3.4.2 Data collection and analysis after AR

When the AR edged towards the end of the semester, the researcher administered a set of tests and a questionnaire of the use of reading strategies in correspondence with the tests and the questionnaire administered in the preliminary work. In addition, a focus group interview was carried out to look into the students' overall experience of the course and their perception of the three stages of AR. The researcher also had the students write an end-of-term essay to reflect on their gains, problems and suggestions after taking the course for a whole semester.

3.4.2.1 Questionnaire on reading strategies

Upon the closure of the AR, the researcher surveyed the students' use of reading strategies again using the same questionnaire used in the preliminary research (See Appendix B). The author imported the results of the questionnaires conducted before and after AR into the *SPSS 17.0* application and compared each student's response to each of the 23 items to see if there were statistically significant changes or improvements in their use of these strategies.

3.4.2.2 Tests administered after three cycles of AR

There were all together three tests administered after AR: IELTS academic reading, IELTS academic speaking and summary writing, in correspondence with the tests. The reading and speaking tasks were all taken from the IELTS official website but different from those used in the tests. As the students had been required to write a summary composition of each unit discussed, their compositions on the text of the last unit (Unit 10) were used as samples of the writing test.

For some reason, the student (S24), who had missed the reading comprehension test, was absent again when the second test was administered. That means the same 38 students took the reading comprehension before and after AR and the results could be compared using pairs samples T test. All of the class participated in the speaking tests before and after AR and hence the results were comparable likewise. As for the writing test, all of the class handed in their summary essays for the last unit. However, six of the class didn't submit their essays for the last unit of the previous semester. So, to make the results comparable, the researcher removed the scores of the five students.

The students' performance in all the tests was rated in the same way as was their performance in the tests before AR. As the speaking and writing tests were not quantitative, each student's performance was scored by two raters in accordance with the speaking and writing rating scales as introduced in Section 3.1.2.4. The correlations of the raters' scoring in all the dimensions (See Table 3-9 and Table 3-10) show that there were no statistically significant differences between the scores given by the raters, which indicates that the rating scales were used consistently.

Table 3-9 Correlation between the raters' scoring of the speaking test after AR

Indicator	Number	Pearson correlation	Sig. (2-tailed)
Fluency and coherence	39	0.816	0.000
Lexical resource	39	0.766	0.000
Grammatical range and accuracy	39	0.592	0.000
Pronunciation	39	0.521	0.001

Table 3-10 Correlation between the raters' scoring of the writing test after AR

Indicator	Number	Pearson correlation	Sig. (2-tailed)
Exactitude of summary	33	0.535	0.001

Continued

Indicator	Number	Pearson correlation	Sig. (2-tailed)
Explicitness of thesis statement	33	0.745	0.000
Clarity of argumentation	33	0.593	0.000
Coherence	33	0.825	0.000
Lexical resource	33	0.700	0.000
Grammatical range and accuracy	33	0.711	0.000
Syntactic complexity	33	0.526	0.002

3.4.2.3 Focus group interviews

Upon closure of the AR, three focus group interviews were conducted on the students' overall experience of the intensive reading course, with a special focus on teacher questions. To see if students of different proficiency levels had different perceptions, each time the researcher invited four students of the same proficiency level to form a group. Each group consisted of four students and the participants of each group were selected by purposive sampling to ensure that they could represent the students of a certain proficiency level. Table 3-11 displays the constituent information of the three groups.

Table 3-11 **Participants of the focus group interview**

Group A (Higher)		Group B (Middle)		Group C (Lower)	
Stu ID	Gender	Name	Gender	Name	Gender
S1	Male	S2	Female	S17	Female
S6	Male	S9	Female	S29	Female
S30	Female	S14	Female	S35	Male
S39	Female	S18	Female	S37	Male

The focus group interviews were held in an audio-video classroom and each lasted about one and a half hour. The researcher prepared a list of questions (See Appendix F) in advance and invited the group members to answer them by turns. The students were welcome to interrupt if they happened to think of anything to add or complement. Unlike the after-class group discussions, which were conducted in English, the focus group interviews were carried out in Chinese in the hope that the students could talk more freely and hence more accurately about their experience with the course.

The interviews were all audio-recorded and afterwards transcribed and analyzed by the researcher himself. While doing the analysis, the researcher read through the transcripts time and again to identify the themes that emerged in them. Should there be any confusing or ambiguous points, the researcher would contact the respondents for clarification or confirmation.

3.4.2.4 Students' end-of-term reflection essays

To further confirm the interview data, the researcher assigned the whole class to write an end-of-term reflection essay. The format of the essay was very much similar to their GPS learning logs, but the students were required to focus their essays on two aspects, one being their own learning and the other the teacher's instruction. They could choose to write the essay either in Chinese or in English and they were given enough time to finish the task as the deadline was 7 days after the publication of the task. Their essays, as with other writing tasks, were collected through *pigai.org*.

All the 39 students had submitted their essays, 9 in English and the others in Chinese. The *pigai.org* platform provides a built-in messaging service through which the teacher and the students can deliver messages. The researcher, after reading each essay, would drop a few lines of comments to the student. Some of the students, upon seeing the researcher's notes, replied and a few of them even elaborated on or added comments to their responses. All the essays and comments were collected and saved in an MS Excel file for further analysis.

3.5 Validity concerns and ethical issues

According to Mills (2011), both quantitative and qualitative data can be categorized into three dimensions: 1) experiencing through observation and fieldnotes, 2) enquiring through asking people for information, and 3) examining through using and making records (Mills, 2011, p. 89). The more the sources of data collected and the more triangulation done among them, the more valid and reliable the AR will be (Sagor, 2005; as cited in Creswell, 2012, p. 590).

In the current study, both quantitative and qualitative data of all the three dimensions delineated by Mills (2011) were collected. The quantitative data were comprised of test scores and results of numerical surveys. Standardized tests were used, as the reading and speaking tasks were taken from the sample tests published by the IELTS official website and the writing tasks were devised imitating the TEM-4 writing module. The speaking and writing tests were rated by two experienced raters independently. The questionnaires used before and after the AR were adapted from validated ones. Hence, the instruments used for the collection of quantitative data secured the reliability of the data collected.

For the sake of triangulation, multiple sources of qualitative data were collected, including transcripts of videotaped classroom instruction, peer observation debriefing notes, the teacher's stimulation reflection journals, the students' learning logs, group discussion notes, transcripts of focus group interviews, and the students' reflection essays. To secure the rigor of qualitative data analysis, the interview transcripts, the learning logs and the reflection essays were analyzed deductively in view of the pre-ordinate themes as well as inductively to identify new themes (Fereday & Cochrane, 2006). Findings emanating from the data analysis were presented to the participants to confirm whether they concurred with any or all of the emergent perspectives (Nowell, Norris, White, & Moules, 2017).

Burns (2010, pp. 152-156) cautioned that four important issues be taken care of to ensure trustworthiness in AR:

1) Keep the pedagogical focus of your research in mind
2) Use more than one source of information
3) Maintain objectivity and perspective

4) Focus on 'practical theory'.

These four issues were all attended to in the current study. First, the pedagogical focus remained consistent throughout the AR, i.e., to improve student learning through teacher's use of questioning sequences. Second, different sources of information were collected, including transcripts of classroom interaction, verbal and written reports from the students, journals of stimulated self-reflection, notes of peer observation, and the forth. Third, measures such as cross-checking of qualitative data were taken to maintain objectivity and perspective. Lastly, the focus of the study remained unchanged throughout the study, that is, to deepen the researcher's 'theories for practice' or his learning about his own teaching contexts and practices.

In respect of ethical issues, all the participants, including the students, the collaborator and the peer observers were all informed of the purposes of the research. At the very beginning, consent was obtained from all the stakeholders. To ensure confidentiality and anonymity, the participants were assured that their identities would be masked as much as possible in the writing up of the thesis. Throughout the research, the participants were free to provide honest answers and the students were assured that evaluations of their academic performance would not be affected. If any of the students refused to take part in the classroom observations, they were allowed to move their seats or positions so that they would not be filmed.

3.6 Summary

This chapter presents the methodology of the current study by mapping out the pathway from the preliminary work, through the design of the three cycles of AR, to the evaluation of the study. The findings of the preliminary work offered implications for the AR regarding the problems to be focused on, the plans to be formed, the interventions to be implemented and the instruments to be used to evaluate the effects of the interventions. The details of the three cycles of AR will be presented in the next three chapters respectively.

Chapter 4 First Cycle of Action Research

This chapter describes the four steps of the first cycle of AR as inspired by the findings of the preliminary study. It first details the problems focused, the plans set up and implemented, as well as the effects observed and evaluated, and then draws implications for the next cycle.

4.1 Focusing

As mentioned in the previous chapter, the biggest problem faced by the researcher was that the students had a very narrow experience with the intensive reading course. Nonetheless, the intensive reading course, according to *the National Curriculum*, is loaded with multiple objectives. Besides the learning of language knowledge, it is also intended to provide opportunities for the training of reading, speaking and writing skills, and the cultivation of critical thinking. Thus, there was a big gap or mismatch between the students' perception of the course and the objectives specified in the syllabus. The preliminary research indicated that the students' narrow perception could be attributed to their previous experience of classroom Q-A interaction, which was mostly oriented towards language points.

On top of that, the researcher was also confronted with some other prominent problems concerning classroom instruction. One was the students' insufficient language proficiency as indicated by the results of the tests. Because of this, many of them were not confident enough to speak English in front of their classmates. That is to say, the students' low level of language proficiency caused their lack of confidence in using the English language which in turn increased their unwillingness to participate in teacher-fronted classroom interaction.

Another problem was the conflict between the students' resounding request for more instruction on language points and the researcher's intention to balance the instruction on the different strands of a language course together with the development of critical thinking. As mentioned in the previous chapter, though the researcher and the students seemed to have adapted to each other by the end of the preliminary research, many of the students suggested in their learning logs that the researcher give elaborate explanations on some difficult words, expressions and structures. In other words, many of the students were dependent on the teacher in regard of the learning of language knowledge.

Bearing the above-mentioned problems in mind, the researcher referred to relevant literature and consulted his supervisor before coming up with a plan of solutions, as will be introduced in the next section.

4.2 Planning

In the light of the literature reviewed in Chapter Two, the researcher realized that the students' narrow experience with the intensive reading course could be expanded through text instruction informed by the notions of learning space and questioning sequences. While the notion of learning space indicates that educational objectives can be formulated as 'act + content', and the learning of a certain objective rests with the learner's experience of variation in the two elements of that formula; the notion of questioning sequences implies that teacher questions, as the most important part of classroom instruction, should be designed and implemented as sequences of questions in correspondence to the educational objectives. Drawing upon Nation's (1996, 2007) work on the four strands of a language course and the educational objectives prescribed in *the National Curriculum*, the researcher established a framework of teacher questions with a view to enriching the students' experience of variation in the two dimensions of content focus and cognitive demand, as demonstrated in Figure 2-5.

The researcher presented to his supervisor the findings of the preliminary work and his idea of applying the notions of learning space and questioning sequences as a guide in designing and implementing teacher questions in order to enrich the students' experience of the intensive reading course. His supervisor approved of the idea and offered suggestions for setting up the AR plan. She suggested that questions for the three stages of instruction, i.e., pre-reading, while-reading and post-reading (PWP) be structured in a way to scaffold the attainment of the instructional objectives.

Based on the supervisor's suggestions, the researcher proceduralized the teaching of a unit as displayed in Figure 4-1. The pre-reading stage was intended to activate students' schematic knowledge relating to the theme of the text; the while-reading stage to involve students in experiencing the text multidimensionally and profoundly, that is, to experience the different strands of language learning (i.e., text comprehension, language-focused learning, and response production) as well as the hierarchical variation in each strand (i.e., the different levels of each strand of learning); and the post-reading stage to bring about an integrated experience of the whole unit. The goals of the first two stages were to be realized by teacher-fronted Q-A interaction and the final stage by group discussion and summary writing tasks constituted by questions. Thus, each phase of instruction was characterized by teacher questions oriented to the corresponding objectives.

Stages	Pre-reading	While-reading	Post-reading
Goals	Schematic knowledge	Multidimensional and profound experience	Integrated experience
Activities	Teacher-fronted Q-A interaction	Teacher-fronted Q-A interaction	Group Discussion Summary writing

Figure 4-1 The general procedure for the teaching of a unit

When the procedure of teaching was decided, the researcher began devising his plan to address the problems as captured in Section 4.1. The plan of actions he devised is as displayed in Table 4-1. To bridge the gap between the students' experience or perception of the intensive reading course and the objectives as prescribed in *the National Curriculum*, the researcher planned to balance the content orientations of teacher questions in accordance with the three strands of input comprehension, language-focused learning and output production. To develop the students' critical thinking, another objective of the course, the researcher planned to design questions of different cognitive levels relating to each content orientation and sequence them hierarchically across different stages of instruction.

To deal with the students' lack of confidence in answering teacher questions in English, the researcher came up with three actions. To help relieve pressure or anxiety, turn allocation was to be dominated by inviting the whole class to answer in chorus or encouraging volunteers to speak up, and the students were to be allowed to switch to Chinese when they could not use English to accomplish their answers.

As for the students' dependence on the teacher's provision of explanations on language points, the researcher planned to make predictions about what language items might be difficult for them and design relevant questions for text instruction. For fear that there might be problems beyond his prediction, he decided to invite the students to raise questions during classroom instruction to complement his questions.

Table 4-1　Solutions planned for the problems identified in AR1

Identified problems	Planned solutions
• Gap between student experience and course objectives of intensive reading	• Balance the content orientations of teacher questions in accordance with the course objectives • Sequence questions hierarchically in each content orientation across different stages of instruction
• Students' lack of confidence in answering TQs in English due to limited proficiency	• Invite the whole class to answer in chorus • Encourage volunteers to speak up • Allow students to switch to Chinese when necessary
• Students' dependence on the teacher for language-related explanations	• Predict possible language problems, design relevant questions, and give self-answers if no one could answer • Invite students to ask questions related to language items in class

4.3 Implementing

To carry out the PWP approach as described above, the researcher collaborated with one colleague of his, Miss Zhou, in identifying the key objects of learning in each unit. They first read the text carefully on their own, noting down problems and/or doubts. Then they met to exchange their understanding of the text and attack the problems they had encountered. Finally, they worked together to identify the key objects of learning to be covered in the upcoming lessons, i.e., to establish the instructional objectives of the unit.

When the instructional objectives were set up, the researcher began designing questions for the three stages. As mentioned earlier in this section, questions for the first stage were meant to activate schematic knowledge, questions for the second stage to involve the students in experiencing the different strands of learning as well as hierarchical variation in each strand, and questions for the final stage were built in the group discussion and summary writing tasks to induce students to integrate what they had learned.

The design and instruction of Unit 3 is described below to illustrate the implementation of the plans set up for the first cycle of AR.

4.3.1 Identifying the objects of learning

The main text of Unit 3, titled *Out of Step*, is an adaptation of a chapter in Bill Bryson's collection of essays titled *I'm a Stranger Myself*. The title of the original chapter is *Why No One Walks*. The chapter describes his anecdotal experiences of walking and driving after his return to the United States after living in England for 20 years and displays his not being able to understand why contemporary Americans were so dependent on cars that they would not think of walking whenever they went. The researcher and his collaborator exchanged their understanding of the text and subsequently decided that the instruction of the text should be focused on:

Interpreting the author's purpose of writing

The editors of the textbook might have speculated that the author's intention of writing the chapter was to reveal his discomfort and maladjustment upon returning to the United States after living in Britain for twenty years and hence they changed the original title into *Out of Step*. The researcher and his collaborator perused the adapted text in reference to the original and conceived that the author's purpose was more to anatomize and criticize contemporary Americans' over-dependence on cars than to expose his uneasiness and bemusement after returning to the U.S. Thus it would be worthwhile to have the students interpret the author's intention of writing the text.

Appreciating the title of the text

As mentioned above, the editors of the textbook replaced the original title—*Why No One Walks* with *Out of Step*, hence it would be necessary to draw the students' attention to the change of the title and have them appreciate which better fits the author's intention: the original or the one given by the textbook compilers.

Identifying the author's humorous and satiric tone

To convey his critical attitude towards Americans' over-dependence on cars, the author described several of his personal encounters in the small town in a humorous and satirical manner. It was deemed necessary to call the students' attention to how humor and satire is achieved through the author's use of language.

Expressing personal responses towards related topics

As the theme of the text has to do with people's overuse of cars in the modern US society and life in a small city in the US, the researcher and his collaborator suggested that it would be advisable to have the students expresstheir own views on the use of cars and life in big cities or small towns.

4.3.2 Designing questions

When the focused objects of learning were decided, the researcher designed the questions for each stage of instruction accordingly.

Pre-reading Questions

Questions for the pre-reading stage are intended to activate the students' schematic knowledge. As the theme of the text has to do with cars in the life of

Americans, the researcher designed two questions as displayed in Figure 4-2.

Pre-reading Questions
1. How has the development of car industry benefited our life? 2. Do you think people are becoming more and more dependent on cars? Why or why not?

Figure 4-2　Pre-reading Questions for Unit 3

While-reading Questions

To help the students get a multidimensional and deep experience of the text the researcher planned to divide the while-reading stage into two sub-stages: global reading and detailed reading. The global reading was to deal with the comprehension questions appended to the text in the textbook, and the students were expected to finish them before class as part of the preview assignment.

For the detailed reading, the researcher brainstormed as many questions as possible relating to each part of the text, including to the title and every paragraph of it. Each question was labeled as CQ (text comprehension question), LQ (language learning question) or RQ (personal response question). The researcher had once thought of assigning each question to a specific level, for instance, text comprehension questions could be categorized into CQ1 (literal understanding), CQ2 (interpreting) or CQ3 (evaluating). However, he had to drop that idea because he realized that it was almost impossible to determine what level of cognitive effort a question would stimulate before its actual enactment. In other words, the level of question can only be determined by examining the interaction initiated by it.

Detailed Reading (Para. 1)
RQ: Can you imagine living abroad for 20 years and move back to your hometown? How would you feel in that case? LQ: Think of other words similar to 'venerable' in form. LQ: Why does the author use three adjectives to describe Hanover: 'pleasant, sedate and compact'? CQ: Why did Bill Bryson decide to settle down in Hanover? RQ: Do you like living in a large city, or a small town? Why? RQ: What kind of person do you think Bill Bryson is?

Figure 4-3　Questions designed for Para. 1 of Unit 3

Figure 4-3 is the screenshot of a slide displaying a list of questions for Para. 1 of the text. For the whole text, the researcher designed 29 questions, including 14 LQs, 12 CQs and 3 RQs. While in most cases LQs were placed in front of CQs followed by RQs on the slides, in practice, the order might be shifted because the instruction was to be conducted on a line-by-line basis.

Post-reading questions

The post-reading activities comprised questions aimed at shaping an integrated experience of the whole text. For Unit 3, two group discussion activities and one summary writing task were designed as demonstrated in following screen-shots of slides (See Figures 4-4, 4-5, and 4-6). The first discussion activity was intended to have the students appreciate the textbook editors' change of the title of the text from the original *Why No One Walks* into *Out of Step*; the second to have them exchange personal ideas on the traffic problem confronting city dwellers. The summary writing task was aimed at integrating the students' comprehension of the textual messages and appreciation of the meta-textual messages of the text with a focus on the critique of the title.

Discussion on the title of the text

What do you think of the textbook compilers' changing the original title "Why No One Walks" into "Out of Step"? Is it reasonable? Or which do you think better fits the central idea of the text?

Figure 4-4 The first group discussion activity for Unit 3

Discussion on public transportation vs private cars

Sit in groups of threes or fours and have a discussion over the following questions:
- What is the situation of traffic in large cities in China?
- What are the causes for this situation?
- What are possible solutions to the problem?

Figure 4-5 The second group discussion activity for Unit 3

> **Summary writing**
>
> Read the text carefully and then write your response in NO LESS THAN 200 WORDS, in which you should answer the following questions:
>
> 1) What is the main message of the text,
> 2) How is the main message developed in the text, and then
> 3) Which better fits the text as a title, "Why NO One Walks" or "Out of Step"?
>
> You can support yourself with information from the text.

Figure 4-6 Summary writing task for Unit 3

4.3.3 Enacting questions

Considering that many of the students were not so willing to be directly nominated to answer questions in front of the class, the researcher organized the classroom interaction around the pre-designed questions first by inviting the whole class to respond, and then nominating particular students to give specific answers. In the process of instruction, the number of questions asked by the researcher was more than that of the pre-designed ones, for he would not only probe for further responses after students giving their initial answers to those pre-designed question but also ask spontaneous questions from time to time as well.

As the instruction around the text was carried out by asking and answering the pre-designed questions, the variation in the dimension of content focus was secured. In other words, in comparison to the students' previous experience of the course, which was merely focused on learning language points, the researcher's designing and asking questions pointing to the variation in the three aspects of content focus, i.e., textual messages, language points and personal responses, would guarantee that the students have a richer experience in the content dimension of learning. What should be of particular concern in the implementation of the pre-designed questions is the hierarchical variation in the focused content aspects. Hence, it would be necessary to demonstrate how the focused learning objects of this unit, as listed in Section 4.3.1, were realized through questioning sequences as conceptualized by Marzano and Simms' (2014).

As the focused objects of learning were intertwined during the process of instruction, it would be awkward to draw them apart in describing how they were enacted. In order to better demonstrate the development of questioning sequences, however, the researcher opted not to follow a chronological order but to collate episodes of classroom interaction pointing to one object of learning spreading across different phases of the instruction of an entire unit but bringing about space for experiencing hierarchical variation. As presented below, three of the identified objects of learning were enacted through questioning sequences.

Interpreting the author's intention of writing

In respect of the first object of learning, i.e., interpreting the author's intention of writing the article, the questions asked at the pre-reading and while-reading stages formed a sequence which could offer the space for the students to experience hierarchical variation. In the pre-reading stage, after inviting two students to give their brief answers to the question on the development of car industry, the researcher moved on to the question on the consequences of car dependence in the modern society.

As displayed in Extract 4-1, the researcher first asked the class whether they thought people would become more reliable on cars (L1), a question which initiated a choral response from the whole class. When the researcher asked for elaboration on their positive answer (L3), one of them—S3 offered a reason: "Because we are lazy". Inspired by S3's answer that probably people would become more and more lazy due to the convenience brought by cars, which is touched upon in the text, the researcher shifted the content focus of the question to the consequences of car dependence (L11). He then nominated another student—S39 to give an answer. After repeating S39's brief answer, the researcher probed her to elaborate her response. While S39 remained silent, some of her classmates were yielding their own answers but unclearly. Then two students offered their answers almost simultaneously: S9 and S17 both spoke of traffic problems (L17, L18). After rephrasing S17's utterance with "crowded or congested traffic" and confirming that the students know the word 'congest' (L21), the researcher proceeded to elicit further response from the class and nominated S10 to give her answer. Seeing that S10 was not talking on consequences directly relating to human beings, the researcher rephrased the question into "Can you think of some problems that it will bring to ourselves" (L37). At this point, it seemed that the students understood the researcher's intention of questioning as S13 offered an answer after a few seconds of unclear talk of the whole class: "We will be fatter" (L39) and "I am right" (L49), which stimulated a burst of laughter in the classroom. Though S13's answer was brief, the researcher was contented to see that she talked to the point and gave her a positive feedback before expanding her words with a complex sentence (L50).

Extract 4-1 On the consequences of car dependence

1	T	OK, the car industry has definitely benefited us a lot, but do you think that people will become more reliable on cars in the future?
2	Ss	((The class answer in chorus)) Ye::s=
3	T	=Why↓
4	S3	Because we are lazy.
5	T	Yes? Jennifer, because what?
6	S3	Because I think (.) people nowadays are very lazy.
7	T	Oh people are <more and more lazy.>
8	S3	And car are (.) very convenient to us=
9	T	Yes=
10	S3	=And in the future people are rich enough to (.) afford a car.
11	T	Yes? In future people well be rich enough to afford cars. Yes: OK: Thank you:. (0.5) And what will that bring to us if we are more reliant on cars.
12	Ss	((unclear answers))
13	T	Yes- S39.
14	S39	((in very low voice)) air pollution.
15	T	Air pollution (.) yes heavier air pollution. (0.5) And?
16	Ss	((students producing unclear answers 3.0))
17	S9	The traffic [will be terrible.]
18	S17	[((XXX)) transportation.]
19	T	What transportation?
20	S17	Crowded transportation.
21	T	Crowded. Yes- or congested (.) traffic. (1.0) Do you know the word congested?
22	Ss	Yes.

Chapter 4 First Cycle of Action Research

23	T	Other consequences? (3.0) S10.
24	S10	(1.0) Eh just like the traffic jam and people will put more time eh put more time on road.
25	T	Yes?=
26	S10	=Because of the traffic jam (.) more people will work late
27	T	Work late?
28	S10	(1.0) Be late for work.
29	T	Oh yes? Be late for work.=
30	S10	=It will do more harm to environment.
31	T	Yes
32	S10	Because people use more cars and there will be more gus.
33	T	More what?
34	S10	Gus- gas- harmful gas.
35	T	Yes.
36	S10	(4.0)
37	T	Can you think of some problems that it will bring to ourselves.
38	Ss	((unclear answers))
39	S13	We will be fatter.
40	T	OK, thank you. Then (.) S13.
41	S13	We will be lazy and lazy=
42	T	=Yes?
43	S13	And be fatter.
44	T	OK, yes, we will be ((laugh)) fatter=
45	Ss	=((laugh))
46	T	and fatter
47	S13	I'm right.
48	T	And what?
49	S13	And I'm right.
50	T	You're right ((the whole class laugh 2.0)) I see. OK. Yes you are. (2.0) So if we are over dependent on cars: (.) probably- we will become physically weaker. Right?

The interaction displayed by Extract 4-1, though originally intended to focus on the students' personal response towards car-dependence, foreshadowed the interpretation of the author's purpose of writing the text, which was formally picked up at the beginning of the global reading. The first text comprehension exercise was a multiple-choice question on the author's

purpose of writing:

Decide which of the following best states the author's purpose of writing.
A. Pointing out the fact that Americans walk too little today.
B. Introducing an alternative to car-driving as a means of transport for an average American.
C. Complaining about inconvenient traffic conditions for pedestrians in America.

(Textbook, p. 42)

Extract 4-2 shows the Q-A interaction around the above question. After reading aloud the question, the researcher invited the whole class to give their answers but met with silence. He then simplified the task into a yes/no question (L1) while walking down the isle of the classroom and checking whether the students had done the exercise before class. Seeing that many of them had not done it, he chose to explain the meaning of possible new words in each statement of the choices. After that he employed a DIU (L2) to elicit responses. Hearing S21's answer, he uttered "Yes?" (L4) as a confirmation check but met with silence again. Finally, he announced the correct answer (L6). At this point, he thought of the interconnection between the author's purpose of writing and the title of the text, and shifted the topic of interaction to the textbook writers' changing the original title *Why No One Walks* into *Out of Step*.

Extract 4-2 On the author's purpose of writing during the global reading

1   T   The author's purpose of writing? it should be (0.5) Is it A? (0.5) Many of you didn'tdo this. ((T began explaining possible new words in the choices 30))
2   T   So the answer should be-? (1.8)
3   S21 A.
4   T   Yes?
5   (2.0)
6   T   It should be (.) A↓ right? But- then let's come to the title of the text. If the answer to this exercise should be A, then (0.3) the title of the text should be chan:ged back into (0.2) Why No One Walks. Right?
7   (1.0)

8	T	It seems that Out of Step is better than Why No One Walks. It's kind of eh it's kind of like a <u>pun</u>. Right?
9		(2.0)
10	T	It's something like a pun. 就有点像<u>双关语</u>，对不对?
11	S33	对啊!
12	T	But the author's original intention was (0.8) to criticize the situation in America, right? Almost no one walks, they are too much car-dependent, right?
13	S21	[Yes many Americans don't walk]
14	T	[so he's not trying to tell the reader] that he himself is out of step with Americans in life right? He is (.) [criticizing], OK?
15	S33	[criticizing]

When the detailed reading came to Para. 8 of the text, where some details on a man's car-dependence were chopped out by the textbook writers, the researcher picked up again the question on whether the author's purpose of writing the article was to describe his being unable to re-adapt himself into the American society or to criticize average Americans' over-reliance on cars. Extract 4-3 shows how the researcher engaged the class in thinking about what was intended in the details in the original article which were removed by the textbook writers. After explaining the word 'dash' in Chinese, he pointed out that the author spent more details on the man's going into and coming out of the post office. He then asked the class whether they had read the original article. Hearing a positive answer from several students, he threw them into thinking about the author's intention of giving a detailed account of that man's movement (L3). After S21's brief response (L4), He repeated some of the details in the original article and then took recourse to the question on the author's intention of writing the article (L5).

Extract 4-3 On the author's purpose of writing during the detailed reading

1	T	You see the expressions used by the author to describe the man's movement? popped outside↑ (.) and dashed inside. dash 就像飞镖一样 (.) 很快 (.) 对不对？其实作者的原文 (.) 有更多的细节 (.) 描写这个. Have you read the original article I delivered to you?
2	Ss	((several students answer in a low voice)) Yes
3	T	Then what (.) do you think the author wanted to do (.) wi:th those details. (2.0)

4	S21	To ridicule that man.
5	T	Yes? To criticize Americans right? Americans even don't walk a distance of 16 feet. That man left the engine <u>on</u> when he went into the post office and when he came out of the post <u>o</u>ffice? (.) he drove again- only 16 feet to the next general store. (1.0) So (.) once again what do you think of the author's purpose (.) of wri:ting this article (.) Mhm?
6	S21	To criticize why Americans don't walk.
7	T	Yes- Do you agree? 所以为什么美国那么多人有肥胖症 - obesity- obese- 对吧 hehe
8	Ss	((the class laugh mildly))
9	T	你们觉得作者在原文中描写的 (.) eh 那个人没有熄火的细节 (.) 要不要删掉啊
10		(2.0)
11		我觉得还是保留比较好 (.) 因为那样可以更准确地反应作者的写作意图 (.) OK uh Para. 9

If the question asked at the pre-reading stage on the possible consequences of car-dependence (Extract 4-1) was a preface for the interpretation of the author's purpose of writing, the question asked at the global reading stage (Extract 4-2) constituted a preliminary check of the students' global understanding of the whole text, and the question asked at the detailed reading stage (Extract 4-3) further engages the students in evidence-based interpretation of textual messages. Though, as displayed in Extract 4-3, only one single student (S21) participated in the episodic interaction while the others remaining silent, the researcher's bringing up the topic again at this point during the detailed reading might have enhanced the students' awareness of how to interpret the author's purpose of writing by "reading between the lines" (Manzo & Manzo, 1993). In short, these questions spreading across different instructional stages formed a sequence which offered the space for the students to experience hierarchical variation in their learning acts.

Appreciating the title of the text

During the process of instruction, the researcher developed a sequence of questions that focused the students' attention on the second object of learning, i.e., appreciating the title of the text.

The first question relating to the title was asked after a brief introduction to the author, including his academic and literary career and the background information of the text (especially where the text was adapted from). As shown in Extract 4-4, the researcher told the students that the original title was 'Why No One Walks' instead of 'Out of Step' and that probably the textbook writers had changed it into the present one for better or worse. The students repeated his words (L2) to show their curiosity or surprise about why the textbook writers should have done so. The researcher then spent a few words recapitulating the author's uneasiness upon moving back to the U. S., and asked the class which title they thought better fits the author's intention of writing the article, but a second thought made him modify the question into another one on the meaning of 'out of step' (L3). Two students gave their answers simultaneously (L4, L5): One student (S3) answered "不走路" (not walk) and the other (Sx) said "没有脚" (without foot/legs). The researcher took S3's answer and incorporated it into a confirmation check (L7) and waited for 49 seconds, allowing the students to look up the phrase in dictionary APPs. One student (S2) then uttered the meaning of the expression: "步调不一致" (not using the same foot when parading or dancing) (L9). The researcher repeated S2's words and then slowed down his speed of speaking when employing a DIU (L10) to prompt further explanation of 'out of step'. The DIU was filled up by S39 with "不合拍" (off the beat) (L11). Right after the researcher confirmed S39's words (L12), S21 interrupted by saying "Eccentric". The researcher hesitated a little bit in taking up S21's words and thought it acceptable to understand 'out of step' as similar to 'eccentric'. He then proceeded with his own comments on the textbook writers' changing the title (L14) but was cut in by S3 (L15) who thought that 'out of step' could mean '走路' (walking), which was beyond the researcher's expectation. The researcher hedged for a short while before accepting her answer and telling the class to read the author's original article after class and contemplate on which title better fits the author's intention (L16).

Extract 4-4　On the meaning of the title

1	T	So, eh, the original is "Why No One Walks". Original title of that essay? 原来的标题啊 (.) 在书里边是 Why No One Walks=
2	Ss	=Why no one walks ((students repeating with a curious or surprising tone))
3	T	对．当他回到美国的这个小镇的时候 他发现人们不愿意走路了．他自己之所以选择到这个小镇居住 就是因为地方很小 他只需要步行就可以解决他日常要做的任何事情 (.) 可是呢 别人认为他很怪异 老是走路 对不对？可是编者在选用这篇文章的时候 为什么要把原：来的标题改成 Out of Step (.) 大家想一想 哪个标题更好．Why No One Walks? 还是 Out of Step 更好．(0.5) Out of Step 什么意思？
4	Ss	[((some students answering unclearly 2.0))]
5	S3	[不走路 不走路的意思]
6	Sx	[没有脚　没有脚] ((The student who answered was a freshman who came to observe my class for fun))
7	T	Out of Step 是不走路的意思吗？
8		((Some students took out their mobile phones and checked the meaning of the expression 49))
9	S2	步调不一致
10	T	步调不一致 对不对？(0.5) 所以 就像我们说 (.) < 人和人 >=
11	S39	= 不合拍
12	T	对．不合拍 eh=
13	S21	=Eccentric
14	T	有一点 (.) 这个意思 en (.) eccentric. 有这个意思．所以 我觉得编者把课文的标题改成 Out of Step 是有道理的 为什么呢？因为作者在英国 (.) 生活很长时间 再回到美国以后 发现跟美国人已经不合拍了 =
15	S3	= 走路也可以啊 因为他喜欢走路啊
16	T	哦 — 走路也可以．他喜欢走路 不喜欢开车 是吧．所以编者还是用了心的 把标题修改了．但是 课文里边 — 我们的课文 只有 913 词 (.) 但是原文有 1290 多词 删节了 300 多将近 400 个词 我觉得删节得并不是很好 (.) 比如说 作者 Bill Bryson 在原文里边 多次提到了他的 wife 但是这里只是开头提到了 作者在原文还提到了他的 children (.) 我已经把原文发给大家了 请大家看了改编的课文 再看一下他的原文 看有什么不同 然后思考一下 (.) 哪一个标题更好。

As the above stretch of interaction shows, four students offered their answers in front of the class and many others participated in the whole-class interaction. It seems that the question on appreciating the title of the text was of interest to the students. At the beginning of the next class, which was held ten days after the previous one (due to the National Day Holiday), the researcher brought up the question on the title again mainly for the purpose of checking whether the students had read the original article and come up with their own answers to the question left to them. At least some of them did what they had been assigned to, as several students directly engaged themselves in the interaction prompted by the question, as displayed in Extract 4-5. The researcher initiated the interaction with a DIU (L1) which was filled up by S9 (L2). When he asked the class whether they had weighed about the two titles (L5), only one unidentified student (Sx) gave a positive answer (L6). Hearing this response, the researcher continued with an alternative question (L7) and Sx expressed her favor of 'Out of Step' over the original. When the researcher probed for an explanation, S33 took over the turn and offered her reasoning (L10). Noticing that S33 made use of 'out of step' in her statement, the researcher probed to see whether she remembered the meaning of the expression (L11). After that, he asked the whole class whether they all considered 'Out of Step' as the better title (L13) and hearing several students respond with "yes" (L14) he suspended the interaction with "We will come back to this later" (L15).

Extract 4-5 On which title is better

1	T	I remember last time I asked you a question, a question about the title. The original title is?
2	S9	why no one walks.
3	T	Right. Why no one walks. But the textbook writers changed Why No One Walks into Out of Step.
4	Ss	Yes.
5	T	Then (.) what do you think about this change made to the title? Why No One Walks into Out of Step. (1.5) Have you thought about this? mhm? (0.5) No?
6	Sx	Yes.
7	T	You like the original title? Or. (.) you like the present one.
8	Sx	The present.
9	T	The present one? Why do you like the present one?
10	S33	Because the author told stories about why he was out step with his neighbors.
11	T	Yes? What does Out of Step mean?

12   S33   It means 不协调
13   T   OK. Thank you. You all think Out of Step is better than Why No One Walks?
14   Ss   ((several students answer in a low voice)) Yes
15   T   OK. But- We will come back to this later.

As mentioned earlier, the objects of learning were interconnected and could not be treated separately. It was especially the case with interpreting the author's purpose of writing and appreciating the title of the text. Extract 4-2 was presented above to demonstrate how the researcher continued to draw the students' focal attention on the author's intention of writing the article. The transcript is pasted below and labeled anew (as Extract 4-6) as part of the interaction was meant to address the appreciation of the title. After checking the students' answer to the text comprehension exercise on the author's purpose of writing, the researcher redirected the students' attention to the title again. After expressing his own understanding that the original title better captures the author's intention (L6), the researcher did stop for a second, but did not invite the class to speak out their own ideas. Instead, he shared with the students his speculation that the textbook writer might have borne the thought that 'Out of Step' could create the effect of a pun (L8). Noting that the students might not know the word 'pun', he repeated the previous statement after a two-second pause and then translated it into Chinese before uttering a confirmation check (L10). One student (S33) made an affirmative answer (L11). Though the mention of the title of the text was more like a flashback or an interlude in the global reading, it did serve to draw the students' attention to the effectiveness of the original title and the one selected by the textbook writers. The researcher's speculation that 'Out of Step' could be understood as a pun led the students to *categorize* it as a figure of speech.

Extract 4-6 On the change of the title

1   T   The author's purpose of writing? it should be (0.5) Is it A? (0.5) Many of you didn't do this. ((T began explaining possible new words in the choices 30))
2   T   So the answer should be-? (1.8)
3   S21 A.

4	T	Yes?
5		(2.0)
6	T	It should be (.) A↓ right? But- then let's come to the title of the text. If the answer to this exercise should be A then (0.3) the title of the text should be <u>chan:ged</u> back into (0.2) Why No One Walks. Right?
7		(1.0)
8	T	It seems that Out of Step is better than Why No One Walks. It's kind of eh it's kind of like a <u>pun</u>. Right?
9		(2.0)
10	T	It's something like a pun. 就有点像<u>双关语</u>，对不对?
11	S33	对啊!
12	T	But the author's original intention was (0.8) to criticize the situation in America, right? Almost no one walks, they are too much car-dependent, right?
13	S21	[Many Americans don't walk]
14	T	[So he's not trying to tell the reader] that he himself is out of step with Americans in life right? He is (.) [criticizing] OK?
15	S33	[criticizing]

Approaching the end of the instruction on the text, the researcher once again set the students to think critically about the textbook writers' changing the original title, as displayed in Extract 4-7. He assigned the students to discuss the question in groups: Which title better fits the author's intention of writing, *Out of Step* or *Why No One Walks*? The discussion lasted for about 6 minutes. The researcher then invited the students to present their ideas. Two seconds after the researcher's invitation, S21 spoke up, saying that he favored Why No One Walks. But when being probed for a reason, S21 did not come up with one and simply answered that the researcher had told them so (L5), which provoked a burst of laughter among the students. S21 then produced a longer stretch of utterance which appeared to be an acceptable reason (L8, L10). The researcher thought that simply giving a reason would not be sufficient and probed S21 to provide examples to illustrate his point. This time, S21 replied with "I don't know. I can't find it." (L14). The moment the researcher was going to say that he had talked about the details of the author's personal encounters in the neighborhood, S21 cut in with "in the first paragraph" (L16). Seeing that S21 did not give any further evidence, the researcher doubted whether he had figured out the meaning of the title given by the textbook writers. To the researcher's question on the meaning of the title, S21 answered "步调不一致", probably reading his notes (L18-21). The researcher acknowledged S21 and then nominated S39 to speak up (L22). S39 began talking after a pause of five seconds and gave two reasons: one is that Out of Step better reflects the theme of the text, i.e., criticizing car dependence; the other is Out of Step is "an advanced expression" (L23). After the researcher made a reformulation of her words, S39 continued to present her speculation about the textbook writers' motivation for the change of the title (L27) and then argued that as the text is an adaptation from the original article and some pieces of information were chopped out so she deemed *Out of Step* might be better from the editors' point of view (L31). After acknowledging S39's contribution, the researcher went on to reorganize her reasoning and argument (L32, L34). In the meantime, he also suggested that the textbook editors might have over-interpreted the author's intention.

Extract 4-7 Further discussion on the title

1	T	OK. That's the discussion. So which one do you think better fits the author's intention?(2.0)
2	S21	why no one walks.
3	Ss	((laugh))
4	T	why?(3.0)because?(3.0)
5	S21	Because you told us.
6	Ss	((laugh))
7	T	yes I told you this hahaha(2.0)
8	S21	because the details of the text are against the title out of step.(5.0)
9	T	S21ijian pardon please?
10	S21	because some details of the text are against the title of the textbook, out-out of step.
11	T	some details, they are against the title- out of step.
12	S21	yes
13	T	for example.
14	S21	Eh(19) uh, I don't know. I can't find it.
15	T	you can't find it- but=

16	S21	=In the first paragraph (5.0)
17	T	what is the meaning of out of step.
18	S21	(3.0) 步调不一致
19	T	[((laugh mildly))]
20	Ss	[((laugh mildly))]
21	S21	you have told us.(8.0)((in a low voice)) 就是步调不一致
22	T	OK. Thank you. some details of the text. they are against (0.8) what is conveyed in the title out of step. Mhm. Uh S39.
23	S39	(5.0) Out of step it's an explanation that probably there's (.) certainly there is car dependence em (7.0) because they're dependent to the cars they don't like walk and another reason is (.) out of step is an advanced expression.
24	T	mhm (.) so you prefer out of step=
25	S39	=yeah
26	T	to why no one walksand you think out of step is better because out of step means the author makes a suggestion right?
27	S39	Yeahand out of step is the author's opinionmaybe (.) he thinks he is a little ((XX)) to complain about the phenomenon (.) about car-dependence. so (0.5) the editor em used out of step instead of why (.) no one walks to present author's opinion
28	T	OK to present the author's opinion
29	S39	Yeah
30	T	I see (.) to better present the author's opinion
31	S39	because we cut pieces of the (.) the article, eh, it is further the whole article. if we can use the whole article, we can use no- why no one walks. and we just select some sections. so, maybe out of step is better.
32	T	OK. Thank you.So S39 thinks that out of step is better than why no one walks but- a moment ago (.) we said probably why no one walks is better than why no one walks right? My suggestion is that you check out of step in your dictionaryand you can find out of step- probably the editors- they think that out of step can be a pun. right? it can have a double-fold meaning.right? one is eh the author Bill Bryson and his wife they are out of step with-
33	Ss	((several students answer)) other Americans
34	T	Yes, other Americansand the other meaning is (. .) it is Bill Bryson's suggestion that Americans should walk more, right? they should use their legs. Probably that is what the textbook editors thought about the author's intention. but when we check out of step in a dictionary we can find that it has nothing to do with using one's legs to walk , right? It seems that out of step is something like an idiom, OK? a set phrase or a fixed phrase, right?it simply means that ehwe are not in agreement with each other or we are not in correspondence with each other, right?out of step- So (.) that could be an over-interpretation by the textbook editors.

The four extracts presented above were all oriented towards the appreciation of the title. The Q-A interaction displayed in Extract 4-4 and Extract 4-5 was meant to recognize the literal meaning of the title as well as its role in the whole text. The interaction displayed in Extract 4-6 led the students to compare the two titles in relation to the author's intention of writing. The interaction embodied in Extract 4-7 induced the students to draw upon what had been discussed previously and think critically and appreciatively about the change made by the textbook compilers to the title of the text. In addition to the sequence of questions involving different cognitive efforts at different phases of instruction, the researcher assigned the students a summary writing task where they were required to summarize the text and then to demonstrate which title better fits the text, *Why No One Walks* or *Out of Step*. The writing task constituted an opportunity to further extend the students' appreciative reading of the text.

Expressing personal responses relating to the text

Among the 39 questions designed for the while-reading stage, 3 of them belonged to the category of personal response and all of them centered around the first paragraph. Though these pre-designed questions might not orient to a central theme and hence not form a sequence that could offer the space for hierarchical variations, the enactment of such questions, as embedded in the instructional process, played a positive role in enriching the students' experience of learning.

The questions asked at the pre-reading stage could largely be taken as personal response questions. Nevertheless, they were designed and enacted in a way to construct or activate relevant schemata to foreshadow the instruction of the text. The first question asked during the while-reading stage to that end was a hypothetical one topically related to the author's return to the U. S. after living in England for 20 years: *Can you imagine living abroad for 20 years before coming back to your hometown? How would you feel in that case?* As displayed in Extract 4-8, after bringing up the question, the researcher waited for eight and a half seconds, and then nominated S2 to answer that question. As S2 was sitting in the far back of the classroom and her voice was not loud enough to be captured by the camera, her words could not be transcribed verbatim. Whatsoever, she did seem to have made some contributions to the interaction as elicited by the researcher's probing questions and clarification requests (L5-L17). After summarizing the main points in S2's contributions (L19), the researcher redirected the question to S32 (L41). Due to her limited language proficiency, S32 did not contribute much in English before switching to Chinese. The researcher went a little bit off the track for a moment and then also switched to Chinese to keep the conversation going (L33). When S32 said that she went home at least once every half month, the researcher turned to the whole class and asked whether there was any one who had left their home for over half a year. Seeing that no one spoke up after a pause of 18.7 seconds, the researcher modified the question into "So when you went back home did you feel strange?" (L41). The researcher did not notice that S32 again was still standing till she made a two-word utterance (L42). The interaction ended up not so successful in eliciting lengthy and complex student output, but it did stimulate the students to think about the hypothetical question.

Extract 4-8 On being away from home for a long time

1	T	then let's come to the text. OK paragraph one I have some questions for you? first can you imagine living abroad for 20 years before coming back to you hometown (2.3) yes how would you feel about that?
2		(8.5)
3	T	OK S2 what do you think about this?
4	S2	(5.0) maybe feel strange
5	T	yes feel strange? You feel strange about what?
6		(2.0)
7	S2	((unclear 2.2))
8	T	Surroundings?
9	S2	((unclear 3.1))
10	T	neighborhood?
11		(2.0)
12	S2	((unclear 6.0))
13		(2.2)

14	T	Friends?=
15	S2	=yes
16	S2	((unclear 4.0))
17	T	a lot of old friends you mean.
18	S3	((unclear 1.0))
19	T	Yes? the neighborhood changed. You feel strange about the surroundings, about the neighborhoo:d (.) about your friends.
20		(5.5)
21	T	S32. (1.3) OK. S32 you're there. mhm How would you feel?
22	S32	change
23	T	OK. change. yes.
24	S32	everything 那个 everything change
25	T	E:verything-
26	S32	[change]
27	T	[chan:]ged
28	S32	Yes yes
29	T	Twenty years later Yes. mhm
30	S32	(1.0) the change small town
31	T	Small town wha:t?
32	S32	小地方要发展的嘛
33	T	mmh 小地方发展快，所以变化很快 =
34	S32	= 对啊
35	T	嗯，离开家最长的时间，有没有半年？
36	S32	没有
37	T	没有半年？半年都没有啊？
38	S32	我半个月回一趟家
39	T	有没有离开家比较长时间的
40	Ss	((students talking unclearly 18.7))
41	T	Yes? So when you went back home did you feel strange?
42	S32	not strange=
43	T	=not strange=
44	S32	=just so so
45	T	Oh ↓ just so so because nothing changed?
46	S32	Yeah
47	T	OK I see.

The next personal response question was intended to elicit the students' views on living in a big city or a small town. As can be seen in Extract 4-9, five students were engaged in answering the question in front of the class. The first student nominated to speak up was S34 who replied that she would prefer to live in a small town out of consideration of distance from home and transportation. The next student nominated was S35 whose reply set the whole class laughing. After recapping S35's contributions, the researcher redirected the question to S20 (L25) and then re-allocated the turn to S11 (L43). Seeing that the students involved in the interaction did not contribute much except S35, the researcher opted to remind the class of the importance of giving elaborated replies to personal response questions (L51).

Extract 4-9 On living in a big city or a small town

1	T	OK uh S34.(0.8) Where is S34. Yes where do you prefer to live (.) in a big city or in a small town.
2	S34	Small town.
3	T	Why do you prefer to live in a small town.
4	S34	I live in a big city distant from my home and (.) transport is too far.
5	T	((laugh mildly 3.0)) Yes you're considering the distance between where you work and where you live.
6	S34	Yeah.
7	T	I see. Yes S35. What do you think about this?
8	S35	Uh the large city.
9	T	Why?
10	S35	Uh just the big city is convenient uh
11	T	Convenient. in what ways.
12	S35	(2.0) in many ways uh transporta:tion:
13	T	Transportation yes?
14		(5.2)
15	S35	Secondly ((unclear 2.0)) I mean in a big city you can hide yourself ((unclear 3.0)) eh
16	T	You can <u>hide</u> ↑ yourself [in a big city.]
17	Ss	[((students laugh loudly))]
18	S35	Yeah.

19	T	Why do you have to hide yourself (.) in a big city?
20		(2.0)
21	S35	Eh living in a big city, if someone live in a big city uh if you do something no one can=
22	Ss	((noise))
23	T	OK. I see.
24		(2.0)
25	T	Two reasons one is transportation the other is you can hide yourself in it aha?= =yes. I see. Thank you .Anyone else: who prefers to live in a small town? Hmm? S20.
26		(2.0)
27	T	Small town. or big city.
28	S20	Big city.
29	T	Big city also?- and why.
30	S20	I can have ((XXXXX))
31	T	you have what?
32	S20	((in a very low voice)) More opportunities.
33	T	opportu:nities (.) yes? what kind: of opportunities.
34	S20	((unclear 2.9))
35	Sx	income
36	T	[In:come]
37	Sx	[收入]
38	S20	yes.
39	T	So: living in a big city: you can have a higher income. That's true. probably @hehe@
40		(6.0)
41	T	Yes opportunities (.) it's easier for you to get job opportunities right?
42		(2.8)
43	T	So: you need to elaborate your answers to a question like this. you need to give reasons (.) Let's see another one? S11. Yes? You are going to answer the second question.
44	S11	I like living in large city.
45	T	Large city (.) >Beijing or Shanghai.<
46	S11	Eh Beijing uh (.) shopping.

47	T	Oh shopping ((laugh mildly)) because (.) yes it is easier for you to do shopping in large cities but you don't have to right? you can sit at home and use Taobao right? You can do anything.
48	S11	(0.6) I think uh in store uh
49	T	I see. you want to do window shopping=
50	Ss	=((students laugh))
51	T	not online shopping right? OK. (0.5) OK. Thank you. Eh 像这样的一个问题 ((T began talking in Chinese on the importance of giving reasons to support one's answer to a question on liking or disliking something 35))

The third personal response question was designed to involve the students in making inferences about the author's personality based on the first few sentences of the paragraph. As demonstrated in Extract 4-10, the question was asked (L10) after interaction around a content question. The question might be too general to be answered so that no one took over the turn after two long pauses (L11 and L13) till S21 broke the silence with a one-word utterance (L14). Some other students seemed to agree with S21 as they first echoed with "怪人" (L16) and continued talking for a while (L18), though indiscernible to the researcher. Realizing that the question was too general and inspired by S21's answer, the researcher invited the students to explain the word 'eccentric' and then shifted the topic to the satiric tone used by the author (L25), which was identified as the third object of learning.

Extract 4-10 On the author's personality

1	T	So the next question- why did Bill Bryson and his wife decided to move back to the United Stages and to settle down in a small town like Hanover. Have you thought about this?
2		((students murmuring))
3	T	OK. Let's see S27. (2.0) What is your answer to this. yes?
4	S27	Sorry I don't know
5	T	Haha you were not listening Ha?
6		(5.4)
7	T	Why did they choose to live in Hanover? (.) Because-
8		(9.0)
9	S27	He wanted to ((unclear 20))

10	T	Yes? Because Hanover is a small (..) town or (.) a small city. right? where they can yes they can walk to the business district. OK thank you. And then what kind of person do you think Bill Bryson is.
11		(5.0)
12	T	After reading reading the essay- reading the text. Mhm?
13		(7.0)
14	S21	Eccentric.
15	T	Yes?
16	Ss	怪人
17	T	怪人
18	Ss	((students talk unclearly 5.0))
19	T	Eccentric. Eccentric is a word used to describe- behaviors- to describe himself right? Eccentric probably his neighbor would think that Bill Bryson is: eccentric right? Eccentric means?
20	Ss	怪人
21	T	a person with strange behaviors right? Cent- cent- center right? Ec or ex means out of the center right? So you're not living a conventional life right? not conventional not like others. That is the meaning of eccentric that means you have so strange behaviors.(3.7)Do you think he is eccentric?
22	Ss	No
23	T	(3.8)By using the word eccentric the author actually he is (0.8)
24	S21	((XX))
25	T	(8.7)he's self mocking 在自嘲 right? hehe OK he's mocking at himself.(1.5) We can also say that he's criticizing the reality sarcastically right?
26	Ss	Yes.

Among the four objects of learning identified by the researcher and his collaborators, two of them, i.e., interpreting the author's intention of writing and appreciating the title of the text, were enacted through sequences of questions that appeared to have created the space for the students to experience hierarchical variation in the cognitive acts. Appreciating the title of the text was brought to prominence in particular as the researcher brought it up four times during the instruction plus a summary writing assignment. It was expected that the students would have been aware of that object of learning by the end of the unit.

The third object of learning, i.e., appreciating the author's satiric tone, was not enacted through sequenced questions as it does not reside in a certain language item but spreads across or permeates the whole text. Nevertheless, the author did call the students' attention to it, as can be seen in Extract 4-10, and to enhance the students' awareness of this object of learning, the researcher asked them to detect other sentences where satire could be identified when talking about rhetorical features of the text.

The fourth object of learning, i.e., expressing personal responses to topics related to the text, was touched upon while the first paragraph was being addressed during the while-reading stage. The three pre-designed questions were seemingly not sufficient to form a sequence where hierarchical variation could be experienced, whereas they had a role to play in invoking effective responses from the students.

As presented earlier, the researcher designed two group discussion tasks, one on the appreciation of the title of the text, the other on traffic problems in China. Due to time constraint, however, the latter task was not enacted in class.

4.4 Evaluating

To evaluate the effectiveness of first cycle of AR, analysis of qualitative data collected on the instruction of Unit 3 is presented as follows.

4.4.1 Students' learning logs

The format of the students' learning log for the second cycle of AR was changed from that used for the first cycle. The new log consisted of four parts: 1) the most impressive questions, 2) gains from Q-A interaction, 3) self-evaluation of performance in classroom interaction, and 4) suggestions about teacher's questions. A few students failed to notice the change of the format of the learning log and wrote their log as they had done for the first two units, which meant that not all data collected were exploitable at this stage. Thus, what is presented below is based on the logs written in the new format.

4.4.1.1 Most impressive questions

As the students wrote their learning log after the instruction of the whole text, their memories of teacher questions might not closely correspond to what the teacher actually asked in class. Hence the questions they reported to be impressive, though converged around several elements, were not uniformly formulated. Table 4-2 shows the distribution of the elements of the most impressive questions reported in the students' learning logs.

Table 4-2   Most impressive questions reported in students' logs of Unit 3

Element of impressive questions	Number of students
• The title of the text	23
• To live in a small town or a large city	7
• Language details (synonyms, potential meaning of certain details, meaning of 'virtually')	3
• Traffic in the future	1

As the numbers show, twenty three of the whole class reported that they were most impressed with the question on the title of the text. Some of them even reported their answers to the question though they had not participated in the episodes of Q-A interaction around the title. It can thus be said that the sequence of questions was successful in bringing about hierarchical variation in the students' learning experience. If not so, then it could be that the researcher's bringing up the question time and again during the instruction contributed to the students' awareness of the title.

Seven students mentioned that they were most impressed with the question on living in a small town or a large city; three of them referred to some language details (like "the question on the meaning of 'virtually'" by S21, "questions on how to differentiate synonyms" by S23, and "questions asked to dig into the potential meaning of certain details" by S10); and one reported to be most impressed with the question on traffic in the future.

4.4.1.2 Gains from Q-A interaction

The students' reported gains were found to cluster around some general benefits of classroom Q-A interaction. Some students mentioned that Q-A interaction helped them learn some language details:

- From those questions, I learn a lot about the passage, especially the details. Like the set phrase"I had this brought home to me". It is new for me before. (S38)
- I realized sometimes we could get deeper meaning from some simple words. When we do some reading, we should not only stay on the sentence the text gives us, but also to explore more information. (S12)
- And when I was in classes, I found you would pay attention to some very small details and extend widely. I learned a lot from it. For example, you asked us which of the two titles of the article is better. Before you ask the question I never thought about the question. (S14)

Some students wrote about the importance of participating in Q-A interaction for such reasons as follows:

- I can practice more and speak more. (S4)
- I can improve my poor spoken English. (S13)
- I need try to answer more questions. (S35).
- I much impressed by my classmates' answers logical and fluent. (S11)
- I like my classmates' funny answers. (S17)
- It is important to listen carefully to teacher questions and classmates' answers. (S33)

Most students indicated that Q-A interaction carried out in the current unit brought light to them the value of critical thinking or deep thinking, as demonstrated by the following extracts from some students' logs.

- I agree with that interaction initiated by questions, so that we are able to spend time to think and to learn about the topic. (S3)
- We are learning from each other by sharing ideas. (S8)
- Interacting with classmates can get a wide variety of ideas, we can open our eyes. What's more, it can also improve the ability of logicality and organization. (S9)
- Teacher questions are important to cultivate the ability of studying on our own and thinking from different dimensions (S10)
- My classmates' answers make me have deeper understanding of the passage

and more critical thinking. (S21)
- We should have an open mind and careful thought. (S22)
- We need to think and rethink about why the writer writes in such a way instead of another. (S26)
- There is non-existence of standard or correctness. (S36)

4.4.1.3 Self-evaluation of performance in classroom interaction

Most of the students were negative about their performance in participating in classroom interaction. The main reason accounting for their negative evaluation is that they perceived themselves as being insufficient in language proficiency, as demonstrated by excerpts from their learning logs:

- I didn't feel so satisfied with my own performance about your questions. Because sometimes I couldn't think so perfectly until you give me some tips. I think it's my problem. (S10)
- I am not so satisfied with my performance in answering some questions. Maybe sometimes I can't speak out what I want to express in English and can't make others understand me clearly. (S18)
- In fact, I am not satisfied with my performance in answering the questions. Because I am so busy for work and activities that my study time is not enough. So, my English lacks practice and it is poor. As a result, I can't say English frequently and sometimes I can't express my meaning. (S4)

4.4.1.4 Suggestions on future teacher questioning

The students' suggestions on future teacher questions clustered around three issues. One is that more open or deep questions should be asked in class:

- I want you give more question to develop our critical thinking abilities. Because that answer does not depend on your English, but on your mind. (S29)
- And I think you should ask questions which can lead us to think more dimensions and think more deeply, it will help us to develop the ability of thinking. (S10)
- the suggestions that I want to deliver to the teacher are increasing the group discussion within the progress of lessons over some opening questions.

Maybe, our will gain some diverse points from the public. (S34)

Another issue had to do with the distribution of questions or allocation of turns in organizing Q-A interaction:

- About classroom interaction, I think everyone should be given the chance to give their view for your questions, but time is limited, you could still ask some students to answer it. (S10)
- you can let others answer the question if one couldn't in order to avoid embarrassment. (S18)
- The teacher can ask the students in class who are not serious or sleepy to answer the questions. (S15)
- In the following teaching, in my opinion, I think teacher should question some students who is quiet in class. This will adjust class atmosphere. And it is better to ask question from easy to difficult. (S38)

The third prominent suggestion made by the students was about time for discussion or preparation before answering a question:

- The question about classroom interaction, I like the link of discussion. On the one hand we can focus, on the other hand we can be more quickly follow the classroom rhythm, master the focus. Furthermore, students can communicate and share ideas more effectively. This is helpful for innovation and expansion. (S31)
- Thirdly, as to the teacher's question, I hope the teacher can give us some time to discuss each other. The preparation will give us more confidence in our teachers' questions. (S36)
- My suggestion is to give the students some time to discuss. (S32)

4.4.2 Peer observation feedback

The researcher invited two different colleagues to observe his teaching of the two units. Both colleagues observed two class hours where the instruction fell on the while-reading stage. The observers were asked to fill in the field note form as shown in Appendix D while observing. A short post-observation conference of about 20 minutes was held immediately after each class.

The colleague invited for Unit 3 was Miss Li who had been teaching at university for 5 years. She commented that the classroom atmosphere was fairly good as most students appeared willing to participate in classroom interaction and that some students were very active despite their limited language proficiency. When it came to the teacher questions, the observer expressed that she was deeply impressed by the researcher's courseware, for it was nearly a list of questions designed for each part of the text. In respect of the content focus and cognitive demand of the questions, the observer replied that they were well designed in general: the questions were text-based and helpful in developing a deep understanding of the text. As for turn allocation, the observer confessed that for a class of such size, she would do the same as the researcher did, that is, inviting the whole class to respond or nominating individuals to answer. In regard of feedback to students' answers, the observer said the researcher did not seem to spare time to correct students' mistakes explicitly as he mostly either repeated or rephrased their answers with mistakes or expanded their fragmentary utterances into complete sentences. The observer thought the classroom atmosphere was rather good, for she felt that the researcher was humorous and had a good rapport with the students. She did not give suggestions on how to improve classroom interaction but she did suggest that the researcher consider spending a little bit more time on explaining some language points. She expressed her concern that the students might not tackle the language points on their own so that it would be necessary for the teacher to spend time giving detailed explanations on them.

The other colleague, Miss Ding, a teacher with only months of teaching experience, observed a while-reading session of Unit 4. In the post-observation conference, she expressed her approval of the researcher's instruction in the manner of asking and answering pre-designed questions. She even said that she would like to borrow that mode in her teaching. She did not comment much on the quality of the questions and the efficiency of Q-A interaction, neither did she give suggestions on improvement. However, she did mention that the classroom atmosphere had left her a deep impression and she observed that the researcher had taken opportunities to ask questions in close relation to students' life or the real world and also questions concerning encyclopedic knowledge. An example she gave to illustrate this was the researcher's asking the students the question on the meaning of 'puritan' and exemplifying it with the story of Benjamin Franklin.

4.4.3 Group discussion notes

When the instruction of Unit 4 was completed (i.e., by the end of the first cycle of AR), the researcher organized the first after-class group discussion where four students were involved in exchanging their feelings of living on campus, doing their English major studies, and attending the intensive reading course. When it came to the last topic, all the four students expressed first talked about the difficulties they were faced with, such as in memorizing new words, in enhancing their grammatical knowledge, in pronouncing words correctly, etc.

When requested to make a comparison between the course experience of the current semester and that of the last, they all indicated that they had now adapted themselves to the new teacher's style of teaching and had started to feel that they need to depend on themselves rather than on the teacher. During the discussion, they also pointed to their awareness of being critical while learning the intensive course and other courses in general.

> S10 made a comparison between the style of teaching of the two teachers of the two semesters, saying that the teacher of the last semester demonstrated to them everything on the textbook, and the teacher of this semester, only elaborates some of the contents in the textbook and even doesn't require them to finish all the exercises. She was positive of such an adaptation because she felt that she had become more self-dependent and critical-thinking than before. The other students expressed that they had similar feelings as S10 did.
>
> (Group discussion note, Oct. 30th, 2017)

4.4.4 Stimulated reflection journals

After each class, the researcher would review the video-tape of that class and reflect on his own teaching. On the whole, he felt comfortable with the design of instruction in a manner of asking and answering questions designed in correspondence with the identified objects of learning. What upset him by the end of this cycle was how to organize the Q-A interaction effectively. He found it difficult to match each student's name with their faces and thus not easy to nominate those who were in need of opportunities to participate but often reticent in classroom interaction. To put it alternatively, he was dissatisfied with the turn allocation in his organization of interaction. This problem seemed to have improved during the instruction of Unit 4 as some less proficient and chronically silent students were nominated to answer some less demanding questions.

What was satisfactory was that the identified objects of learning were enacted during instruction and the Q-A interaction created the learning space for the students to experience variation in the dimensions of content focus and cognitive demand. As the students reported in their learning logs, what they had learned was more than discrete language points but also the value of close reading and critical thinking, respect to peer classmates, exchange and sharing of ideas, autonomous learning, etc.

4.4.5 Implications

The evaluation, as presented above, proved that the first cycle of AR, i.e., trialing questioning sequences, was successful in that the sequences of questions designed before and enacted during the classroom instruction created the necessary conditions for the students to experience variation in the two dimensions of content focus and cognitive demand. Analysis of the data collected through the students' learning logs, group discussion notes and the researcher's reflection journals showed that the first cycle of AR contributed to enriching the students' experience of the intensive reading course. They began to realize that the intensive course was not merely for the learning of language points or the accumulation of grammatical and lexical knowledge, but also for the development of integrated skills, including the improvement of language proficiency as well as critical thinking. In other words, the questioning sequences were effective in extending the space for the students to experience the intended objects of learning.

However, some problems loomed large as the first cycle proceeded. Firstly, as the students wrote in their learning logs, whereas most of them explicitly expressed their preference of open questions relating to their own life over closed questions associated with the textual information, there were quite a few of them insisting that more questions be asked to address language points. Secondly, many of the students found it pressed to answer the teacher's questions in class and expected to have more preparation time before answering the teacher's questions. Furthermore, turn allocation remained a problem as some students suggested in their learning logs that those reticent students should be mobilized to speak up in class and the researcher noted in his reflection journals that it was difficult to match all the students' names with their faces which made it hard to nominate those less active students at ease.

Noting the feasibility of designing and enacting questioning sequences in consideration of the intended objects of learning as well as the new problems, the researcher decided to make modifications to the plan for the next cycle of AR.

Chapter 5   Second Cycle of Action Research

This chapter gives a detailed account of the second cycle of AR with adaptations made on the basis of the first cycle. The major adjustment adopted is the researcher's having the students preview the text before class in reference to a list of teacher questions so as to make sufficient preparation to answer them in class.

5.1 Focusing

In view of the findings of the first cycle of AR, the researcher decided to focus on how to further extend the learning space for the students through the design and implementation of questioning sequences. The major problems remaining to be resolved, as identified in Section 4.4.5, can be recapitulated as follows:

1) how to balance the proportion of comprehension, language and response questions as some students requested for more response questions and others more language questions?

2) how to relieve the students of pressure or anxiety when organizing Q-A interaction as some students reported to feel nervous to answer questions due to insufficient preparation time? and

3) how to involve chronically reticent students in classroom interaction as some students complained that some of their classmates always sat back in the classroom?

5.2 Planning

To tackle the problems listed above, the researcher consulted his supervisor and his colleagues for possible solutions and negotiated with the students before setting up a plan of solutions for the second cycle of AR (See Table 5-1).

To address the first problem, the researcher decided to design more open response questions relating to the students' campus life and engage more students in interaction initiated by such questions. In addition, to help tackle language problems, the researcher requested the students to bring to the class their own questions relating to any language points and raise them any time they would like to.

As for the second problem, the students suggested in their learning logs that more preparation time be given before nominating a respondent. However, the researcher found it not realistic to provide extensive waiting time in all cases and instead decided to hand out to the students in advance the list of questions he designed for the forthcoming unit. It was assumed that, by so doing, the students could fully prepare themselves for answering any questions listed in the hand-out.

The third problem was a matter of turn allocation and would be easily resolved by deciding in advance on the chronically silent students to be involved in the interaction initiated by certain questions. The researcher thus made a list of the students he had observed to be silent most of the time in class so that he could nominate them to answer questions with precision.

Table 5-1 Solutions planned for the problems identified in AR2

Identified problems	Planned solutions
• Some students' request for more response questions and some others' request for more language questions	• Design more response questions • Invite students to raise language questions
• The lack of sufficient preparation time before answering teacher questions	• Hand out the list of teacher questions days before classroom instruction
• Some students were chronically reticent	• Make a list of the students who always keep silent and occasionally nominate them to answer questions

Upon the completion of Unit 4, the researcher broke to the whole class the modified scheme of teaching as described above. The proposal met no disagreement, though some few did grudge about having to spend much time in previewing the lesson and preparing for the questions.

5.3 Implementing

As with the first cycle, the researcher first collaborated with his colleague in identifying the objects of learning to be focused upon, and then designed and enacted questioning sequences accordingly. What distinguished the current cycle from the previous one was the researcher's handing out to the class the questions he had designed so that the students would have sufficient time to prepare their own answers and to come up with their own questions which the researcher had not thought of. What follows is the implementation of the plan during the instruction of Unit 5.

5.3.1 Identifying the objects of learning

The main text of Unit 5, in the title of *The Real Truth about Lies*, is an article on how telling lies, even small white lies, can do harm to the humane communion. After reading through the text carefully, the researcher and his collaborator had sessions of discussion to exchange their understanding and decided to focus on the following objects of learning.

Interpreting the author's attitudes towards lying

The author does not explicitly show his attitude towards telling lies at the very beginning of the text. Instead, he illustrates it with statistical figures, stories and quotes. Hence, it would be necessary to have the students read between the lines and infer the message conveyed behind them. Throughout the text, the author uses a variety of words and expressions to refer to lies and the act of lying and the practitioners agreed that the author conveys with those words and expressions his attitude to the act of lying. Thus, it would be worthwhile not only to draw the students' attention to the words and expressions, especially the subtle differences between them, but also lead them to interpret the theme of the text.

Appreciating the author's use of figures in demonstrating the ubiquity of lying

The text begins with findings of surveys conducted by psychological professors and/or researchers on the prevalence of lying in everyday life. Such a writing technique was considered of significant value to English learners. Thus, the teachers decided that the students should be called to interpret the author's intention of citing those figures and to appreciate the value of such a technique.

Appreciating the author's misquoting of Mark Twain's words

While discussing the author's intention of ending the text by citing Mark Twain's words— "When in doubt, tell the truth. It will confound your enemies and astound your friends.", the two teachers found it hard to connect the quote with the preceding part of the whole text and hence attempted to look for the original text where the words were used. It turned out that it was a misquote wrongly attributed to Mark Twain, who had never written such but only entitled one chapter of his non-fiction travelogue *Following the Equator* as "When in doubt tell the truth". The two teachers thought it worthwhile to take advantage of this misquote as an opportunity to cultivate the students' critical awareness in reading any given texts.

Expressing personal responses towards lying

Lying is not uncommon in real life. No one could be immune to telling lies or being lied to. The author of the text perceives lying, even telling small white lies, as an ethical problem. The teachers both conceived that such a perspective should be exploited to stimulate students' personal responses.

5.3.2 Designing questions

Bearing all the five objects of learning in mind, the researcher began to design questions for the three stages of instruction.

Pre-reading Questions

The researcher designed four questions for the pre-reading stage, as displayed in Figure 5-1. The first three of them were intended to stimulate the students' schematic knowledge relating to the theme of the text; and the last questions was intended to foreshadow the discussion of the use of figures in demonstrating the ubiquity of lying.

Pre-reading Questions
1. Do you remember lying to anyone? Why did you tell the lie?
2. Have you ever been lied to? If someone lies to you for your own good, how would you feel?
3. Search at Yahoo.com "survey lies lying", read one of the returned reports on lying, and retell the major findings of the report to your class.

Figure 5-1   Pre-reading Questions for Unit 5

While-reading Questions

For the while-reading stage, the researcher prepared two sets of questions, one for global reading and the other for detailed reading. To supplement the text comprehension questions provided in the textbook, the researcher devised four global reading questions (See Figure 5-2) to help students further understand the general textual messages of the text.

As for the detailed reading, the researcher came up with 34 questions, including 11 CQs, 16 LQs and 7 RQs. The proportion of the three types of questions was moderated in accordance with the students' feedback about teacher questioning in the instruction of the preceding units. Figure 5-3 is a screenshot of the slide displaying the questions designed for the instruction of paragraph 3.

Global Reading
1. Do you remember lying to anyone? Why did you tell the lie?
2. Have you ever been lied to? If someone lies to you for your own good, how would you feel?
3. Search at Yahoo.com "survey lies lying", read one of the returned reports on lying, and retell the major findings of the report to your class.

Figure 5-2   Global Reading Questions for Unit 5

Detailed Reading (Para. 3)
1. LQ: Translate the first sentence.
2. LQ: What kind of clause is "what most of us would call earth-shattering"?
3. CQ: For what purposes do men and women lie respectively in general?
4. RQ: [discussion]Is it the case in real life? Do you tell different lies to people of different gender? Why?

Figure 5-3   Detailed Reading Questions for Para. 3 of Unit 5

Post-reading questions

The post-reading stage was comprised of a discussion activity and a summary writing task, both constituted by concrete questions. The discussion activity was designed to have the students comment on the film *Good Will Hunting*, where the orphaned hero named Will lied to his girlfriend about his family background. The activity was meant to stimulate the students' personal responses towards cordiality or candidness in romantic relationships. Figure 5-4 shows the discussion activity consisting of three questions. The summary writing task was meant, as usual, to develop the students' integrated learning of the text. Figure 5-5 is a screenshot of summary writing task consisting of three questions.

Discussion

Watch the film *Good Will Hunting* after class, and discuss with your classmates the following questions:
- Why did Will lie to her girlfriend (Skylar) about his family?
- Do you think Skylar would forgive Will if she discovered about his lies?
- Suppose you were Will or Skylar, what would you do in that situation?

Figure 5-4 Discussion activity for Unit 5

Summary Writing

Read the text carefully and then write your response in NO LESS THAN 200 WORDS, in which you should answer the following questions:
- What is the main message of the text?
- How is the main message developed in the text? and
- Is it acceptable to tell small white lies?

You can support yourself with information from the text.

Figure 5-5 Summary writing task for Unit 5

5.3.3 Handing out the questions as a guide for preview

The researcher handed out the questions designed for the three stages of instruction to the whole class three days ahead of tapping into Unit 5. The students were required to come up with answers to the questions while previewing the text. The researcher also voiced his expectation that the students bring their own questions to the classroom and that questions of any sort would be welcome. Furthermore, during the process of instruction, the researcher would stop at appropriate times to invite students' questions. The assumption for doing so was that students' questions would help enrich their experience of learning, or extend the outcome space of learning in Marton and colleagues' words (Marton & Booth, 1997; Marton & Tsui, 2004), because by so doing the individual students' needs could be better catered to.

5.3.4 Enacting questions

During classroom instruction, questioning sequences were enacted to carry out the identified objects of learning to ensure that the students could experience variation in the two dimensions of content focus and cognitive demand. What follows is a detailed description of how each object of learning was addressed through teacher-fronted Q-A interaction.

Interpreting the author's attitude towards lying

The first object of learning, i.e., interpreting the author's attitudes towards lying was carried out through several episodes of Q-A interaction in the phase of while-reading, both global and detailed. The researcher first picked up the topic by having the students look for words and expressions concerning lying used by the author, and then had them think about the author's attitude towards telling small lies (L5 to L14), as demonstrated in Extract 5-1.

Extract 5-1 On the words and expressions concerning lying

1	T	OK the first thing to do is (..) en find in the text all the words and expressions about lying or telling lies. See how many you can find
2		(5:55.05)
3	T	mhm there are many. right? like in the first paragraph-
4		((locating and explaining related words and expressions in the text paragraph by paragraph 19:12.00))
5	T	所有的 课文中出现的这些 和 lying 相关的词 都是一些无伤大雅的谎言 是吧 (2.17) They are harmless falsehoods (1.0) small white lies or little white lies or white lies and small untruths (3.30) 还有吗 好像就这些吧 所有这些和 lying 相关的词汇 其实表示的都是一些 <harmless (..) little white lies> right? 你觉得这些可以接受吗
6	Ss	可以啊 / 可以接受

7	T	mhm? I think the author tries to answer this question. whether it is acceptable or moral to tell small white lies. (1.40) Do you think it is acceptable?
8	Sx	mhm. yeah.
9	T	What is the author's answer (..) to this question
10	Ss	((unclear 2.30))
11	T	uhuh?
12	S13	Maybe not
13	T	maybe yes maybe not?=
14	S13	=maybe not.=

To help the students get a further global understanding of the text, he led them to divide the text into specific parts, as displayed in Extract 5-2. In the process, questions were asked about the author's intention of writing the article, like the DIU in L7 about the commonality of lying, the elicitations in L13 and L15 about the consequence of lying, the interrogative in L19 about the author's way, and another DIU in L31 about the author's suggestion on whether to tell a lie or not. The interaction did not arrive at a specific solution to the part division of the text before the ringing of the bell but did induce them into interpretive reading of the text. Despite the limited student responses, quite a few students engaged themselves in the interaction.

Extract 5-2 On the division of the text

1	T	and then yes (..) so: how many parts do you think (.) the text can be divided into.
2	Ss	((unclear 5.70))
3	T	You cannot see the screen clearly right?
4	Ss	yes/yes
5	T	When we're doing intensive reading? I guess we must answer two questions. The first question is? what is the main message of the text right or what does the author wants to tell us (.) and the next question is how (2.10) first is what ↓ right? what is the main message. main idea. main argument. and the second is how does the author convey this message (11.10) I told you that mhmh the author writes the text in order to answer that question that is whether it is acceptable to tell small white lies. (0.85) and how does he answer that question. first?
6		(6.60)
7	T	First yes he tells us- (4.55) he tells us that-

8	S21	even the small lies hurt
9	T	(0.65) <lying is (..) very common>
10	S6	ridiculous=
11	T	=yes lying is very common in our everyday life and people (.) who lie or have ever lied. do not give attention to such deceptions right and then yes uh uh when he shows us how commonplace lying is he uses- he uses a lot of figures- that is why last time I asked you to search on Yahoo- to search for reports reports on lying surveys right? >and you found a lot of figures in those reports< right? <one in five or three out of five or eight in ten> reported that they have told lies and they also reported that they are not worried about such deceptions right? (0.95) so many figures and then (0.5) in the next part (.) the author (.) tells us mhm?
12	S21	((unclear 9.80))
13	T	Yes first (..) lying is common? and second-
14	S21	((unclear 6.10))
15	T	yes about- mhm?
16	S21	((unclear 5.50))
17	T	yes ↓ the consequence right? the consequence or the consequences of lying.
18	Ss	((several students pronouncing the word consequence in low voice 3.35))
19	T	and (2.95) how does the author (2.5) account for the consequences of lying.
20		((unclear 7.00))
21	T	he gives us some examples right? a typical example is a person called Tom right? mhm?
22		((unclear 2.10))
23	T	Yes a corporate executive whom I'll call Tom right Tom is an example (2.85) or the pumpkin pie example- @hehe@ pumpkin pie- what is pumpkin pie?
24	Ss	南瓜饼/南瓜饼/南瓜饼
25	T	你们喜欢吃南瓜饼吗
26	Ss	((students answer in chorus)) 喜欢
27	T	我们食堂里有 有没有发现？
28	Ss	有啊/有啊/有啊
29	T	and then in the last part the author-
30	S21	uh just the answer to why people should not tell small white lies
31	T	yes the authors (..) recommendation (.) or suggestion for (1.0)
32	S21	whether we should [tell the truth]
33	T	[people who are] confronted with such a question right? yes whether to tell the truth or not. and the author's suggestion is: ? (1.0) he quoted or he cited (0.5) he cited Mark Twain right?=
34	Ss	=yeah/yes

35	T	to answer that question- <when in doubt tell the truth yes when in doubt tell the truth (1.55) it will confound your enemies and astound your friends> (2.35) it seems that his suggestion is
36	Ss	tell the truth/tell the truth
37	T	to tell the truth right? you don't have to tell lies otherwise you will have to tell more lies to cover up the first lie right He cites Walter Scott's words right <what a tangled web we weave when first we practice to deceive>
38		(4.10)
39	T	OK (.) we have a little more than three minutes (.) and then ((T comments on students' summary writing of Unit 4, 3:15.00))

At the beginning of the next class, the topic was picked up again regarding the division of the text and the interpretation of the author's attitude towards lying (Extract 5-3). Seeing that some students provided different answers to the question (L8 and L10), the researcher led them to review the main points of discussion on that issue in the previous class (L19 to L39). As can be seen in the transcript, the students did not verbally contribute much as with the previous episode of interaction. Nevertheless, they probably arrived at a clearer line of thought of the author's writing, which might have strengthened their interpretative reading of the text.

Extract 5-3 On the division of the text

1	T	OK (.) where did we leave off last time?
2	S21	(14.45) eh how can we separate- (2.5) 怎么把 - 分成几个部分
3	T	mhm?
4	S21	the structure of the passage
5	T	OK the structure of the <u>whole</u> (.) text
6	S21	yes
7	T	(1.05) how many parts do you think the text can be divided into
8	Sx	I think it's three
9	T	Yes three:: or four. (1.5) yes S1
10	S1	four
11	T	you think it's four=
12	S1	=yeah
13	T	why do you think (1.5) it can be divided into four parts?
14		(10.70)

15	T	mhm?
16		(7.10)
17	T	where do you lay the dividing lines and what is the main idea of each part
18		(6.05)
19	T	yes last time I said (1.46) I think the text can be divided into=
20	S21	=three
21	T	yes the first part is about (2.25) lying is common- place in our daily life right? and then the second part (.) is about the consequences of lying or telling lies (.) and the last part (1.30)
22	S21	the standard-
23	Ss	the truth/tell the truth
24	T	(1.25) the standard? or criteria? (4.25) what- what kind of standard- the standard for what.
25	Ss	((unclear 2.10))
26	S21	en::
27	T	(9.25) mhm the last part is it about any standard?
28		(3.75)
29	T	the last part is the author's suggestion=
30	Sx	=yes=
31	T	=right?
32	S21	yes
33	T	en when you're (0.5) in doubt: right whether to tell the truth and the author's suggestion is: =
34	Ss	=tell the truth/tell the truth/tell the truth
35	T	what?
36	Ss	[It will confound your enemies]
37	Ss	[When in doubt tell the truth]
38	T	yes the quote by Mark Twain when in doubt tell the truth (1.35) mhm?
39	Ss	((T and students read together)) It will confound your enemies and astound your friends.

Seven minutes after reviewing the part division, the researcher repeated the question "What is the author's attitude towards telling white lies?" and invited the whole class to give their answers (Extract 5-4). Hearing the different answers of S21 (L2) and Sx (L3), the researcher confirmed that of Sx and asked further about the situations where one can tell white lies (L4). After S21 pointed out the paragraph in which the answer could be found (L9), the researcher confirmed S21 by reading the relevant words (L12) and steered the interaction to the translation of "the exchange of the principle of trust for the principle of caring" (L17) and then to the word explanation of 'ethicist' (L25) before raising another question on the author's suggestion for the dilemma of whether to lie or not (L31).

Extract 5-4 On the author's attitude towards small white lies

1	T	what is the author's attitude towards- towards telling white lies. What do you think the author means. small white lies?=
2	S21	=should be avoided=
3	Sx	=it depends
4	T	mhm it depends yes S33 said it depends mhm in what cases can one lie or cannot tell white lies
5	Sx	((unclear 3.90))
6	T	uhuh?
7	S21	((unclear 3.00))
8	T	S21 uhuh?
9	S21	uh: paragraph (.) sixteen
10	T	paragraph six<u>teen</u>? (0.85)
11	S21	lying is ((unclear 2.0)):
12	T	yes? yes the principle of trust for the principle of caring (1.00) The most understandable lies ↑ are an exchange of what ethicists refer to as the principle of trust for ↓ the principle of caring. So (.) here is the exchange of A for B. right?
13	S21	yeah=
14	T	=mhm that means-
15		(2.70)
16	S21	trust and caring
17	T	(3.30) the exchange of the principle of trust for the principle of caring 这个怎么翻译 this is a big question right?=
18	S21	=yeah (4.25) 最 最 最 - (1.5) [最可以理解的]
19	Sx	[用呵护代替信任]
20	T	用呵护代替 (..) 信任 . 对 . 用呵护代替信任 很好 是不是 the principle of trust for the principle of caring
21		(4.80)
22	S21	((unclear 1.50))
23	T	呵护或者关爱 是吧 (10.20) ethicists 是什么？
24	Sx	伦理学家

25	T	yes 伦理学家
26	Ss	yes/yes
27	T	伦理学家主要是研究 -
28	Sx	[伦理]
29	T	[人与人] 之间的关系的 是不是？是吧 mhm. so it depends yes some white lies are acceptable some others are damaging (.) right? to the society and they should be avoided (..) and then- what does the author suggest we do if we are not sure about whether to tell the truth or not- the author's suggestion is-
30	Sx	tell the truth=
31	T	=yes. (..) tell the truth mhm

  As can be noted in the above presentation, the object of learning was enacted through a sequence of questions spread across different episodes of classroom instruction. The interaction displayed in Extract 5-1 mainly dealt with looking for details concerning the author's description of lying, Extract 5-2 reminding the students of interpretive or inferential reading of those details, Extract 5-3 dividing the text into parts and figuring out the main idea of each part, and Extract 5-4 interpreting the author's attitude towards telling lies. In other words, the questions initiating the four episodes of interaction constituted a sequence relating to the first object of learning. The interaction initiated by those questions made it possible for the students to arrive at the interpretation of the author's attitude. That is to say, the sequence of questions, spreading across different phases of instruction and varying to some degree in content focus and cognitive demand, afforded the space for the students to experience the object of learning.

  Appreciating the author's use of figures in demonstrating the ubiquity of lying

  The second object of learning was addressed in the pre-reading and the while-reading. Extract 5-5 demonstrated the Q-A interaction in the pre-reading phase. In L5, the researcher called the students' attention to the use of figures in the reports they had been assigned to read before class. S3, S21 and S10 engaged themselves in identifying figures in the reports they had read. The researcher did not raise the key question till L49, where he invited the students to figure out the function of the numbers or figures in the report surveys.

Extract 5-5 Pre-reading question on the use of numbers as evidence

1	T	Can you tell us the major findings of the reports yes the lying survey (2.5) S3 have you finished reading the report? (1.65) mhm? tell us the findings
2	S3	((unclear 27.5))
3	T	yes what is the- (..) conclusion of that (.) report.
4	S3	(6.20) en the finding is that it is common to see deceptions in romantic relationships and marriages
5	T	mhm yes deception- deception is very common in relationships and marriages hehehe (9.15) are there any figures? (2.30) 数字 mhm? (5.10) eight out of ten? (.) or seven out of ten?
6	S3	just some examples
7	T	oh some examples uhuh for what- reasons do lovers lie to each other. (21.35) you didn't get (..) the reasons?
8	S3	(6.75) just saw the results
9	T	only the results OK?
10	S21	((unclear 9.35))
11	T	what?
12	Ss	pardon?/pardon?
13	S21	uh 就是说他们为了避免讨论有问题的问题 所以他们就对 (.) 互相之间撒谎
14	T	有 example 吗？
15	S21	(1.25) example (3.40) 好像没有
16	T	(4.10) They lied to each other to avoid (.) avoid the discussion of some problematic issues
17	S21	yeah
18	T	(2.70) especially there is tension between the two right? (3.05) S10 mhm? (3.05) the major findings of the report you have read
19	S10	(0.5) here is uh (1.5) about four in ten said their lies are justified sometime
20	T	four in ten. yes?
21	Sx	yeah
22	S10	jus- just over half fifty two percent said it is never justified
23	T	[mhm?]
24	S10	[and] (2.0) and about two thirds said that under certain circumstances they lie trying to protect someone's feelings
25	T	(1.35) to protect someone's feelings yes. two thir::ds.

26	S10	(0.5) and (.) another four in ten at times choose to exaggerate the story to make it more interesting and one in two about lying to a <child> about a parent (XX) is also acceptable
27	T	mhm? is also OK
28	S10	(0.95) yeah
29	T	mhm
30	S10	(0.75) and eh about a third say it's OK (..) at times to lie about one's age (.) and- lying about being sick to take a day off- off work
31	T	to take a day off work
32	S10	and eh very few thought it's- it was OK to lie in a relationship ↓ and treat on a spose or to cheat in classes
33	T	Cheat?
34	S10	Treat.
35	T	on what?
36	S10	on a spose- S-P-O-U=
37	T	=on a spouse
38	S10	spouse
39	T	to cheat on a spouse- you know cheat on someone? what does it mean- cheat on somebody. when we say cheat someone- it's different from cheat on someone.
40	Sx	(1.15) 偷情
41	T	hehe 偷 -yes if you cheat on someone it means you have a love affair- you have extramarital relationship (4.15) is it also justified?
42	S10	(1.25) oh no I think it is not justified
43	T	according to the report is it justified?
44	S10	(5.25) let me see (1.5) very few thought it acceptable
45	T	yes very few (.) mhm
46	S10	not the report=
47	T	=yes most people thought it unacceptable right?
48	S10	yeah
49	T	(5.70) Thank you. survey- this is a survey. A survey should have a lot of figures or digits right? (4.95) for what. (3.80) why do they use these (.) digits. figures. for what purpose (9.45) to support his or her=
50	Sx	=argument=
51	T	argument right. yes (2.0) the results in the form of figures and digits are evidence right?

The question was picked up again in the detailed reading but was specifically directed to the author's use of figures, as displayed in Extract

5-6. As can be noted in the transcript, S21, who had been actively engaged previously, was the only student who contributed fragments to the interaction. However, S21's fragmentary answers and Sx's confirmation (L8) were proof that the students had realized that figures or digits are not only evidence for arguments but can serve the author's purpose of demonstrating the ubiquity of lying in everyday life (as in L6).

Extract 5-6   On the use of figures

1	T	OK then let's come to the text (0.8) uh I have some more questions here uh (1.20) first the second question is about the first part that is the first five paragraphs the author uses [many]=
2	S21	[figures]=
3	T	=yes figures right. (0.85) so why do you think the author uses these figures? (1.30)
4	S21	uh eh (0.5) to demonstrate
5	T	to demonstrate yes to demonstrate that lying is commonplace [right?]
6	S21	[it is] ubiquitous.
7	T	All these figures- they constitute the evidence for the author's argument right?
8	Sx	yes
9	T	so you remember the first: time we came to this unit right I asked you to search at Yahoo.com some reports on=
10	S21	=lying surveys
11	T	right all these reports (2.0) quote figures from the surveys like eight out of ten or or three quarters right? mhm. (0.55) the reporters (1.5) report that they would lie OK.

The questions in the two episodes of interaction presented above, with the first projecting the second, made up another sequence. While the questions in the first episode called the students' attention to numbers and figures in survey reports and hence set them into thinking about their function, those in the second episode led them to appreciate the use of figures in the text under discussion. The researcher could have arranged more time to have the students compare the rhetorical effects of other types of evidence in argumentation, for example, quoting authoritative statements, to help them have a deeper learning about the rhetorical feature of the author's writing.

Nevertheless, it can be said that the sequence of questions had its effect in creating the space for the students to experience the intended object of learning.

Appreciating the author's misquoting of Mark Twain's words

Extract 5-7 displays a long stretch of interaction initiated by the question on the author's misquoting of Mark Twain's words. After reading the paragraph aloud, the researcher called the students to speculate whether Mark Twain had written the words quoted by the author (L1). Noting the students' doubts, he shared the result of his searching for the original words in Mark Twain's works (L8 to L26). Then S21 asked if the researcher had found the original passage of the text (L30), suspecting that the textbook writers might have made adaptations to the original. In L33, the researcher remarked on the misquoted words elsewhere and recalled his discussion with his colleague, Miss Zhou, the intensive reading teacher of the other class, on how the misquoted words could be misleading to the readers. He closed that episode of interaction by reminding the students of possible serious mistakes in the texts.

Extract 5-7 On Mark Twain's misquoted words

```
1    T    (2.0) Do you think that is by Mark Twain?
2         (0.80)
3    Sx   maybe=
4    T    =you can search the internet for (.) the original source
5         (1.20)
6    T    yes or no?
7    S21  nope
8    T    I searched it and I didn't find
9    Ss   ((students laugh 2.0))
10   S21  尴了个尬
11   Ss   ((several students laugh mildly 0.75))
12   T    yes [it was] wrongly attributed to Mark Twain.
13   Sx       [embarrassment]
14   T    yes [I only]
15   S21      [attributed to]
```

16	T	yes I only found the first part of the quote (1.05) when in doubt tell the truth this is by Mark Twain in Following the [Equator]
17	S21	[you mean]
18	T	the author is wrong and then I found in Wikipedia. Wikipedia says it was wrongly attributed to Mark Twain because he had never written such a sentence.
19	S21	so who wrote this sentence=
20	T	=Oh who wrote this sentence I don't know @hehe@ yes uh I (.) found it in Wikipedia OK? (2.0) The teacher of the other class. she asked me this question why did the author quote Mark Twain especially the latter half of the quote (0.80) It will confound your enemies and astound your friends. but I tried to search for the source of that quote and I failed
21	Ss	((several students laugh mildly 2.0))
22	T	(3.05) OK I will forward (1.45) the two pictures OK (1.30) to our group WeChat. (4.45)
23	Ss	((several students giggle 3.05))
24	T	(6.35) Yes the first picture (.) this is the screenshot of the Gutenburg books OK (2.80) from (.) Mark Twain's <Following the Equator> yes the title of the second chapter is <when in doubt tell the truth> and that's it there is no It will confound your enemies and astound your enemies right and then let's come to the second picture OK the second picture (..) are you using your cell phone?
25		((T and students laugh 3.10))
26	T	yes the second picture (0.5) you see this is from Wikipedia yes Wikiquote wikipedia mhm (1.10) uhm some quotes of (0.8) Mark Twain. from this book. Following the Equator. (0.70) chapter one. (1.30) uh- no chapter two right- when in doubt tell the truth. it appears in the very beginning? uh of chapter two of that book. and the sentence it will confound your enemies and astound your friends which does not appear in the text. (1.25) and here it was: attributed to Henry Wotton. (0.95) who advised a young diplomat? to tell the truth and so puzzle and astound his enemies so such a sentence is by another author [not by Mark Twain]
27	Ss	[((several students laugh))]
28	T	right but it was attributed to Mark Twain mhm this is ridiculous right?
29		((T and students laugh))
30	S21	do you have the original uh (2.0) passage
31	T	the original passage of this quote? no. I don't have it mhm
32	S21	((unclear 8.0))

33	T	if you search at Yahoo.com you can find that ma:ny writers quote this sentence and they attribute it to Mark Twain but actually it was not written by Mark Twain so this is a common error right (1.85) so we simply need to delete the last sentence of this text. (1.80) so when in doubt: tell the truth. that's it right mhm? (6.60) yes Miss Zhou said she could not understand the last sentence of the text because it is not connected to the rest of the text? who is the enemy and who is the friend? (6.25) Does the author mention? (0.85)
34	S21	[no]
35	T	[that] any people are our enemies or friends? no. at all right?=
36	Sx	=yes
37	T	(11.55) so we need to- we need to be careful when we do the reading (1.55) There are mistakes. serious mistakes OK.

The interaction displayed above could be seen as a 'side sequence' (Jefferson, 1972) or simply off-topic talk. However, put in a larger scope, the seemingly irrelevant episode, designed in advance in actuality, helped to open up the space for the students to reflect on their habituated reading experience, that is, being ready to accept whatever is presented in a text. In other words, the question designed to call the students attention to the misquoted words and the interaction initiated by it made it possible for the students to learn to read critically.

Expressing personal responses towards lying

In response to the students' suggestion that more open questions be asked to personalize the theme of the text, the researcher designed seven personal response questions for detailed reading. Besides the increasing number of RQs designed for the while-reading stage, three of the pre-reading questions were meant to elicit such personal responses as well.

Extract 5-8 displays the interaction evolving around the first pre-reading question. As can be seen in the transcript, the students were actively engaged in the interaction. The researcher first allocated the turn to S17, who then talked, with the aid of S13, about how she "cheated" her mother for a "running reward" every day. The interaction went well till S21 cut in with a plausible account (L18) for S17's not feeling so guilty of lying to her mother. The researcher brought the interaction back to the topic and allocated the turn to S19 (L23), who asserted that she had never lied (L26, L28). After a burst of laughter from her classmates, S19 proceeded to modify her assertion into not remembering any lying experience (as confirmed by the researcher's utterance in L32). After giving a brief talk on the ubiquity of lying, the researcher directed the same question to S28 (L35), a mostly reticent student. S28, after S3's jocular cut-in (L36), talked about how she played a joke on her roommates (L47). At the moment, the researcher took the opportunity to initiate further but brief interaction on lying on the April Fool's day.

As can be noted, a light classroom atmosphere was created as evidenced by the bursts of laughter in the wake of the researcher's probing for further responses, rephrasing students' words and re-interpreting the plausible accounts for their responses.

Extract 5-8 Pre-reading question on telling lies

1	T	S17, do you remember lying to anyone?
2	S17	I told my mother that I run every day.
3	T	Oh why did you lie to your mother?
4	S13	eh her mother (..) gave her (.) fifty yuan.
5	S17	@Hehehe@
6	T	OK (.) @hehe@ you pretended that you were=
7	S13	=running
8	S17	yeah
9	Ss	((students laugh 0.93))
10	T	and your mother would give you fifty yuan- [yeah] as a reward right
11	Ss	((students laugh 5.51))
12	T	Do you feel- (.) guilty?
13	Ss	((student laugh very loudly 3.91))
14	S17	maybe a little=
15	T	[oh a little]
16	Ss	[((students laugh 3.07))]
17	T	So it seems that you- it doesn't bother you right lying to your mother is not=
18	S21	=not if she is your mother
19	T	(0.53) what? S- S21 what did you say.
20	Sx	he is a mother

21	T	eh? (1.74) you're a mother.
22	Ss	((students laugh 1.33))
23	T	(3.20) en yes anyone else? (2.0) S19 do you remember lying to anyone last time?
24	Sx	((unclear 1.42))
25	Ss	((students laugh 0.98))
26	S19	(1.46) I've never lied.
27	T	Really you've never lied.
28	S19	en (2.5) no.
29	Ss	((students laugh 2.0))
30	S19	eh ((unclear 7.38))
31	T	oh you can't remember (.) probably because you lie too often
32		((T and student laugh 2.36))
33	T	or I have told too many lies ↓ (.) as a result I can't remember anything
34		((students laugh 2.13))
35	T	(1.29) may:be. right? we lie very often (.) it is very hard for us to remember how many times we have told lies. Anyone else who remember: ? mhm? (0.8) S28 You're laughing
36	S3	lie too much
37	Ss	((students laugh 2.0))
38	S28	not
39		((T and students laugh 1.11))
40	T	(0.94) yes what is your last lie.
41	S28	(3.20) en I've lied to my: (..) roommate heh
42		[((students laugh 1.65))]
43	T	[ah you lied to your roommate]
44	S28	eh yes=
45	T	=What was the lie: .
46	Sx	((unclear 2.31))
47	S28	I lied to my roommate eh I lied to her- she (.) that I had a boyfriend
48		((students laugh loudly 5.20))
49	T	Why did you do that. uhuh?
50	S28	funny
51	T	oh you- you- funny- you did that for fun
52	Ss	((students laugh 3.06))
53	T	(1.20) to amuse yourself and your roommate (4.66) eh there is April the first right? called=

54	Ss	愚人节 / 愚人节 / 愚人节
55	T	April Fools' Day right? so hehe (1.15) did you lie (..) in the last April Fools' Day?
56	Ss	yeah/no
57	Sx	((unclear 1.69))
58	S17	No I think that festival is very boring
59	T	Oh that day ↓ is very <u>bo</u>:ring.
60	S17	no that- 那个 就那个
61	Ss	((students laugh loudly 2.35))
62	S17	that- that day is very boring
63	T	oh that day is very boring (..) because you failed to lie to anyone
64	Ss	((students laugh 1.33))
65	T	(4.23) ((seeing that S3 was talking to her neighbor)) S3 huh?
66	S3	what.
67	T	What is your interesting story.
68	Ss	((students laugh 1.64))
69	S3	we were talking about April Fool's Day

In continuation of the interaction on prior experiences of lying to others as presented above, the researcher raised another question— "Have you ever been lied to". As displayed in Extract 5-9, the researcher directed the questions to students other than those involved in Extract 5-8. The first nominated student, S4, responded that she did not remember having been lied to (L2); the second nominated student, S37 talked about lying to the girl he liked with some difficulty and an equal amount of humor (LL4-30), which plunged the whole class into laughter. After that, S13 offered to share with the class something (L32): her feeling of being lied to whenever her desk mate S17 said to her things like "I love you", which brought more fun to the class. What came next was even more interesting as S33 cut in (L41) and switched the topic to being lied to during childhood by parents about the red packet money.

Extract 5-9 Pre-reading question on being lied to

1	T	Have you ever been lied to? (6.27) S4 (9.56) I mean (.) have you ever been lied to by anyone?

2	S4	((unclear 8.67)) uh I don't remember it.
3	T	(0.5) oh you don't remember it mhm (2.18) maybe you failed to know the truth @hehe@ OK (.) S37. (5.74) Do not look at the screen. The question is: have you ever been lied to by anyone?
4	S37	(unclear 5.65)
5	T	too many times?
6	Ss	((students laugh loudly 2.84))
7	S37	(2.40) I think eh (1.0) it- it is- it was- a fib yeah
8	Sx	Fib huh?
9	S37	fib (..) little- little lie. a little lie
10	Ss	fib/fib/fib
11	S37	en because en (3.0) eh we- we just eh eh talk something about eh (1.5) ((unclear 16.57)) and and I like the- I like her en I she want to talk with me but I I like her- I have something to do yeah it is a=
12	T	=you you mean you lied to someone else
13	S37	yeah
14	T	OK
15	S37	uh but- but- but- but not I not know I like she always sometimes she know eh eh I lied- I lied to her yeah (1.0) I don't I don't know why
16		((T and students laugh 2.0))
17	Sx	(0.5) 第六感
18	T	you wanted to lie to her hehe
19	S37	((unclear 1.73))
20	T	So if someone lies very often and then he or she will be called (.) a liar right?
21	Sx	yes
22		((T and several students laugh 2.53))
23	S37	but I but eh I'm- I'm em (1.29) she- her- she won't- doesn't care- doesn't care
24	T	uhuh uhuh OK?
25	S37	you know- you know.
26		((students laugh loudly 5.60))
27	T	she didn't take it seriously
28	S37	yeah
29	S21	you know? I don't know.
30	Ss	((students laugh loudly 5.16))
31	T	(2.5) OK (2.0) thank you
32	S13	I have something to say

33	T	Yes?
34	S13	S17 says he loves me very much (.) every day he tells me that he- that she
35	Ss	((several students laugh 2.0))
36	S13	(1.29) she every day tells me: she she loves me but eh just now she I think she's a liar
37		((several students laugh 2.0))
38	S13	he- she is a liar
39	S17	I'm not.
40		((T and students laugh 2.0))
41	S33	你们被爸爸妈妈骗过红包吗？
42	T	被爸爸妈妈骗红包
43	S33	对啊
44		((several students laugh 1.24))
45	Sx	Ohoh=
46	T	爸爸妈妈骗你们 是不是？
47	S33	是 hehehe
48	T	把你们的红包给我是吧？
49		((students laugh loudly 7.07))
50	S8	对啊 从小骗到大啊
51	T	从小骗到大 =
52	S8	= 对 大了就不骗了
53	T	哦 是啊 爸爸妈妈总是说帮你保管
54	S33	= 拿过来吧 =
55	T	= 等你想花钱的时候 =
56	S33	= 拿过来就不还了 =
57	T	= 就不太好办了

Extract 5-10 is the transcript of Q-A interaction that exploited further into the students' prior experience of being lied to for their own good. After bringing up the topic, there was a long break of 21.6 seconds. Conceiving that the students were not ready to answer the question, the researcher called their attention to cases where a family member being diagnosed with a serious disease (L3, L5) and met with mixed responses (L6). When the researcher started to talk about how doctors in the west and those in China might react to such cases (LL8-10), S3 responded in Chinese that Chinese doctors' decision to lie or not to lie is determined by the patient's family members (L11, L14).

Extract 5-10 Pre-reading question on being lied to for one's own good

1	T	The last question- yes- if someone lies to you for your own good (.) how would you feel.
2		(21.6)
3	T	for example (.) a family- suppose yes (.) a family member got a serious disease (.) like cancer=
4	Sx	=tumor=
5	T	=yes or tumor or any incurable disease (3.47) would you tell- him or her the truth (4.36) or if you meet the doctor (3.33) will you expect the doctor to tell you the truth
6	Ss	(1.47) yes/no/no
7		((T and several students laugh 1.79))
8	T	(3.20) in the west. like in America (.) the doctor is required to tell the truth he or she (.) cannot prevent the patient from=
9	S21	=from knowing truth
10	T	yes from knowing the truth
11	S3	中国怎么做 家属说了算
12		((T and students laugh 2.0))
13	T	Yes in China uh=
14	S3	doctor lies
15	T	Yes when the patient is diagnosed with a serious dis<u>ea</u>se the doctor (.) would choose to say that I- I need to see your family right?
16	Ss	yeah/yah
17	T	yes I need to see your family @hehe@ that means he or she is not going to tell the patient the truth.

The interaction initiated by the first three pre-reading questions, as demonstrated above, were organized to stimulate students' schematic knowledge about lying. These questions were picked up later with the intention to further elicit students' responses.

Extract 5-11 displays the interaction initiated by the researcher to check whether the students would agree with the author that men and women tell lies for different reasons.

Extract 5-11 On why men and women tell lies

1	T	yes another question is? do you think it is the case in real life that men lie to other men to propo- to promote themselves and women=
2	Sx	=yes=
3	S21	men tell lies for his=
4	T	=mhm well S21
5		(3.70)
6	S21	uh for example my father
7	T	your fa:ther
8	S21	yes uh my father always tell their- his uh brothers that how great my brother is
9	T	=you have a brother=
10	S21	=yes. elder brother
11	T	mhm
12	S21	but in fact uh my elder brother is not so good
13	T	mhm
14	Ss	((students laugh 1.10))
15	S21	uh he just to demonstrate that his- eh- son is very cleverest=
16	T	=mhm=
17	S21	in the world yes so I think it is self-promoting
18	T	yes self-promoting (1.5) do women also promote themselves?=
19	S18	=sometimes.
20		((T and S21 laugh 0.70))
21		(1.50)
22	T	sometimes. (.) S18 Do you like promoting yourself
23	S18	no.
24	T	no? @hehehe@
25	S18	((unclear 2.25))
26		(2.55)
27	T	what about men lying to women
28		((students laugh 2.95))
29	T	and women lying to men (1.65) for what.
30		(1.05)
31	S3	for face I think=
32	S21	=what's the relationship=
33	T	=aha for face ↓ S3 said face ↓ =
34	S3	=[perhaps]

35	S21	=[看什么关系]
36	T	噢 要看什么关系 如果是情侣呢 @hehe@
37	S33	[吃惊]
38	S1	[情侣]
39	T	吃惊
40		((students laugh 1.45))
41	S21	maybe @hehehe@
42	T	所以 情侣关系有时候 会很脆弱 是不是

The pre-reading questions on lying to someone for their own good was picked up when the text instruction was at paragraphs 16 to 18. As can be seen in Extract 5-12, S33 offered to answer the question (L2) and shared with the class an interesting story of hers. The teacher nearly gave the floor to her except for occasional confirmation checks (e.g., L4, L11) and sporadic flashbacks (e.g., L9, L30).

Extract 5-12 On lying for someone's good

1	T	Paragraphs 16 to 18 yes (3.0) yes first uh let's see this question. have you ever told lies to children for their own good or to set them up for a surprise party. have you?
2	S33	ehm
3		(5.25)
4	T	Never? (1.5) [mhm?]
5	S33	[certainly.]
6	T	certainly. yes S33 what is the lie that you have ever told
7		(1.20)
8	S33	When I am acting as a baby sister en en I should take care (0.5) for my en younger cousin cousins
9	T	mhm
10	S33	and he he keeps crying and he wants he wants his mother (1.0) he don't he don't want anyone except his mother so so I lied to to him (1.75) en as long as he can eh eat lunch by himself then I take him to look for his mother (0.80) but I di- I didn't and en when he finished his lunch I take him en to go for a nap
11	T	oh a nap ↓
12	S33	yeah
13		(0.95)

14	T	Yes (0.85) and then what happened?
15		(0.80)
16	S33	he- he forgot he forg=
17	T	=he forgot her mother=
18		=((students laugh 2.00))
19		(2.15)
20	S33	and I plays this kind of tricks on my: en cousin brothers and sisters many times and they forgot every time.
21		((students laugh 1.15))
22		(0.55)
23	S3	too young too naive=
24	T	=OK poor little brothers @hh@ thank you but do you feel (..) guilty for (.) doing that?
25	Ss	never/no/no
26		((students laugh 0.90))
27	Sx	of course not
28	S33	no\ and I'm proud of-
29		((students laugh 2.75))
30	T	Oh you are proud of yourself=
31	S33	=no I'm proud of my time that he can finish his lunch or breakfost uh usually they they have difficult to eat by themselves
32	T	OK I see you tell lies as incentives for the children right? to encourage them to eat faster
33	S21	liar
34	T	a liar? @heh@

Right after S33's story, the researcher proceeded with another question, as he had done in the pre-reading stage, to elicit the students' response towards lying to seriously ill family members about their illness. As Extract 5-13 shows, the researcher nominated four chronically reticent students—S12, S7, S19, and S35—to answer the question.

Extract 5-13 On lying to seriously ill family members

1	T	and what about the second one suppose (..) a family member of yours is seriously ill. (2.0) what would you do. would you tell him or her the truth
2		(13.80)
3	T	S12

4		(2.60)
5	S12	uh (1.0) if- uh if it was bad I will (.) tell the truth
6	T	oh ↓ you will tell the truth
7	S12	if it wasn't I will cover it up.
8	T	OK you will cover it up
9	S12	yeah
10	T	uhuh it depends that means. right? depends on whether the disease is fatal. right?
11		(3.40)
12	S12	yes
13	S21	yes that matters if the disease is serious
14	T	yes seriously ill
15	S21	so it may be 没有
16	S3	you will know it
17	T	eheh sooner or later you mean yes?
18		(2.40)
19	T	What about S7
20		(1.50)
21	S7	I will tell the truth yes every one has the right to know the truth
22	T	yes everyone has the right: ↑ to know the truth.
23	S7	yes
24		(1.40)
25	T	thank you OK (1.5) S19.
26		(6.65)
27	S19	If there is hope I will tell the truth
28		(0.80)
29	T	if there is hope uh (1.0) hope for what.
30		((students laugh))
31	S21	maybe he can recover from the disease
32	T	Ah yes
33	S19	if he has the opportunity to recover and you will tell the truth (0.90) if not then probably- will you tell the truth?
34	S21	maybe he will know
35		(7.20)
36	S19	if there is no hope to recover I won't tell the truth but eh if he is dying I will tell the truth

37	T	you will (3.0) you mean- if you know that he is dying then you will tell him the truth?
38	S19	yes
39	T	mhm. OK I see. (1.0) Thank you. S35
40		(2.05)
41	S35	I'll tell the truth
42	T	you will tell the truth mhm
43	S35	because I think every people choose can choose uh (2.5) they can decide to tell it
44		(1.40)
45	T	Yes yes
46	S21	they're privileged to know the truth
47	T	(1.0) it is up to them. (..) yes what to do after they have known the truth yes? thank you.

As with the pre-reading stage, another question, on the feeling of being lied to by family members about one's own illness, was asked in continuation of the question on lying to family members on their illness. As shown in Extract 5-14, the researcher directed the question once again to some less active students, namely S20, S37 and S23, before redirecting it to S21, one of the most active of the class.

Extract 5-14 On being lied to by family members

1	T	so then let's move to the next question so what if you yourself (.) are seriously ill right @hehe@ and your parents and siblings choose to cover up the truth. (..) how: ↓ would you feel
2	Sx	pretend I don't=
3	T	=and you [find out]
4	Sx	[pretend that I don't]
5		(1.80)
6	T	S20 yes
7		((several students laugh 1.0))
8		(3.06)
9	S20	((in very low voice, unclear 0.70))
10	T	you will what?
11	S20	I will anger
12	T	you will feel angry if you know the truth.

13		((students laugh 2.20))
14	S20	((in very low voice, unclear 4.45))
15	T	you will feel that your parents and siblings they don't love you
16		((students laugh 2.95))
17	T	if they don't tell you the truth that means they don't love you
18		((T and students laugh 1.40))
19	S21	maybe is they love you so they cover up the truth
20	T	yes maybe it is simply because they love you so much that they choose to cover up the truth en (..) thank you any way (.) yes S37
21		(4.95)
22	S37	I- (..) I (..) I think eh maybe but I am not angry- angry and but- (1.0) I think eh (1.5) (1.8) eh
23	T	do you think it is understandable?
24	S37	Yeah (.) yeah (.) yeah
25	T	(2.0) although you will feel (.) upset right about that?
26	S37	because eh (2.0) if I was seriously ill em they- they they lie to me (.) I feel very possible (.) to do it eh I know I know they lie to me but eh I- I think eh I just think eh (1.5) think that's the time yes
27	T	seize the rest of time
28		((students laugh 4.40))
29	T	(1.0) OK good good seize the rest of time thank you uh S23? yes what's your response to this question.
30		(1.25)
31	S23	I will pretend not to know
32	T	OH:: ↓ >you see? she has a very typical answer< I will pretend <u>not</u> to know the truth
33		((T and students laugh 2.70))
34	S3	((unclear 1.25))
35	T	but why ↓ yes (.) because they lie to you? >and you want to lie to them<
36		((students laugh loudly 2.10))
37	S23	because they try to protect me
38	T	yes
39	S23	um they want me to be better so: they just encourage me (.) so: >I just- I just-< I suppose to pretend. so I will pretend
40	T	you will also pretend that you don't know the truth. OK that is very interesting. yes? S21.
41	S21	uh let met think about- yes I will feel very?- uh furious
42	T	<u>furious</u> uhuh

43	S21	and I will think that (.) choice. why not they choose to tell me the truth (.) but choose not to tell
44	T	you will also cover it up?
45	S21	(0.5) no. I- I think. why not they choose to to tell me the truth. but they choose to cover the truth up and eh maybe I will angry with my parents and then gradually I may understand their thought their uh ?? and eh maybe I will choose to cherish my- cherish my rest life I will maybe do something that I have never do.
46	T	OK you will do something you have never <u>done</u> ↓
47	S21	yeah

The questions asked in the while-reading and post-reading stages were not simple repetitions of the ones asked in the pre-reading stage though the content focus seemed to be the same. Rather, the latter questions required the students to make contributions based on what they had learned previously both inside and outside the classroom. That means, the cognitive efforts required to answer the questions asked in the different stages were accordingly of different levels. In other words, the personal response questions asked across the pre-reading, while-reading and post-reading stages of instruction formed a questioning sequence, offering the students the opportunity to make varied personal responses towards the theme of the text.

What can be easily observed in all the episodes of interaction displayed above in comparison to those presented in Chapter 4 is that the students were more ready to participate in the interaction and the utterances they contributed were of higher quality in terms of complexity, accuracy and fluency (CAF). Such a change can be attributed to the pedagogical treatment of having them preview the text in reference to the list of teacher questions, as will be discussed in the next section.

5.4 Evaluating

As with the evaluation of the first cycle of AR, the pedagogical effectiveness of the second cycle is to be accounted for by looking at the data collected through students' learning logs, peer observation feedback, group discussion notes and the researcher's reflection journals.

5.4.1 Students' learning logs

What was reported in the students' learning logs showed that the pedagogical intervention carried out in the second cycle brought about the intended consequences. Most of the students felt impressed with the personal response questions that had been focused upon during classroom instruction, gained from contributing to classroom interaction and listening to others, had positive perceptions of their own performance in A-Q interaction, and confessed that they could hardly think of any suggestions for teacher questioning in future classes.

5.4.1.1 Most impressive questions

As the students had been given in advance the list of questions designed for classroom instruction, they were able to identify the impressive questions in their original form, and so did many of them. However, as many of them also reported without referring back to the hand-out, and rephrased the questions in their own words, it would be wise to focus again on the elements of the questions. What should be noted here is that some students reported more than on impressive questions. Table 5-2 displays the elements of the questions reported to be most impressive by the students.

As presented in Table 5-1, the questions impressive to the students after learning Unit 5 seemed to be more varied than the ones they reported after learning Unit 3. As mentioned earlier, the researcher, in consideration of the students' request for more open questions, increased the number of personal response questions, and enacted some of them repeatedly across different stages of instruction. The results show that the researcher's intention was successfully materialized.

Table 5-2 Most impressive questions reported in students' logs of Unit 5

Elements of impressive questions	Number of students
• Feeling of being covered up by family members if seriously ill	18
• Whether to tell seriously ill family members the truth	12
• Prior lies one has ever told	8
• The author's misquote of Mark Twain's words	7

Continued

Elements of impressive questions	Number of students
• Explanation and translation of "The most understandable and forgivable lies are an exchange of what ethicists refer to as the principle of trust for the principle of caring"	4
• How to conduct a survey project concerning lying	2
• Explanation and translation of Sir Walter Scott's quote	2
• Words and expressions used to refer to lying or telling lies.	2
• The author's suggestion on whether to tell the truth or not	1
• The difference between doubt and suspect?	1
• Men's and women's purposes of lying	1
• Paraphrase questions	1
• Translation questions	1

The students gave various reasons for what was most impressive to them. Those who reported on the questions concerning lying and being lied to mostly commented that those questions were thought-provoking and closely related to their everyday life:

> It makes us think about the principle of trust and the principle of lying. (S5)
> Through the teacher didn't ask me, but I thought it deeply. (S4)
> It's a reality question for us to consider, and I will cover it up. (S10)
> It's really thought-provoking. (S12)

Some students who had not been nominated to answer these questions provided lengthy answers in their logs as well:

> You didn't ask me to answer the second question [on the feeling of being covered up by family members if seriously ill]. But actually I would like to answer that one, my answer is the same as one of the students who answered you. Her answer was that she would pretend that she didn't know the truth. Now that my family don't tell me the truth, they have their own reasons. They just didn't want to upset me, it's also a way to show love and care. But you said that answer is interesting. (S19)

In my opinion, I will tell the truth if he is an adult for the reason that he knows himself very much and has his own thoughts. However, I will choose to cover up the truth if he is a child who is too young to accept it. Additionally, I remembered whose answer is that she will tell the truth due to every one has the right to know about themselves. (S18)

Interestingly, quite a few students reported to have been deeply impressed by the question on one's feeling of being covered up if seriously ill and attributed their deep impression to S23's answer:

The answer from S23ueyu that she will pretend not to find the truth was so different. I think it's very interesting to know others' thoughts. (S21)
The question is worth discussing, the teacher asks lots of classmates. But only S23ueyu's answer depress [impressed] me a lot. Her answer is "I'll pretend not knowing the truth", I never thought about it and I think it's too cruel to the patients because it's hard to do that when the patients are seriously ill. (S20)
But the most impressionable answer is the S23ueyu's answer. She said: "I'll pretend to not find out the truth. Because her answer is the same as mine. (S27)

Most of those who mentioned about the question on prior lying experiences also admitted that they were impressed with some funny answers:

The most impressive question is "Do you remember lying to any one? why did you tell the lie?", because the answer of S17, she said "I lied to my mom I ran every day to keep fit. Then my mom gives me a red packet to reward me." (S29)
For example, the teacher asked us "What's lies did you say?" I was thinking a few minutes at that time, but I can't miss anything lies. However, when I heart a classmate' answer, she said she lie to her young cousin. I recalled something. I want to be more positive in class and open my mind. (S11)
The most impressive question raised by my teacher was that "when did you lie to somebody last time?" My answer was the same with the one who was questioned by my teacher, to be exact, her answer was "I can't remember." "We told so many lies that we can't even remember" my teacher responded humorously. (S39)

Those impressed with the question on the author's misquoting Mark

Twain's words wrote that the teacher's pointing out the author's misquote made them realize the importance of reading critically, i.e., not being ready to accept every word in print:

> The most interesting question is whether the idiom was said by Mark Twain. Usually we do not think twice because it is a textbook, however, it did made mistakes, that surprised me a lot. (S37)
>
> Third, Mark Twain just said "when in doubt, tell the truth", but not "it will confound your enemies and astound your friends". I think it is funny. After all, we should not be careless when we write a text. (S7)
>
> The last sentence in this passage is half from Mark Twain and half from another people. From which, I learned we should not believe author totally, we need prove it by all means through ourselves. (S10)

In addition, some of the students attributed their deep impression of particular questions to their having been nominated by the teacher to answer them:

> As far as I am concerned, the most impressive question is that "Did you lie recently?" Because I answered this question, I remember it deeply. (S17)
>
> There is also an array of questions gaining my attention: the sick questions. Coincidentally, I was nominated to answer one of this question. (S23)
>
> You asked me to answer the first question, my answer was if there had hope for him to recover from the disease, I would not tell the truth. Others also have their own answer, some said they will tell the truth, because they have the right to know the truth. Some said if he is going to die soon, they will tell the truth. It's depends, what we can do best is to comfort them and company with them. (S19)

In sum, the impressive questions, as reported by students, partially proved that the intended objects of learning had been successfully enacted, especially the ones pointing to the students' personal responses towards lying and the appreciation of the author's misquoting Mark Twain's words.

5.4.1.2 Gains from Q-A interaction

What the students reported to have gained from the classroom interaction throughout the instruction of Unit 5 mainly centered around inspirations from listening to their classmates' answers to particular response questions.

Many wrote of how they had benefited from listening to their classmates' answers as they began to realize the value of exchanging different ideas:

- Apparently, the attitudes vary from person to person, some of my classmates choose to blame or complain a majority of students is same with mine. (S8)
- what I learn from my classmate is that everybody has his own idea and position. (S6)
- Most students gave their answers. Some said they will tell the truth, while some said they won't. And I think there is no true or false in these answers. (S12)
- The answer from S23 that she will pretend not to find the truth was so different. I think it's very interesting to know others' thoughts. (S14)
- But from the students' answer, we will learn how to change an angle to answer questions, sometimes feel that they understand better, this will be a better understanding of the text. (S15)
- So above all, I realize truth is a complex issue. And whatever we talk about it from any aspect it has its logical reason. (S24)
- Through those questions and classmates' answers, I learned that thinking is very significant. (S30)
- The atmosphere in class was active at the time. There are many answers from my classmates. (S31)
- I learn much from S23, she said every means is the method that parents protect us. that is touching for me. (S34)

Some wrote of the recognition of critical thinking in reading and writing, an inspiration generated by the teacher's question on the author's misquote of Mark Twain's words:

- After all, we should not be careless when we write a text. (S7)
- The last sentence in this passage is half from Mark Twain and half from another people. From which, I learned we should not believe author totally, we need prove it by all means through ourselves. (S10)
- Then I learn that what on books can also be wrong, and we should check the truth by ourselves. (S14)

- I was taught that never take everything for granted via this question. (S23)
- From those, I realize that I should be more careful and patient to read and enjoy the passage like the interesting questions I listed. (S26)
- it makes me realize that we can't just trust the book again. And We need to get the truth by ourselves. (S35)

A couple of students also made some general comments on what they had learned from the teacher fronted Q-A interaction:

- And, sometimes the interaction initiated by teacher questions are not only funny but also can let us gain a lot. (S4)
- [After listening to someone's answer to that question,] I recalled something. I want to be more positive in class and open my mind. (S11)
- From those questions, I learned lots of new words and knowledge. And we can think more. I can learn how this passage developing and what is the author's thoughts. (S38)

The gains reported by the students, as demonstrated above, constituted further evidence for the successful enactment of the intended objects of learning through the questioning sequences. The classroom interaction initiated by teacher questions not only led to the students' learning of new contents and/or ideas but also the improvement of their critical thinking. Additionally, a light and joyous classroom atmosphere was created as the students took active part in the teacher-guided interaction.

5.4.1.3 Self-evaluation of performance in classroom interaction

The students' self-evaluation of their performance in classroom interaction was much more positive than before. What was of greatest relief to the researcher was that some students indicated that they were satisfied with their performance in classroom interaction because they had made good preparations before class with the guidance of the hand-out:

- I feel a little satisfaction with my performance, because I have made some preparations for the class before. (S6)
- There is no denying that we are fully absorbed in the class via these provoking

questions. Also, I am content with my performance in that I have a crystal-clear perception to the questions you ask. (S8)
- At first, the third question of mine is "the white lies is at expense of in losing trust and caring "However, after I search[ed] the Baidu to find the translation, I realized that I misunderstood the sentence. It should be "the white lies is to make care at expense of trust" Now, I [am] satisfied. (S9)
- I <u>fell</u> [felt] satisfied with my performance in answering this question, because I had made <u>well</u> [good] preparation[s] to express my true thought. (S12)
- I think my performance is better than ever before, because I can consider questions before class and follow the teacher's way in class. (S13)

Though some students confessed that they were not satisfied with their performance, few of them attributed their dissatisfaction to their low levels of language proficiency. Instead, they thought the problem rested with ill preparation or lack of confidence:

- To tell the truth, I'm not satisfied with my performance in the class, becauseI always keep silent when teacher ask us to answer his question, because I'm afraid of making mistakes and I'm poor at expressing my thoughts correctly in English, I'm progressing in my speaking English. (S2)
- I was not satisfied with my performance during answering teacher's questions. The reasons were that I hadn't prepared to answer the question and I was a little out of mind and my mind was empty that time. (S3)
- I am not satisfied with my performance. Because I am not active enough in answering these questions. And I am not active in thinking. (S5)
- I feel not vary satisfied with my own performance in answering teacher's questions, because sometimes I have no idea about teacher's questions or I can't answer the questions of teacher quickly and rightly. (S7)

It could be understood that the more the students, though of low proficiency, get involved in classroom interaction, the less likely they would attribute their poor performance in classroom interaction to their insufficient language proficiency. What matters most is not how well the students are linguistically prepared for answering teacher questions, but rather whether they have been given sufficient preparation time and how well they are prepared to participate in classroom interaction. As noted earlier, it is not realistic or practical for the teacher to give lengthy wait time after asking a question during classroom interaction. Nor is it realistic or practical for the students to think profoundly and prepare fully to answer teacher questions within the limited given preparation time. This cycle of AR offers an alternative to this dilemma, that is, to have the students make preparations before class.

5.4.1.4 Suggestions on future teacher questioning

Many of the students left the suggestions section blank in their learning logs for Unit 5. Some students explicitly wrote that they could not think of any suggestions:

- I really can't figure out more suggestions. (S23)
- I don't have any suggestions for the teacher. (S36)
- Last but not least, there's no more suggestion can give for you after repeating this question for so many times. (S18)

Some others did leave some words for this section, but the words were more like praises than suggestions:

- For the suggestions, I like the relaxed atmosphere. Some simple and helpful questions can create a good learning environment. (S31)
- In unit 5, the teacher does a little bit of good work that makes the lesson plan in advance. It is my hope that the teacher can continue to do this. (S15)
- When it comes to the suggestions, specifically in classroom interaction, I do believe that my teacher does a good job. In terms of interactions initiated by teacher's questions, it is apparent that those questions provoke us to think critically. (S39)

There were a few of them who suggested that the researcher reconsider his allocation of turns during Q-A interaction as they observed some of the students were not active or motivated enough in answering teacher questions:

- I think you did quite well in interaction, next time you can try to interact with students who seat at back and ask questions which can make everybody think. (S1)

- Finally, my suggestion is that teacher could ask questions to a certain student, and ask more difficult question to whole [all] students. (S7)
- Maybe the students need a little improvement. Like some are not devoted or active enough. We should motivate ourselves in answering teachers' questions and interact more positively. (S5)

On the whole, the students were approving of the adjustment in the action plan, i.e., handing out the pre-designed questions days ahead of instruction so that they could make full preparation to participate in classroom interaction. However, what arose as a new problem was that two students ended their learning logs with the expectation that the researcher would help them resolve some puzzlement about the text:

- I have something else to say: I still don't know how to paraphrase sentence well, I hope you give me some advice and paraphrasing skills. (S22)
- Besides, I hope you can explain the difficulty in grammar's work, for example, the "Verbless clauses", you could give some tips for us because I deem it's a little complex. (S10)

As introduced earlier, right before the onset of this cycle of AR, the researcher invited the students to bring their own questions to the classroom; and during the text instruction, the researcher would stop to check whether they were catching up with the progress and request them for unresolved questions. Conceiving that these two students might have forgotten to raise their questions in class during the instruction of Unit 5, the researcher reiterated to the whole class that questions of any kind would be welcome and that they could interrupt the teacher whenever they came up with one. Yet, during the instruction of Unit 6, none of the students raised any question in class. Amazingly, more students left questions in their learning logs, hoping that the researcher could help them out. The students' unwillingness to raise questions in class was to be taken into serious consideration, as will be discussed in Section 5.4.3 below.

5.4.2 Peer observation feedback

Two colleagues came to serve as peer observers at the researcher's invitation. Miss Ding, who observed the session covering the pre-reading and part of the global reading. In the post-observation conference, she showed her approval of the researcher's design and enactment of pre-reading questions to stimulate the students' responses towards lying, which she thought not only helped personalize the theme of the text, but also built up an amusing classroom atmosphere. She was impressed with the researcher's giving more chances for the students to speak up during the pre-reading stage as she observed that more students were involved in answering teacher questions than she had observed previously. She didn't talk much about the other aspects of the researcher's organization of Q-A interaction other than some general comments or kind words on how she would like to learn from the researcher.

The other observer, Miss Zhu, came to observe the session which covered the last part of the detailed reading and part of the instruction on the exercises. By the fall of 2017, she had had nine years' experience of teaching English majors and had taught intensive reading course for several semesters. Theoretically, she was more capable of viewing the researcher's teaching from an insider's perspective. She indicated that she was deeply impressed with the classroom atmosphere which was "humorous, enjoyable and thought-provoking". She did not comment much on the content focus, cognitive demand and turn allocation of the Q-A interaction. But she did suggest more content feedback to the students' responses because she felt that the students might be in need of guidance in judging their own beliefs or values. She pointed out that during the Q-A interaction, though the researcher offered opportunities for the students to express their ideas or thought, he seldom gave them content feedback, that is, sharing his own ideas or thoughts towards the same issues.

5.4.3 Group discussion notes

Four groups (Groups #2 to #5) of students were involved in the after-class group discussion during the second cycle of AR. Each group consisted of four students. When the discussion came to the intensive reading course, two girls of the second group complained that they had a heavy learning burden because they had to preview the texts, write summaries and learning logs. However, the other two girls disagreed and said that previewing the text by trying to answer the questions handed out to them made it possible to follow the teacher's steps in class, and writing summaries and learning logs were also effective in strengthening their learning.

The third group comprised four boys. They did not talk much about the intensive reading course; neither did they give much feedback on the researcher's style of teaching. However, two boys did mention that they had a more profound understanding of Unit 5 because they had read the text carefully and tried to answer all the questions handed out to them.

The four girls in Group 4 told the researcher that they felt very uncomfortable at the beginning of the semester because they had to adapt to his "freestyle" of teaching which was so different from the two teachers who had taught them in the first academic year; nonetheless, as time went by, they got used to his particular way and were able to catch up with him. Someone put the researcher's and the other two teachers' approaches of teaching in comparison and said that the other two teachers would explain every detail of the text and check the answers to all exercises, whereas the researcher chose to cover less in classroom instruction but forced them to learn more and as a natural consequence they felt their horizon expanded and autonomy improved under the guidance of the teacher's focused teaching.

The fifth group, made up of four girls, seemed not having the motivation to major in English as all of them said that English was not their first choice when they were enrolled for college. They made some complaints on the English major curriculum for the reason that they were not allowed to choose courses on their own. They did not talk much about the intensive reading course except that they felt the researcher's teaching was OK to them. S22, by the end of the discussion, asked the researcher a question concerning a language point in Unit 6. Before answering the question, the researcher took the opportunity to ask S22 why she had not raised the question in class. Her reply was that she had feared that the question would sound silly to her classmates, which enlightened the researcher on the reason why the students would sit back and lower their heads when the researcher invited the class to ask questions.

5.4.4 Stimulated reflection journals

In his reflection journals on the teaching of Unit 5 and Unit 6, the researcher wrote that he was generally satisfied with his organization of Q-A interaction. He felt relieved that the major intervention implemented in this cycle of AR, i.e., handing out to the students the list of teacher questions in advance, was effective in deepening the students' understanding of the texts and promoting their willingness to participate in classroom interaction. On top of this, more RQs had been designed and some of them were enacted repeatedly across different stages of instruction, which left a deep impression on the students as reported in their learning logs. In the meantime, more students, especially some chronically reticent students, were engaged in Q-A interaction and quite a few of them reported apparent gains.

However, there were some discomforting matters. For instance, the researcher observed, while reviewing his own lessons, that only a few students had been directly engaged in the interaction around the author's misquote of Mark Twain's words, and reflected that he should have involved the students in more profound thinking instead of simply pointing out the misquote. Likewise, the students had not been induced to 'appreciate' the author's use of figures demonstrating the prevalence of lying in everyday life. The researcher could have done so by asking some subsequent questions, such as "what if the author didn't quote the figures from survey reports?" In other words, the learning space could have been further extended for the students to experience the variation in the dimension of cognitive demand.

As mentioned earlier, approaching the end of Section 5.4.1, the students were not so willing to raise questions in front of their classmates in class as they were willing to answer the teacher's questions. The researcher conceived that the students were more inclined to communicate with the teacher in private, either face to face or through online devices, like such Apps as WeChat and Pigai. The fact that the students asked their teacher questions concerning the textbook revealed that the teacher's questions did not cover all the students' needs. Though the researcher adjusted the proportion of the three categories of questions designed for text instruction, like increasing the number of RQs and LQs at the students' request, the questions were devised mainly either according to the objectives prescribed in the curriculum or according to the teachers' perception of what to focus in classroom instruction.

Miss Zhu's suggestion that the researcher give more content feedback, as mentioned in Section 5.4.2, was definitely pertinent and could be taken as an echo of Cullen's (2002) call for more 'discoursal feedback' in teacher talk. However, the researcher assumed that the language teacher's role lies more in providing students opportunities to think for themselves and to express their thoughts and ideas than in sharing his own. Whilst it can be argued that the teacher's content feedback could serve as input to the students, in view of the limited time for classroom instruction, it would be wiser to guide the students to take advantage of the practice opportunities (Allwright, 1984; Allwright & Bailey, 1991).

5.4.5 Implications

On the whole, the second cycle of AR was successful in further extending the learning space for the students to experience the two dimensions of variation: content focus and cognitive demand. All the three problems, as identified in the Focusing section, were resolved or alleviated to a large degree. Firstly, the proportion of comprehension, language and response questions was balanced as more response questions were designed and some response questions were carried out repeatedly across different stages of text instruction. Secondly, the students' pressure or anxiety of being involved in Q-A interaction was considerably relieved as the extracts of classroom interaction demonstrated that the students were better prepared to answer the teacher's questions and more students volunteered to offer their answers. Lastly, more chronically reticent students were mobilized to participate in Q-A interaction and some of them rendered more contributions than before.

In a nutshell, by handing out to the students the list of questions pre-designed for classroom instruction, the researcher allowed the students to make full preparation for answering the questions. Thus, not only the ones directly engaged in Q-A interaction had the opportunity to experience the text, those not directly engaged, by listening to the teacher and their classmates, were also interactively and cognitively involved, as all of them were better prepared for the 'multilogue' (Schwab, 2011) or 'multi-party spoken interaction' (Walsh, 2011).

Nonetheless, there emerged some new problems to be addressed in the next cycle of AR. First, the students were not so willing to ask their teacher questions in class even though they were puzzled by, usually, language problems. Second, it was hard for the teacher to predict what questions the students might encounter or to make decisions as to what the students might want to learn. Third, some few of the students did not preview the text or answer the questions handed out to them as required, and consequently failed to take advantage of the learning space offered to them as reflected in their learning logs. These problems should be focused on in the next cycle of AR so as to improve the students' learning.

Chapter 6   Third Cycle of Action Research

This chapter presents the third cycle of AR with the major pedagogical treatment being researcher's incorporating student questions into the questioning sequences to further extend learning space.

6.1 Focusing

As introduced in the last section of Chapter 5, three problems were to be focused on in the third cycle of AR:

1) the students' unwillingness to raise their own questions in class despite their puzzlement with the text;

2) the teacher's inability to predict the students' needs or wants in regard of text instruction despite his efforts in collaborating with other teachers in designing teacher questions and evaluating classroom interaction;

3) some students' ill preparation before class despite the teacher's explicitly delivered requirements.

6.2 Planning

Some researchers have attributed Chinese students' unwillingness to raise questions in front of peer classmates to the influence of such cultural factors as the doctrine of means and the value of face protection (e.g., Li Qingsheng & Sun Zhiyong, 2011; Wang Jian & Zhang Jing, 2008), whereas others have counter-argued with empirical evidence that students' willingness to raise questions could be improved by some innovative classroom management strategies, such as heterogeneous grouping (Qu Sheming, 2006) and the introduction of some enjoyable entertaining activities (Lin

Huihua, 2012). Qu Sheming (2006) and Lin Huihua (2012) investigated how the change of questioning role from teacher to students could impact classroom interaction and both found that giving students opportunities to initiate interaction with their own questions is effective not only in improving the quality of classroom interaction but also in strengthening students' motivation for learning. Nonetheless, they both acknowledged that the effect of changing questioning role depends on the students' language proficiency and the cognitive level of their questions. In other words, innovative classroom management strategies may help students break through the restrictions of some cultural conventions or doctrines and hence improve their willingness to raise questions, but whether such strategies are effective or not largely depends on some individual factors, such as the students' language proficiency level and the depth of their thinking.

As observed earlier, the students would be more willing to get engaged in classroom interaction if they were better prepared before class. The researcher thus conceived that it might be viable to have the students raise their own questions while previewing the text and deliver them to the teacher in private before class. He assumed that by so doing all the three problems could be alleviated: by raising questions and delivering them to the teacher before class, the students could relieve themselves of face-threatening concerns, inform the teacher of their learning needs and wants, and have deeper engagement with the text.

The researcher broke to his supervisor such an intervention and his supervisor suggested that it would be worthy of a try. She added that having the students prepare their own questions while previewing the text might be effective in promoting the students' autonomy in learning and sharpening their critical thinking.

Hence the plan for the third cycle of AR was incorporating student questions into the design and enactment of questioning sequences. It was expected that the researcher could know better of the students' understanding of the text and their needs and wants of text instruction by reading the questions raised by them before class, and that the questioning sequences designed and enacted in consideration of their needs and wants could further extend the learning space for them to experience the variation in the dimensions of content focus and cognitive demand. Table 6-1 summarizes the planned solutions to deal with the identified problems.

In the midst of the instruction on Unit 6, the researcher told the class the plan for the next cycle of AR, that is, for the two upcoming units, the students were to preview the text of each unit carefully, come up with their own questions concerning each part of the text and then deliver their lists of questions to the researcher two days ahead of text instruction so that he would have time to incorporate their questions into his list of questions.

Table 6-1   Solutions planned for the problems identified in AR3

Identified problems	Planned solutions
• Students' unwillingness to raise questions during classroom instruction	• Have the students raise their own questions while reviewing the text before class • Incorporate student questions into the sequences of teacher questions
• Teacher's inability to predict all the students' needs and wants	
• Some students' lack of preparation before class	

6.3 Implementing

Like before, the researcher collaborated with his colleagues in identifying the objects of learning after exchanging their understanding, interpretation and puzzlement of the text. When the objects of learning were identified, the researcher proceeded to design questions for the text instruction. After receiving the students' questions on the *Pigai* platform, he exported each student's questions to an MS Excel file, pooled all the questions together and cataloged them in order of the serial number of the paragraphs of the text. By so doing, he was able to pick out the questions that were different from the questions designed by himself, thus supplementing them into his courseware. What follows is a detailed account of how the plan was implemented in the instruction of Unit 7.

6.3.1 Identifying the objects of learning

The main text of Unit 7 is a short story written by John Collier. The story begins with a young man, named Alan Austen, going into an old building in the Chinatown of New York, looking for an old man who sells a magic love potion. The plot of the story evolves as the dialogue proceeds between the young man and the old man whose words reflect totally different perspectives towards romantic love and marriage.

The researcher and his collaborator, as usual, negotiated about what to focus on in the instruction of the unit after exchanging their understanding of the text. They decided that the following objects of learning should be carried out.

Understanding the development of the story

As mentioned above, the story evolves around the dialogue between the two main characters, i.e., the old man (the love potion seller) and the young man (the love potion buyer). Thus, the two teachers thought it necessary to draw the students' attention to the particular development of the story as reflected in the dialogue.

In addition, the story ends with the old man seeing the young man off with "Au revoir" (French for "See you later") which leaves readers with a suspension on what will happen to the young man and the old man afterwards. It would be worthwhile to have the students further develop the story in sequel to the text.

Appreciating the author's description of the main characters

The dialogue not only displays the selling and buying actions between the old man and young man, but also contributes to the characterization of the two as their perceptions of romantic love and marriage are revealed as the conversation unfolds. In addition to the words spoken by the two characters, the author gives vivid accounts of their psychological status. To better understand the text, it would be advisable to induce the students to interpret the two characters and to appreciate the author's particular way of characterizing them.

The two protagonists are characterized by their words and their psychological activities. Whilst the old man appears aloof and self-poised throughout the story, the young man's mental state changes drastically from skeptical and hesitant to excited and overwhelmed. The two teachers conceived it especially necessary to involve the students in analyzing the young man's emotional change as the story develops.

Expressing personal responses to issues related to love

The theme of the story is closely related to college students' life. Considering that all the students would be confronted with difficulties or problems in establishing and maintaining romantic relationships, the two teachers decided to induce the students to exchange their opinions and beliefs towards love-related issues, especially how couples should treat each other.

6.3.2 Designing questions

As with the previous units, the researcher went about designing questions for the three stages of text instruction after identifying the objects of learning.

Pre-reading Questions

Altogether three questions were designed for the pre-reading stage. As displayed in Figure 6-1, all the three questions were intended to stimulate students' prior experience or schematic knowledge of love.

Pre-reading
1. Have you ever loved anyone? Or have you been loved?
2. What is the feeling of being in love or being loved?
3. What do you think is the right way for people in love to treat each other?

Figure 6-1　Pre-reading Questions for Unit 7

While-reading Questions

For the while-reading stage, the text comprehension questions were to be employed as questions for the global reading and a total of 41 questions, including 21 CQs, 14 LQs and 6 RQs, were designed for the detailed reading.

Chapter 6　Third Cycle of Action Research

Detailed Reading (Para. 1)
RQ: The first paragraph is made of one single long sentence without only one pause. How do you feel when you read it?
CQ: Why was Alan Austen "as nervous as a kitten"?
LQ: Can you think of more expressions like "as nervous as a kitten"?
LQ: What's the difference between peer, peep, and peek?
LQ: Can you think of other words similar to "dim" in meaning?

Figure 6-2　Questions designed for Para. 1 of Unit 7

Post-reading questions

The post-reading stage consisted of two optional discussion activities and a summary writing task. Both the discussion activities and the summary writing task were comprised of questions in relation to the theme of the text, as displayed in Figure 6-3 and Figure 6-4.

Discussion
Sit in groups and have a discussion over one of the following topics.
- What do you think would happen after Alan goes back with the love potion? Make up a story as a sequel to that of the text.
- What is love? How should people in love treat each other? You can make a list of dos and don'ts.

Figure 6-3　Discussion activity for Unit 7

Summary Writing
Read the text carefully and then write your response in NO LESS THAN 200 WORDS, in which you should answer the following questions:
1) what is the main message of the text?
2) what is love in your opinion? and
3) how should people in love treat each other?
You can support yourself with information from the text.

Figure 6-4　Summary writing task for Unit 7

6.3.3 Incorporating student questions

Thirty-four of the students delivered in time through *pigai.org* the questions they had come up with while previewing the text. A total of 882 questions were collected, which means each student raised 23 questions on average. Most of the students' questions pointed to language problems and many of them were overlapping. Nonetheless, some students' questions were unique and thought provoking. A few of them not only raised questions for the paragraphs of the text, but also put forward questions for discussion. One student, S12, made a list of questions under the title of "Discussion":

1. Do you think the love potion is useful?
2. What's your opinion about Alan's behavior?
3. How to evaluate the old man?
4. What is love? What would you do if you fell in love deeply with a person?

Another student, S39, prepared four questions in the name of "Other questions":

Q1 What is Alan's understanding of love?
Q2 What's the plot of this passage?
Q3 If you fell in love with someone, and you could not get any response from him or her, would you insist on your love?
Q4 Marriage is a tomb of love, do you agree or disagree, list your reasons.

Several students had the inclination to raise questions that were very interesting at first sight but might be too open or big and hence not so practical to be carried out in class. What follows is a list of such questions raised by S20:

Para. 24:
Have you ever been persuaded to buy something?
Para. 25:
Have you ever been jealous when some handsome guys or charming ladies talk to your girlfriend or boyfriend? How did you deal with that?
Para. 26:
Q1: Can you accept the truth that your boyfriend or girlfriend can not live without you? Why?
Q2: Do lovers need personal space? Reasons?

Chapter 6 Third Cycle of Action Research

Students' Questions (Para. 1)
1. How to understand "before" in this sentence? What will happen if Alan finds that the name is wrong? (S33)
2. What does "certain" imply? (S1)
3. From Alan's performance what do you think of his personality? (S3)
4. What kind of atmosphere does the author paint in this paragraph? (S23)

Figure 6-5 Students' questions for Para. 1 of Unit 7

After exporting all the students' questions from *pigai.org* to an MS Excel file, the researcher sorted out the students' questions around each part of the text (from the title to all the paragraphs), filtered the overlapping ones and those that were too big or unpractical, and supplemented his courseware with the rest of the students' questions that were connected, either tightly or loosely, to the objects of learning identified earlier by the two teachers but beyond the researcher's own preparation. Figure 6-5 is a screenshot of the slide that displays the students' questions for the first paragraph of the text.

6.3.4 Enacting questions

As usual, the three stages of text instruction were carried out by means of Q-A interaction. In addition to the questions the researcher had designed in advance, he also raised questions selected from the collection of students' questions. The objects of learning were focused upon during text instruction through questioning sequences, comprised of the questions designed by the teacher and those raised by the students.

Understanding the development of the story

To check the students' global understanding of the text, the researcher first asked them to think of a possible ending of the story and answer the first text comprehension question. As displayed in Extract 6-1, the students seemed not quite ready to answer the question as they only gave fragmentary responses.

Extract 6-1 On the possible ending of the story
```
1    T    what do you think is going to happen?
2         (2.24)
```

3	Sx	C/C
4	T	it should be C why?
5	Ss	((unclear 2.20))
6	T	you know the word stifling?
7	Ss	not breathing/ 窒息
8	T	yes Diana loves him in a sti:fling way that means (.) Diana's way of loving him makes him feels stifled right?
9	Ss	yeah/right
10	T	it makes him feel like he cannot breathe
11		(6.96)
12	T	if you are asked to write a story in sequel to this story that means to continue yes write a continuation of that story (3.40) you will (1.28) what kind of story will- will you develop yes?
13	S21	the boy goes to the rocking chair (..) it makes a different ending
14	T	如果让大家续写 - 续写这个故事 (..) 你会 (.) 写一个什么样的故事出来
15	Ss	有暗示啊 / 结尾有提示啊
16	T	嗯 他暗示了 - 但是一定要按他的暗示来写吗?
17		(1.20)
18	Sx	uh?
19	S3	结尾是必然的
20		必：然的吗?
21	S3	对啊
22	T	世上有这么多必然的事情?
23		((unclear 2.80))
24	T	好 大家可以想一想这个问题 到最后我们来做一个 discussion 看看你们能想到什么样的结尾哈

After checking the answers to the text comprehension questions, the researcher called the students' attention to the title of the text ("The Chaser"), asking them about its meaning in relation to the text. The question is closely related to the development of the plot in that it foreshadows the ending of the story. As can be seen in Extract 6-2, there was a long stretch of interaction initiated by the question, and quite a few students shared their answers or guesses to it. At first, some of the students referred to the note given in the text and said that the title means a strong liquor (L9) or some mild drink (L10 and L12). After some short off-topic talk (LL22-24), the researcher suggested that the students look up the word in their dictionaries and introduced to them the meaning of 'someone who pursues someone admirably' (LL25-30), which stimulated them to have a short discussion on the possible translation of the word (LL34-48) despite the researcher's attempt to draw their attention to the possible use of the word as a pun (L2). To further elaborate the meaning of the title, the researcher then displayed the Wikipedia entry of 'chaser' (LL49-51), which led to a lengthy discussion (LL52-96) till the researcher's reiteration that the title is a pun (L97).

Extract 6-2 On the title of the text

1	T	Have you (1.0) referred to any dictionary about the meaning of this word? (1.28) huh?
2		(13.48)
3	T	there is an entry for this word in the words and expressions right?
4	Sx	yeah
5		(2.72)
6	T	Let's see the explanation for chaser
7		((T and students read the explanation of chaser given in the textbook 9.96))
8		(2.92)
9	Ss	((students translate the English explanation into Chinese)) 烈酒 / 醒酒的 / 威士忌
10	Sx	解酒水
11	Ss	((several students laugh doubtfully))
12	Ss	醒酒的酒 /milder drink
13		((unclear 2.16))
14	T	在喝了烈酒之后还有再喝一点更温和的酒
15	Ss	((unclear 8.52))
16	T	do you drink? @hhhh@
17	Ss	mhm. /yes
18		(0.52)
19	T	alcohol I mean (.) right?
20	Ss	((several students respond in chorus)) waah
21	T	strong drink of liquor
22	Sx	老师你能喝多少
23	T	我不喝酒我不知道
24		((students talk about drinking 15.08))

25	T	but (0.5) if you (.) check the dictionary. you will find another (.) sense of chaser right? chaser is a person who:- (1.0)
26	Ss	<admires ↑ > admires someone
27	S21	yeah? who ↓ admires someone
28	T	yes pursues someone right?
29	Sx	追求 =
30	Sx	= 追求者
31		((students repeat the teacher's words 4.20))
32	T	chaser. So do you think this is a pun? right?
33	Ss	yeah/yeah/yes
34	T	the title could be a pun.
35	S33	撩妹的人
36		((T and students laugh 2.40))
37	T	@haha@
38	S33	撩妹的人
39		(1.32)
40	T	chaser 和撩妹的人 -
41		(1.60)
42	S3	不一样 [撩妹撩很多人] 追只追一个人
43	Ss	[不一样 / 不一样]
44	T	噢这样是吧 =
45	S33	= 追也可以追很多人啊 =
46	Sx	= 那个 是啊
47	T	(0.80) 哦 . 追也可以追很多人
48		((students talk in Chinese about the difference between 撩妹 and chase 13.36))
49	T	yes? if you: (2.0) turn to (1.0) Wikipedia (.) you can find an entry for the chaser the story OK? 在维基百科上面有一条 - 有这个词条 就是 the chaser 的 词条 eh because it has been adapted into several movies yeah there is an introduction uh (..) for the story or the plot of the story and there is such a line that is first the stimulant and then the chaser.
50		((students read aloud "the stimulant and then the chaser" 2.0))
51	T	first the stimulant then the chaser so: (0.5) it's eh (.) a little hard to understand ↓ right? whether- uh in this text the chaser will be followed by a strong drink of liquor probably. right? because there is the life ↓ cleaner (1.0) life cleaner is much stronger than the chaser
52	Sx	yeah
53	T	Yes- but (1.5) uh according to that line of the movie OK? first the stimulant then the chaser (1.80) so what does it mean.

54		(5.84)
55	T	is it the life cleaner that is the chaser?
56		(6.16)
57	T	the love potion (0.5) do you think the love potion is the chaser (0.5) or the life cleaner is the chaser
58	Ss	love potion/life cleaner
59	T	probably the love potion is: (.) the stimulant right?
60	Ss	stimulant/stimulant
61	S21	yes and the life cleaner is the chaser
62		(5.64)
63	T	That's my guess OK @hhh@
64	Ss	yes/yes/yes
65		(1.32)
66	S21	so it's very interesting
67		(3.20)
68	T	This is from the Oxford dictionaries OK? the first sense- the first sense of- of chaser in the oxford dictionary. (.) is person or thing that pursues someone or something for example. promotion chasers
69		(1.0)
70	S33	感情追求者
71	Sx	promotion
72		(2.0)
73	T	what does promotion mean?
74		(3.32)
75	T	promotion chaser should be (.) someone who is seeking to get promoted right?
76	S6	往上爬?
77	T	对 对 想要往上爬的
78		(2.32)
79	T	and (0.5) sense number three is a strong alcoholic drink. it is not a <u>milder</u> alcoholic drink right? but a strong alcoholic drink after a weaker the weaker is taken first. right? and then the strong. and the strong is the chaser (0.5) so eh it's weird right?
80		(1.36)
81	Ss	((unclear 3.12))
82	T	yes it's kind of contradictory=
83	Sx	=yeah

Questioning Sequences and Extension of Learning Space: An Action Research Study

84	T	right? but this is Oxford dictionary. I don't know uh where the explanation given in the textbook is taken from.
85		(2.0)
86	S3	((in a very low voice)) I don't know either
87	T	yes it's- it's weird
88		(2.36)
89	T	我们书上是温和的 但是牛津词典上说的是 =
90	Ss	猛烈的 / 烈性的
91	T	猛烈的 对不对 所以按照词典上的释义的话 - the chaser 应该是 life cleaner 对不对 eh 前面的 love potion 只不过是 -
92	Ss	清酒 / 浅尝
93	T	stimulant 吊胃口的 是吧
94	S17	开胃的 @hehe@
95	T	差不多 you- you didn't raise a question about the title except S33. OK S33 asked eh (0.5) such a question- what is the meaning behind the title chaser (.) how to understand the title chaser (.) the people who try to acquire something: or ↓ the drink that can make you feel sober after drunkenness. probably both=
96	S13	=((in a very low voice)) both=
97	T	=right? (1.0) the people (2.5) the person who tries to (.) acquire something or the drink that can make you sober after drunkenness so it should be both I think it is a pun P-U-N pun yes.

While going through the text in details, the researcher picked one question raised by the students concerning the use of passive voice in mentioning Alan's having been given a card as to where the love potion could be found. The interaction initiated by the question was not long, as displayed in Extract 6-3. However, it reminded the students of the mysteriousness of the seller of the love potion and the suspended ending of the story as well.

Extract 6-3 On someone behind the story

1	T	yes some of you. (0.5) raised the question about (.) as he had been told to do (0.5) this is in passive voice right (1.04) who who told him to do this
2	Ss	Not known/not mentioned
3	T	yes it's unknown right
4	S23	It's a secret
5	T	(0.68) is it a secret? @hh@
6		((several students laugh 2.28))

7	S3	I wonder probable a Chinese.
8	S21	他那个 (1.5) 第三段
9	T	This is it!
10	Sx	[the card had been given]
11	S21	[yes? (0.5) yes ↓]
12	T	yes- also in paragraph three. the card had been given right?
13	Sx	who gave the card to him
14		(1.60)
15	S21	如果没有看那个故事的话
16	T	yes? there must be someone behind the story. @hehe@
17	Sx	yes
18	T	@hh@ OK this is what. this is [kind of suspension] right suspension.
19	S3	[就像打广告]
20	S21	eh 怀疑?
21	T	悬念 right mhm (1.64) Do you feel suspended? @hehe@
22	S13	=of course=
23	T	=yes we're wondering who this person is right?=
24	Sx	=who said that=
25	T	=yes even we don't know his name (1.36) neither do we know the name of the old man. Right?

The question on the possible ending of the story was picked up again by the end of the text instruction. As can be seen in Extract 6-4, a host of students made their contributions to the long episode of interaction. After reviewing the development of the whole story along with Alan's emotional change, the researcher used a DIU in L3 to elicit the students' evaluation of the old man; when hearing S21 had a different opinion, the researcher probed him to give a reason (L10) and then steered the interaction to the possible ending of the story (L12). While S21 held that Diana would die after taking the potion (L15), S3 disagreed (L17) but did not give further elaboration. S6, S33, S3, S10, S39 and S20 were engaged in the coming interaction with fragmentary ideas until S35 who offered to share a different story (L91) as elaborated in L93, and was welcomed by the rest of the class (LL94-109).

Extract 6-4 On the possible ending of the story

1	T	and in the end (..) he got (.) the love potion and he felt grateful for the old man
2	Ss	yes/yeah
3	T	unfortunately (1.0) the old man was- mhm
4	Ss	((unclear 4.57))
5	S21	was a (1.0) evil @heh@
6	T	yes he was evil was wicked was vicious right?
7	Ss	yes/yeah
8	T	Why. (2.0) why. why do you think so.
9	Ss	((unclear 2.57))
10	T	uhuh? you don't think so uhuh. (2.0) S21 you- you think so- why.
11		(3.20)
12	T	because the old man he had another plan right?
13	S21	yes uh he has another purpose the purpose is (2.0) he wanted- he wants to get more money from Alan and he doesn't consider the results of- of his actions
14	T	<yes?>
15	S21	eh (1.0) the end of the story is Diana was dying- eh is dying because of=
16	T	=oh really? Diana died?
17	S3	他只是买了那个 =
18	S21	不是吗？你不是一直这么讲的吗？
19	S3	我也没有那么严重 @hehe@
20		(2.0)
21	S3	imagination
22	Ss	((students laugh 2.0))
23	T	you imagined that Diana would die after taking the love potion
24	S21	eh no the life cleaner
25	T	the life cleaner
26	S21	because Alan eh was sick of Diana
27	T	(0.7) Alan would be sick of Diana
28	S21	yes (1.0) so I think he is a evil wicked vicious
29	Ss	((laugh 0.63))
30	S21	vice. everything.
31	T	>OK thank you< I- I think S6 has another story. (.) different from yours.
32	S6	no (..) the same story
33	T	>the same story?<

34	S33	<[the same] story>
35	Ss	((unclear 0.92))
36	S6	huhuh?
37	T	yes?
38	S6	same story
39	T	Don't you have a story different from S21's after Diana-
40	Sx	taking the love potion
41	T	(0.9) yes
42	S6	ah- (1.5) they will dissent me.
43	S21	dissent you
44	T	>what? what?<
45	S3	@haha@
46	Ss	((laugh 1.49))
47	S3	刺激你们
48	S6	another story?
49	T	uh- yes.
50	Ss	((unclear 5.37))
51	S6	my story is-
52	Ss	((laugh loudly 3.72))
53	S6	uh my story is:
54	S3	my story [is]
55	S6	[Alan] (.) back back to the old man's house and buy life cleaner
56	S3	跟他的一样吗？
57		(1.37)
58	S6	>对一样啊<
59	S3	一样啊？
60	S10	一样的
61	T	the life cleaner (1.0) and then?
62		(1.49)
63	T	Diana died?
64	S6	[no (1.5)]
65	S3	[no no that old man]
66	S6	get cut (2.0) get divorced
67	T	divorced
68	S6	yeah
69		(3.03)

70	T	after taking the life cleaner (2.0) divorce.
71	S21	啊 S1 开始你的表演
72		((laugh 3.09))
73	S20	uh because the old man (.) told Alan to (.) think twice
74	T	Really? when. when did he- when did he-
75	S20	uh in spi- spiritual side.
76	T	oh the spiritual side.
77	S20	yeah think of the spiritual side uh paragraph twenty one
78	T	yes I see
79		(3.03)
80	S20	the old man told- told Alan to think twice but Alan didn't
81	T	you mean that consider the spiritual side is to tell Alan to think twice?
82		(2.91)
83	S39	((unclear 14.86))
84	T	((T explains the distinction between spiritual and sensual aspects 83.54))
85	S21	What's the ending of this story.
86	T	no=
87	S21	=no story? no ending?
88	Ss	((laugh 0.80))
89	T	yes? John Collier (.) <didn't write another story> (1.0) in continuation yes.
90		(0.9)
91	S35	I have a story.
92	Ss	((students clap hands 2.22))
93	S35	Maybe the Diana uh (0.5) Alan get the potion (.) to the Diana (.) then Diana love Alan (.) and then Alan get caught. since this enm (0.5) he not- not love Diana any more. (.) and Diana (.) get some way to (..) meet the old man. and took the love potion to Alan (..) then the same=
94	Ss	=((student talk and laugh 20.46))
95	S3	这个结局很完美啊！
96	T	有没有看到 S3=
97	Ss	=((laugh loudly 3.77))
98		(1.55)
99	T	yes there will be a happy ending
100	Ss	yes/yes/yeah/ya
101	S6	我顿悟了
102	Ss	((students laugh loudly 5.43))

103	S21	为什么不可能这样子啊 - Alan 去找那个 life cleaner 然后 Diana 也去找那个 love potion 然后碰到了
104	Ss	((unclear 2.06))
105	S21	然后就发现了真想 然后就 bye-bye
106	S3	但是她控制不住自己
107	T	噢 这样也很好啊 是不是 如果是这样的话 还不如就 bye-bye 好了
108	Ss	((several students laugh 1.71))
109	S13	算了吧 让他们两个人一起吃药吧

The questions scattered across the above four episodes of interaction constituted a questioning sequence relating to the first object of learning and made it possible for the students to have a profound understanding of the development of the story. The students were at first induced to make wild guesses about the possible ending, then to infer about the implied meaning of the title and the suspension created by the author, and finally to share with the class their imagined endings of the story. Approaching the end of the text instruction, the students, having gone into details of the text, were apparently more willing to give their answers. The possible endings shared by them formed a mosaic, which helped to create a pleasant classroom atmosphere.

Appreciating the author's description of the main characters

The second object of learning, i.e., appreciating the author's description of the main characters, was enacted through Q-A interaction across several sessions of instruction. Extract 6-5 displays the interaction in the stage of global reading where the researcher encouraged the students to think of as many words as they could to describe the two main characters of the story. During the process, each time someone articulated a word, the researcher asked him or her for evidence of that feature. So it went and in the end the whole class came up with two lists of words for the two characters respectively, as shown in Table 6-2.

Extract 6-5 On the characters of the story

1	T	How many characters are there in the story.
2	Ss	three/two/three

3	T	Who are they?
4	Ss	((students pronouncing the names of the characters 4.0))
5	T	yes Alan and the old man: the old man- the author didn't give a name to the old man right
6	Ss	((unclear 2.84))
7	T	just old man old man right
8	Ss	((unclear 7.72))
9	T	eh can you use a few words to describe the characters (1.84) first Alan. what kind of person do you think he is.
10	Ss	(0.5) punished/foolish
11		((students laugh loudly 5.28))
12	T	<Alan is foolish yes> OK (1.40) yes. young man. especially young man. in love are all fools.
13	Ss	((unclear 1.80))
14	T	Don't you think so?
15	Ss	no/no
16	T	girls are not as foolish as (..) boys
17	Sx	yes
18	Ss	((students laugh loudly 3.00))
19	Ss	opposite/yes yes yes
20	T	opposite. (.) really?
21		(2.72)
22	T	foolish. yes: more words?
23	Ss	poor/immature
24	T	immature? OK
25	Ss	((unclear 5.04))
26	T	why do you think he is immature. (.) S23ueyu huh?
27		(4.80)
28	S23	he's young and too:- didn't experience the life
29	T	mhm? he was not experienced mhm. yes in comparison with the old man? right he was immature=
30	Sx	=Narrow-minded
31	T	narrow-minded yes why do you think he is narrow-minded?

Table 6-2 Words the students thought of to describe the characters of the story

Alan (the buyer)	The old man (the seller)
foolish, immature, narrow-minded, naive, poor, insane, selfish, jealous, possessive, crazy, nervous, timid, sensitive, pessimistic, reckless	profound, experienced, sophisticated, insightful, indifferent, wicked, mischievous, crafty, sly, grave, greedy

The author's characterization of the old man was picked up later in the detailed reading, as shown in Extract 6-6. The question was re-specified into one about the old man's room. The students first came up with some adjectives in Chinese meaning shabby or broken (L5 and L6). In L15, the researcher directed the students to the old man's way of talking, which was rather polite and characterized the old man as one being well-educated, and the students came up with another set of Chinese adjectives (LL16-18). In L36, the researcher guided the students on the reason for the author's detailed account of the condition of the old man's room. Hearing a few students' answers that the author's purpose was to create the atmosphere for the story (L40), the researcher reminded them of Alan's asking the question "Is it true?" (L46), indicating that there is a connection between the old man's shabby room and Alan's distrust of the old man.

Extract 6-6 On the old man's shabby room

1   T   So what do you think of the room.
2   (2.72)
3   S23 emmmm shapy
4   T   it's- yes the word right S23
5   Sx   简陋的
6   S21 破落不堪
7   T   eh shabby yes (1.32) the room is very shabby right (0.5) there is (.) almost no. (.) furniture (2.36) but a plain kitchen table (.) plain means- ordinary. it's not beautiful at all ↓ rocking chair?- yes S20un asked? what is a rocking chair ↓ rocking chair is-
8   S20 [摇椅]
9   T   [摇椅] yes
10 T   you can rock sitting on a chair OK (0.5) even rock and roll @hehe@=

11	S13	=that's [fantastic]
12	S20	[it's ordinary]
13	T	yes (1.0) an or:dinary chair. (2.88) and then we see the shelves- a couple of shelves (.) containing in all perhaps a dozen bottles and jars. so not many (.) perhaps a dozen.
14	Ss	((unclear))
15	T	yes many of you (.) noticed that the old man said very politely? I'm glad to make your acquaintance. why make your acquaintance instead of very glad to see you or nice to meet you right?
16	Sx	很像政要
17	T	=yes what's your impression of this old man ↑ when- when you read this. when you read his words ↓ (2.92) the old man must be (.) what kind of person=
18	S33	老江湖
19	T	老江湖？@hehe@ 我们看武侠小说 uh (1.0) 那些各大宗派的教主 他们个个都 谈吐不凡 是不是啊 @haha@
20	Sx	像是有身份的人 =
21	T	= 有身份的人 噢 (1.04) 有地位是不是 @hehe@ (1.24) I guess the old man must be well-educated
22	Sx	well-educated
23	T	in a movie adapted from this story yes the old man is a <u>professor</u> yes.
24		((T and students laugh 1.37))
25	T	(0.72) yes the old man must be well-educated do you think so mhm?
26		other[wise he couldn't greet Alan Austen] in such a polite way- make your acquaintance this is very formal right
27	S21	[so why was he so poor]
28		(1.12)
29	T	[make someone's acquaintance >yes but<]=
30	Sx	[maybe he is a (.) chemistry professor]=
31	T	=>why is he so poor<
32	S21	=I don't know=
33	T	=living (.) in such a shabby room
34	Ss	((unclear 2.92))
35		(5.12)
36	T	and yes another question is why does the author (0.92) em describe (0.5) the condition of the room in such (.) de:tails
37	S21	in paragraph two
38	T	yes in paragraph two right? mhm
39		(2.48)

40	S17	一般 (.) 这种场景描写都是为了渲染气氛
41	T	(0.5) 渲染气氛？[mhm]
42	S17	[是的]
43	T	(0.5) OK=
44	S17	=@ehehe@
45	T	@hehehe@
46	T	Why would Alan ask such a question- is it true ↑ =
47	S3	=because he didn't believe it=
48	S21	=because=
49	Ss	=((several students talk 0.56))
50	T	yes ↓ because Alan didn't (.) believe that=
51	S21	=the house is too shabby=
52	T	yes a man that lives in such a shabby room ↓
53	S21	don't have the magic potion=
54	T	wouldn't be in a position to sell such magic potion right?=
55	Ss	=yeah/yeah
56		(0.96)
57	T	That is why the author described (0.80) the condition of the room in such details=
58	S3	= 不放心吧 =
59	Sx	=yes
60		(0.88)
61	T	otherwise Alan wouldn't have asked such a question right? (1.0) do you think so?

When the instruction came to the old man's words "Young people who need a love potion very seldom have five thousand dollars. Otherwise they would not need a love potion.", the researcher asked the students to figure out the meaning of those words, as demonstrated in Extract 6-7. The students were motivated to think about the old man's opinion of money and love and his judgment of Alan, the poor young man coming for the love potion. Though the researcher closed the interaction with some jocular words on love (L31), his intention was to have the students appreciate the author's characterization of the old man by his words, sharing his own life experience and his insights about the conflict between money and love in a young man's life.

Extract 6-7 On the old man's opinion of money and love

1	T	Young people who need a love potion very seldom have five thousand dollars. Otherwise they would not need a love potion. What does it mean. S35 what does it mean. Otherwise.
2	S35	(1.0) 如果一个 (.) 年轻人有 (.) 五千 (.) eh 的话 他就不再需要那个怀春水了
3		(0.63)
4	T	mhm [mhm]
5	S21	[反了吧]
6	S3	好像反了
7	T	yes. yes. mhm.
8	T	如果他有五千美元 他就不会需 -
9	S35	[不会需要]
10	S3	[不要这种]
11	Ss	((unclear))
12	T	需要怀春水的人 (.) 一般 [都没有那么] 多钱
13	S3	[一般都没钱]
14	Ss	((unclear 3.49))
15	T	那什么意思大概就是说 如果有了前你就不会 需要用怀春水来 -
16	Ss	来吸引 / 来吸引
17	T	吸引吗 - 是吸引吗
18	Sx	来控制 =
19	T	= 控制 对 嗯 是不是 eh 他说的是对的 huh
20	S6	对
21	T	嗯 嗯 thank you yes (0.74) 但是你觉得 (1.0) (1.03) 真的有了钱就不需要控制？
22	S3	可能在 =
23	S2	= 爱情和金钱
24	R	(0.86)
25	Ss	((unclear))
26	T	所以 没钱是 (1.0) 很可怜的 对不对 @hehe@
27	Ss	((laugh 2.0))
28	Ss	((unclear 7.83))
29	T	这个 old man the old man 他也曾经年轻过 是吧 年轻人对爱情没有自信的

30	S3	他曾经也追过 =
31	T	是啊 年轻人没自信的主要原因 就是没钱 但是也不能等到很有钱才谈恋爱吧 (2.0) 不过 我觉得 如果现在还没谈恋爱的话 可能还是太晚了一点哈
32	Ss	((laugh loudly 10.00))

The old man's way of talking was addressed further later as the detailed reading proceeded. Extract 6-8 displays interaction initiated by the researcher's asking one question raised by a student concerning the omission in a sentence uttered by the old man. The student question, in actuality, pointed to the structure of the sentence. However, the researcher took it as an opportunity for the students to further appreciate the author's methods of characterization. That is, the old man's simple words reflected that he knew very well what Alan wanted to buy.

Extract 6-8　On the old man's way of talking

1	T	Alan said I want nothing of that sort. I don't want to kill anyone right
2	Sx	mhm.
3	T	but- the old man said probably it's just as well (0.5)
4	S21	@mhmh@ 一切皆有可能
5	T	(0.69) 噢 你认为是一切皆有可能？ (0.63) 一切皆有可能那句话怎么说的啊？
6	Ss	nothing is impossible/everything is possible/anything is possible
7	T	nothing is impossible 或 者 是 impossible is nothing right? (..) You see probably it is?- just as well ↓ something must be- something must be <omitted> between it is and just as well right
8	Sx	对啊
9	T	(0.5) it is 后面没有东西啊 is 是一个系动词 后面省略掉了 省略掉了什么 大家看一下
10		(3.72)
11	S21	eh life cleaner
12	T	mhm?
13		(1.31)
14	T	Alan 前面说 I want nothing of that sort?
15	S21	[that sort 就是 life cleaner]=
16	Sx	[前面的东西]
17	T	ah ah- it is (0.5)

18	Sx	maybe what you want
19	T	ah it is that sort of thing that you want ↓ (.) probably. Right?
20	Sx	em probably it is that sort of thing just as well
21	S33	it is the thing exactly you want=
22	T	=yes? probably it is something=
23	S21	=something you want
24	T	嗯 说不定 你 可能也需要是不是？
25	S33	说不定你用得到呢
26	T	噢 说不定你用得到 大概也可以 说不定哪一天你用得到 huh

As mentioned in Section 6.3.2, the author characterized Alan (the young man) mainly by describing his emotional changes along the process of his dialogue with the old man. Alan's feeling doubtful whether the old man had the love potion in storage was tapped into earlier, as demonstrated in Extract 6-6. When the text instruction came to Alan's confidence of his fidelity to his girlfriend Diana, the researcher asked the students the question "Why was Alan so confident in himself?" (L1) and stimulated interaction, as shown in Extract 6-9. S21 responded that Alan was confident of his fidelity because he was "in secret love with Diana" (L3 and L5), which the researcher rephrased as "in intense love with Diana" (L6). The interaction was expanded by S17's and S3's insertion that Alan would probably betray Diana (L8 and L9), which sparked discussion on whether Alan would 'slip a little' if he got married to Diana (LL 8-34). The researcher's attempt to end the interaction in L34 was further expanded by S17 who gave a reason by quoting a maxim in Chinese (L35) and the discussion steered into the contradictory feeling of being in love until the end.

Extract 6-9 On Alan's asserted confidence

1	T	Why was Alan so confident of himself.
2	Ss	((unclear 6.57))
3	S21	He said he will never betray Diana.
4	T	That's a good word betray right? He will never betray Diana because he is-
5	S21	in love with Diana @hehe@ in secret love
6	T	he was in intense love with or he loves Diana intensely right?

7		(1.88)
8	S17	[no I but but the girl]
9	S3	[but later he will]
10	S17	will forgive him uh whatever he he do and I think that boy would would never challenge that girl
11	R	(2.23)
12	T	Oh I see mhm
13	Ss	((unclear 12.80))
14	T	challenge
15	R	(9.71)
16	T	Do you think that (1.5) Alan (0.5) will not slip a little?
17	Ss	((unclear 2.91))
18	S17	I think=
19	T	=you don't think so right=
20	S3	yeah
21	S17	maybe maybe not
22	T	mhm?
23	S17	I think if Diana
24	T	mhm
25	S17	love him so much and and will will forgive him forever if he must slip a little
26	T	probably he will be=
27	S39	=he is the true self=
28	T	get sick @he@
29	Ss	yeah/yes/ya
30	Ss	((laugh mildly 1.66))
31	S21	yeah you'll get very sick=
32	T	sick or tired right
33	Sx	yeah
34	T	probably someday in the future Alan will get sick of Diana and tired of the marriage right
35	S17	因为 > 得不到的永远在骚动 被偏爱的都有恃无恐 <
36	T	再说一遍
37	S17	@ehe@
38	Ss	((unclear 5.48))
39	S21	翻译成英语
40	T	得不到的永远在骚：动 =
41	Ss	对 / 对 / 对

42	Ss	((unclear)) 有恃无恐
43	S21	you are always greedy
44	T	uhuh?
45	Ss	((unclear)) 有恃无恐
46	T	<被偏爱的有恃无恐?>
47	Ss	((unclear 2.80))
48	T	被偏爱的是指什么？
49	Ss	就是爱/被爱的一方
50	T	噢 被爱的一方就有恃无恐 想做什么就做什么 比较任性=
51	S17	=对
52	T	得不到的-
53	Ss	永远在骚动
54	T	永远在骚动 哇 两方是不对等的
55	S17	不是 就是他得不到之前 他会 特别骚动 特别想得到 得到了之后 自己被偏爱了就 没那么珍惜了
56	T	(0.8) 每个人都会这样？
57	S17	I think so
58	T	@hehehe@
59	S13	我感觉挺多人这样
60	T	大多数 (0.5) 嗯 那为什么=
61	S17	大多数男人
62		(0.4)
63	Ss	((laugh loudly 18.34))

Though the expanded interaction displayed in Extract 6-9 was seemingly diverted from the central topic, it did open up a space for the students to rethink about Alan's asserted confidence of his fidelity to his beloved Diana. More importantly, it foreshadowed the next question on the words and expressions used by the author to describe Alan's emotions throughout his dialogue with the old man, which initiated another interaction. As Extract 6-10 shows, the researcher led the students to locate those words and expressions in the text and to have a panoramic view of Alan's emotional change as the story progresses, from nervous at the beginning, to anxious in the middle, and to grateful at the end.

Extract 6-10 On Alan's emotions

1	T	yes let's take a look at the words and expressions the author used to describe Alan's emotions.
2	S17	Alan's emotions
3	Ss	((unclear 1.66))
4	S21	rapture
5	R	(2.12)
6	T	from the beginning Alan-
7	Ss	nervous/as nervous as a kitten/very nervous
8	T	then
9	S17	hello kitten
10	Ss	en/em
11	T	yes someone asked that question why not kitty
12	Ss	((laugh 4.69))
13	T	because Kitty is a name right
14	Sx	yes
15	T	kitten means a little cat
16		((small talk about Hello Kitty 17.60))
17	T	and then in para- in which paragraph
18	S21	horrified
19	T	yes he was horrified right Alan was horrified when he heard about-
20	Ss	life cleaner/life cleaner/glove cleaner
21	S21	eh he thinks the thing must be a poison
22	T	yes he thought that must be a poison
23	S21	yeah?=
24	T	=he was horrified because he was not coming for a poison he was coming for the love potion
25	Ss	yes/yeah
26	T	yes and then- in (0.7) in- in which paragraph
27	Sx	twelve
28	Sx	ten=
29	Ss	((some students in chorus))=twelve=
30	T	yes?
31	Ss	((unclear 1.77))
32	T	(1.0) why why did Alan feel apprehensive or anxious
33	Ss	((unclear 5.25))

34	T	(0.5) he was afraid that- the love potion is as. expensive as- [the love potion]
35	Ss	[the love potion]
36	Ss	((unclear 1.26))
37	S21	and he hasn't so many- [money]
38	S3	[money]
39	T	he couldn't afford that right?
40	Ss	yeah/yes/yes
41	S13	he is very poor
42	T	and then?
43	Ss	((unclear 9.48))
44	T	<then paragraph- [twenty]
45	Sx	[twenty]
46	T	yes paragraph twenty
47		((T and students)) attempting a look of scientific detachment
48	T	scientific detachment 超然物外 置身事外 摆出一副 -[置身事外]的表情
49	S21	[置身事外]
50		(1.48)
51	T	我要的不是春药的效果 是不是？
52	TS	((T and students laugh 2.46))
53		((unclear 1.49))
54	T	casual- casual impulse but consider the spiritual side OK
55		(4.18)
56	T	yes and then as the story proceeds
57	S21	paragraph twen:ty- six
58	T	yeah paragraph twenty six
59	S17	in a rapture
60	Ss	((read the text 2.57))
61	T	extreme excitement right?=
62	Ss	=yes/yeah
63	T	he was extremely excited eh when he heard about the: effect of the love potion and then paragraph-
64	Ss	thirty two/thirty two/thirty four
65	T	thirty two yes again he- [cried]
66	Sx	[cried]
67	T	oh that is love that is love
68	Ss	((read the text 7.20))

69	T	and then paragraph thirty- [four <overwhelmed with joy>]
70	Ss	[four <overwhelmed with joy>]
71	T	and paragraph twenty- eh [thirty six]
72	Ss	[thirty six]
73	T	said Alan [fer:vently]
74	Ss	[fer:vently]
75	Ss	((turning pages 12.5))
76	T	and then (1.5) no more
77	Ss	((unclear 1.08))
78	S21	I can't tell you how grateful I am
79	T	oh I can't-
80	S3	paragraph forty three
81	T	I can't tell you how grateful I am [yes]
82	Ss	[yeah/yeah]
83	T	how grateful I am
84	Ss	((unclear 1.60))
85	T	I can't believe it right

Several interaction presented above unfolded around the second identified object of learning, i.e., appreciating the author's description of the two main characters of the story. Despite the limited number of participants directly involved in the interaction and their limited verbal contributions, the questions asked by the researcher constituted a questioning sequence which held the students' focal attention to the author's method of characterization. There was variation in the content focus and cognitive demand in the questions and hence the questions could be said to have opened up a space for the students to experience the object of learning.

Expressing personal responses to issues related to love

The third object of learning, i.e., expressing personal responses to issues related to love, was enacted through Q-A interaction which spread across different sessions of instruction.

As early as in the pre-reading stage, the researcher asked three questions to warm up for the discussion of the text. As shown in Extract 6-11, the first pre-reading question the researcher cast to the students was intended to have them share their previous experience of loving someone. However, the interaction was steered into the Oedipus complex when S21 answered that he had loved his mother (L3 and L6) and S2 uttered the Chinese for the Oedipus complex. The researcher took this opportunity to expand the students' knowledge about the ancient Greek mythological story. It might be said that the post-expansion was off the topic but it did invite some of the students to share with the class their encyclopedic knowledge. Additionally, it constituted the variation of content focus in the personal response questions implemented in the text instruction.

Extract 6-11 Pre-reading question on loving someone

1	T	Three questions for us to have a short discussion. The first is have you ever loved anyone?=
2	S17	=[yeah? @ehehe@]
3	S21	=[my mother.]
4	T	or have you ever been loved ↓
5	S13	[she has lover]=
6	S21	[the mother]=
7	S17	= >no. no. no no<
8		[((students laugh 2.0))]
9	S2	[恋母情结]
10	S29	little secret yeah
11	T	yes? how do we say 恋母情结 in English.
12	Ss	((unclear 14.88))
13	T	Can anyone tell\ us the story of Oedipus or the Oedipus- eh <u>complex</u>. ((T writes on the board))
14	S6	[Oedipus complex] 俄狄浦斯情节
15	S3	[mother complex]
16	T	yes. Oedipus.
17	S6	[俄狄浦斯]
18	S13	[O-di-pus]
19		((students pronounce the word Oedipus))
20	T	Yes in English the pronunciation should be Oe-di-pus
21	Ss	((students follow T in pronouncing the word))
22	Ss	((unclear 6.80))

23	T	Complex
24		((19.8))
25	T	yes can anyone tell us the story about this complex
26		(2.28)
27	S21	S5
28		(1.32)
29	T	ah S5 (1.0) Do you know the story?
30	S17	希腊神话
31	S5	He married his mother
32	T	Yes? Oedipus married <his mother>=
33	S21	=killed his mother
34	S5	and killed his father
35	Ss	((several students talk in surprise)) wa ah
36	S5	but he didn't know-
37	T	yes
38	S5	that is his true mother
39	T	yes you're right=
40	S5	=and when he found out he- he stabbed his eyes=
41	T	=yes=
42	S5	=and- and his mother ended herself
43	T	Yes: (.) his mother also committed <suicide>? yes. (2.0) that is Oedipus complex. seems that Oedipus was doomed to kill his father and marry his mother OK. that is Oedipus <u>complex</u>.

The second pre-reading question was concerned with the students' feeling of being in love. As shown in Extract 6-12, the researcher first called on S6 (whose girlfriend was in the same class) to give an answer and the interaction thereafter sparked rounds of laughter (as in L5, L9, L12 L14, L22 and L27). Upon the completion of S6's answer, the researcher redirected the turn to S21 (L37), one of the most active students of the class, and then to S35 (L55). All the three students gave complete responses to the question though there were frequent pauses and some grammatical mistakes. The interaction contributed to a light and active classroom atmosphere which in turn kept the interaction going smoothly. More importantly, the different feelings verbalized by the students made it possible for the students to experience the

disposition of critical thinking.

Extract 6-12 Pre-reading question on being in love

1	T	S6.
2	S6	en en?
3	Ss	((laugh loudly 2.8))
4	T	how do you feel about being in love
5	Ss	((students continue laughing 2.44))
6		(2.16)
7	T	being in love is not like poetry-
8	S21	Ah! I see.
9		((T and students laugh 4.76))
10	T	is it?
11	S6	you're right
12		((T and students laugh 3.32))
13		(5.28)
14		((several students laugh1.68))
15	S6	what am I to do
16	T	yes. I- I- I mean- have you ever been- (1.0) we're talking about yes these three questions yes have you ever loved- or have you ever been loved by anyone? and what is the feeling of being in love? right?
17		(1.44)
18	S6	feeling
19	T	(0.5) yes feeling
20		(2.40)
21	S6	@hhh@ sometimes happy: sometimes- sad
22		((students laugh loudly 5.2))
23	T	why- why sometimes sad? @hehe@
24	S6	because sometimes have quarrel?
25		(0.64)
26	T	oh quarrel!
27		((T and students laugh 1.44))
28	T	tha- that's normal right?=
29	Sx	=yes=
30	T	=even- [even-]
31	S6	[that's real life]
32	T	Yes (1.72) we quarrel with our brothers and sisters right?

Chapter 6 Third Cycle of Action Research

33	Ss	yes/yeah
34		(4.48)
35	T	happy and sad so being in love is a mixture of happiness and sadness
36	Sx	yes
37	T	OK (.) yes uh anyone else S21
38		((several students laugh in a low voice 2.04))
39	S21	怎么又找我 -
40		((students laugh loudly 2.00))
41	T	what do you think of love!
42	S21	someone told me that if you fall in love with somebody (.) your heart will pump fast
43	Ss	[students laugh]
44	S21	[uh I have never felt this feeling maybe I'm not in love with someone.]
45	Ss	((students laugh loudly and someone claps hands))
46	S3	@henhen@ >he's a sad boy<
47	T	your heart will beat faster @hehe@
48	Ss	((several students laugh 0.96))
49	T	If one is in love=
50	Sx	=have you ever been in love=
51	T	S6 is that true?
52		((students laugh 3.20))
53	T	yes you will have faster heartbeat but some people say like you will miss your heartbeat right? when you're in love with someone you- >when you're in love with someone< you will <miss your heartbeat> (3.08) that's exciting mhm (1.40) @hmhmhm@
54	Ss	((unclear 5.24))
55	T	uh S35? Have you ever been in love?
56	Ss	((students laugh 6.24))
57	S35	(1.84) I think ((in a low voice)) once (..) in high school
58	Ss	high school/high school
59	T	uhuh?=
60	Ss	((several students exclaiming)) =wa oh=
61		((students laugh and clap hands))
62	S3	that's normal
63	T	yes? (1.0) what was the feeling?
64	S3	happy=
65		=((students laugh loudly 4.88))

66	Ss	normal/shocked
67	S35	eh feel more nervous- you feel more- (1.0) a lot nervous
68	Ss	yes/yes
69	Sx	不讨厌吗？
70		(6.68)
71	S35	<feel eh> (16.76) nervous and uh (1.5) sometimes you feel happy and uh uh (5.5) more times nervous
72		((students laugh 6.28))
73	T	oh yes? that makes you nervous. anyway thank you. yes most of the time you're nervous and sometimes happy

The third pre-reading question was connected to the preceding questions in that it went further to elicit the students' personal responses about how people in love should treat each other, as shown in Extract 6-13. Two students, S23 and S33, were called on to answer the question. While S23 shared her own perception of the matter, S33 related it to the Thai movie *Eternity*, which the researcher had recommended to the class previously.

Extract 6-13 Pre-reading question on how to treat the loved one

1	T	OK let's see- S23 OK? Do you have anything to say about this (..) yes how should people in love treat each other
2		(5.56)
3	T	huh?
4	S23	em (0.5) I think (.) it- for a couple in love they should respect each other
5	T	respect OK?
6		(2.88)
7	S23	em (..) mature (1.0) understanding and uh
8	T	need to be understanding
9	S23	Yes (2.28) be helpful
10	T	OK be helpful to each other
11		(2.28)
12	S23	also: (1.56) have the: responsibility for- if they want to have their family they need to have responsibility @hehe@
13	T	OK they should bear responsibilities?
14		(4.12)
15	S23	uh em be equal is very important

16	T	(0.8) O:K.
17		((T writes on the board 20.00))
18	T	mhm
19	S23	that's all=
20	T	=that's all thank you thank you OK: yes- a couple should respect each other (.) they should understand each other uh they should be helpful to each other (1.0) they should be responsible to their family and uh they should be equal to each other or treat each other equally.
21		(4.20)
22	T	Do you have more?
23	Ss	((unclear 3.04))
24	T	Yeah. S33? (.) be independent and eh?
25	S33	(1.00) we can learn that from the movie Eternity.
26	T	indepen:dent? and eh
27	S33	<pree-vate space>
28	T	(1.28) pri- private space yes
29		((T writes on the board 2.0))
30	S33	and trust en and eh (0.5) trust each other we can learn that eh we need common interest
31	T	Yes: trust and common in:terest

In the midst of the detailed reading, the researcher asked the question again on how people in romantic love should treat each other. As displayed in Extract 6-14, the researcher allocated the turn through nomination to S10 (L3), whose answer stressed the importance of keeping private space between the loved ones (L4). In L14, the researcher related S10's answer to the protagonists in the Thai movie *Eternity*, which sparked a short post-expansion and lighted up the classroom atmosphere as well.

Extract 6-14 On how to treat each other in romantic love

1	T	How do you think people in love should behave themselves
2		(9.54)
3	T	S10 you have something to say?
4	S10	(0.5) eh I think people in love should keep certain distance
5	T	(0.5) mh yes? keep certain distance mhm
6		(6.69)

7	S10	and they shouldn't (5.0) think (2.0) um care each other at any time they should have their private space
8	T	yes they should have their private space keep a certain distance and have their own private space
9	S10	em (2.0) and they get along with each other (1.0) for a long time they will (.) hate each other
10	T	uhuh? yes? you mean if they (.) what? if they get along with each other?
11	S10	uh for (.) so long time.
12	T	(1.09) for too long time=
13	S10	=too long time
14	T	and they will begin to hate to each other really? like Sangmong @he@
15	Ss	((laugh 2.22))
16	T	Sangmong and Yupadee right?
17	Ss	((unclear 1.0))
18		(3.94)
19	T	Do you think Yupadee hated Sangmong?
20	Ss	((in chorus)) NO
21	T	No probably that is the difference between men [and women]
22	S3	[yah yah]
23		(2.17)
24	T	Thank you S10 keep a certain distance and have private space right?
25	S10	yes
26	T	(0.6) otherwise they will (.) hate each other.
27	Ss	((laugh 2.0))

The same topic was brought forward once again by the end of the text instruction. This time, as shown in Extract 6-15, the researcher had the students have a group discussion before organizing the Q-A interaction. Then the researcher invited one student out of each group to present their discussion to the whole class within one minute. As can be seen in the transcript, two students, S32 and S21, made their contributions to the interaction by turns before the camera ran out of power. In comparison to the students' responses to the pre-reading questions, the students' contributions elicited by the post-reading question seemed to be of higher quality in terms of verbal fluency, syntactic complexity and grammatical accuracy. S21, for example, was directly involved in the interaction displayed in both Extract 6-12 and Extract

6-15. The two questions both belonged to the type of open personal response questions but the pre-reading question was intended to be less demanding than the post-reading one. However, S21's response to the former question was qualitatively inferior to his response to the latter question. This indicates that the repetition of the same question or the bringing up of similar questions at different stages of instruction is conducive to the qualitative change in learning, as claimed by Marton and associates that repetition with variation can lead to meaningful learning (Marton and Booth, 1997), because the situation of learning has undergone qualitative changes despite the repetition of the task or the question to be answered.

Extract 6-15 On how to treat each other

1	T	OK I want you to have a discussion (1.0) please turn to page 129. (2.0) giving a talk.
2		((T and students turn pages 11.20))
3	T	have a discussion and then make a list of do's and don'ts that is how should people in love treat each other
4		((students discuss 0:07:30.86))
5	T	OK let's start from the last line. present your discussion to the class within one minute.
6	S21	Monica.
7	T	Monica? S32 right?
8	S21	yeah
9	T	OK let's start from the last line S32 please give a one minute talk about the do's and don'ts.
10	S32	do's and don'ts? 就是恋爱的人什么该做什么不该做是不是？
11	T	嗯
12	S32	一分钟啊！?
13	Ss	((laugh 2.8))
14	T	eh less than one minute is also OK
15	S32	uh respect to each other
16	T	respect each other not respect to each other
17	S32	噢 (3.0) eh eh- 对 (2.0)
18	T	that is the do. and the don't is?
19	Sx	respect is everything
20	Ss	((laugh 2.0))

21	S32	and take care of each other
22	T	OK thank you
23	R	((unclear 26.00))
24	T	the last line but one are you a group?
25	S21	we are always one group
26	T	OK who's the speaker yes
27	S21	(2.0) first we need to have our own freedom that is private space and we shouldn't lie to each other
28	T	OK private space but no lies
29	S21	and second is stand of other's point of opinion understand each other and we shouldn't
30	Ss	((laugh 1.66))
31	S21	uh the third is we need to treat the other's friends different that is we need to separate the other from each other's friends or other people=
32	T	=because she is unique.
33	S21	yes he is unique- uh she is unique unique uh (2.0) last. as a boy or as a man (.) we need to give the girls a feel of security not only not only the emotional aspect but=
34	S6	=never slip=
35	Ss	((laugh loudly 2.05))
36	S21	(1.5) but also the ma- material aspect that's all.
37	T	oh security of the material aspect=
38	S21	=yes
39		((the camera was out of power))

The personal response questions employed across the three stages of instruction, i.e., pre-reading, while-reading and post-reading, formed another questioning sequence intended to realize the third object of learning, i.e., expressing personal opinions towards love-related issues. The questions varied in content focus in that the latter questions are more specific than the former ones. They also varied in cognitive demand in that the latter questions require higher levels of cognitive processing than the former ones. Whereas the questions asked in the pre-reading stage requested the students to share their experiences or feelings, those asked in the while reading and post reading stages involved the students in giving their own judgments on the basis of what they had learned as well as their personal experiences.

Simply put, the sequence of personal response questions created the space for the students to experience the variation in expressing their own feelings and opinions, not only in articulating what came to their mind, but also in elaborating what they articulated by relating to their own encyclopedic knowledge or personal experiences.

In addition to the questions presented in the above extracts, the researcher answered the student questions incorporated into the courseware as well and some of their questions were incorporated into the sequences of questions relating to the three objects of learning. As can be noted, the episodes presented above are relatively longer than those demonstrated in the preceding two chapters. One reason for that is the incorporation of student questions into the sequences of questions. Another reason is that the students were better prepared to participate in classroom interaction as they had previewed the text as required by the teacher to raise their own questions. Further discussion is to be made below in the evaluating section.

6.4 Evaluating

6.4.1 Students' learning logs

The students were expected to report in their learning logs how they had benefited from classroom questions in three aspects: 1) raising their own questions while previewing the text, 2) participating in classroom Q-A interaction, and 3) the teacher's answering students' questions. Thirty eight of the class submitted their logs as required and most of them wrote in close correspondence with the given format. Some of the students even provided examples to illustrate how they had benefited from the newly introduced intervention.

6.4.1.1 Benefits of raising questions while previewing the text

What the students gained as a result of raising their own questions while previewing the text clustered around three interconnected themes: 1) a deeper understanding of the text, 2) active thinking, and 3) autonomous learning.

Most of them claimed that they had a deeper understanding of the text because they had to read every detail carefully and otherwise they could not come up with their own questions:

> After raising the questions by myself I can have a deeper understanding of the novel, because we are easily paying attention to the details ... (S3)
> After raising my own questions while reading the whole passage, I have a deeper understanding of this passage. (S6)
> Obviously I have benefited a lot from raising questions on my own. At least I have to go through the whole passage and be familiar with the context. Without the task, I may just walk into a class with knowing nothing about the passage. (S5)
> I was more familiar with this text. While I raising questions, I would want to know what the text mean, what the author wants to tell us? Therefore, I read this text carefully so that I was more familiar with the text. (S17)
> I really have benefited from raising my questions while reading the text. It's effective to urge me to do the pre-reading work. If I want to raise some significant questions, I must read the text at least three times and try my best to get its points. Then, I have to find the author's purpose, try to think about what does him want to express. So, my ability of reading will be improved. After that, it's really useful for me to understand the text better. (S12)

What was of particular interest to the researcher was that S20, a student of low language proficiency level and usually silent unless he was called on in classroom interaction, wrote that by raising questions as required by the teacher he began to realize the value of reading the text carefully:

> In the past, I read the text without questions, I always feel confused by the text and I can't develop my own knowledge. What's more, with time went by I easily forget the details. But when I read the text with questions especially myself questions, I will read the text careful in case miss some details and after finish reading, I discover that I can solve all my questions. (S20)

Most of the students reported that raising questions while previewing the text constituted an opportunity for them to think independently and profoundly about the messages conveyed in the text:

- It was like a brainstorm, no matter the quality of these questions, you just need to think as much as possible. It is a good way to form a thought which can benefit us a lot in the future. (S20)
- [I]t is more significant for us to think, which is different from informed by others. (S3)
- The best way to get to know a person or a thing is to raise questions. During the process, we are driven to think. (S5)
- [A]lthough my question may be shallow and stupid. But at least I totally read the whole text and had more profound thoughts. (S7)
- Raising our own question is a good way to read a text, because when you are raising question you are thinking, if you don't do that you may just finish the reading but get nothing. Raising question make reader think what author think. (S35)

Quite a few of the students mentioned about being 'forced' to take an active role in learning, i.e., to learn autonomously:

- Personally, the request of raising questions about the text we are going to learn forced me to perform actively during the process when we planned to start a new unit. (S33)
- With this task, I previewed this passage again and again. Then I can understand the article more or less, which <u>teached</u> [taught] me that it is of importance to study by ourselves first. Only when we are willing to study, we can study better. (S38)
- I think giving question is a good form for us to dig the passage deeply and lead us to tackle it. And I wish more questions could be solved by ourselves. (S10)
- [I]t makes me prepare for the lesson. (S6)

There was one student who gave a detailed account of how she had benefited from being forced to preview the text and come up with her own questions:

- It is unit, it has a little difference from the former ones. We are ordered to raise our own questions while reading the test.I have an extraordinary different and fresh experience from doing it. I started to pay attention to the details and logic. For instance, I am curious about the reason why the old man could know Alan's name when he just came in. I began to notice the description of environment, such as dirty buff-colored, rocking chair, plain kitchen table and so on. What's more, I learned to connect the whole myself with story's development, from beginning to the end. And most beneficial thing I got from this way is to discover further more than the surface. (S26)

Apart from the three above-mentioned aspects of benefits, two students also indicated that by so doing they were better prepared and hence were in a better position to follow the teacher in the process of classroom instruction:

- Thanks to raising my own questions, I can pay more attention to the point when the teacher talks about those and can also understand the text profoundly. (S16)
- Even if I got absent-minded I can catch up with the teacher very soon because after raising questions I am very familiar with the text. (S29)

6.4.1.2 Benefits of participating in classroom Q-A interaction

The students gave positive feedback about participating in classroom Q-A interaction, i.e., answering questions and listening to their classmates' answering questions. There were two major types of benefits mentioned by the students. One type pointed to the exchange of ideas or thoughts and the other the learning of certain particular details.

Many of them indicated that participating in classroom Q-A interaction was helpful in broadening their horizon or generating new thoughts:

- Listening to my teacher's questions, and the answers by my classmates and the teacher, I learned the other people's viewpoints and how will they think about a particular incident. (S20)
- Besides, I expanded my mind by listening to my classmates' answers. Our answers are different means we could absorb some new thought. And my classmates' points are more comprehensive and more creative. (S4)
- I found that my classmates have lots of good ideas, and the questions they raised were very worth thinking. So I get many different understanding by thinking these questions. (S17)
- Everyone has different thoughts consequently the answer varies from person

to person. We can learn more different views and expand our thinking through communication and discussion. (S18)
- At the same time, I also learnt a lot when listening [to] my classmates' questions. Some other questions from different perspective[s] really make me have a deeper thought. (S38)
- What a person says reflects someone's quality of character to varying degree. We can not lose sight of this point … Views on the question whether lives need cleaning sometimes vary from person to person. Apparently, both reply and questions from my classmates impress me deeply. It is not so much the superficial language as the profound meanings that make the lines meaningful. (S8)

Some students illustrated how they had reached a deeper understanding of certain parts of the text or learned more about certain language points:

- Moreover, we answering or listening to our classmates' answers to the teacher's questions during the class. It is a helpful way to find new details about the text. (S7)
- What impresses me most is that the question raised by S5: why the old man says the subtle words? I don't remember what the answer was given by the teacher clearly, but as far as I'm concerned, I think the old man is trying to show his strength by pretending to be inscrutable in order to convince the young man to buy the love-potion. (S2)
- What's the most impressive question in my mind is your question---what will happen if Alan take the love potion to Diana. There are all kinds of answers among our class: Yours, S21's and S35's answer attract me. I am a strong believer in the idea that "After Diana knows Alan drunk the mixture, she find the old man and drink it for Alan". Finally, they deeply fall in love with each other. It's fabulous answer. I like happy ending. (S9)
- Then, through answering the teacher's questions, I believe it is also a thinking process. When the teacher asked about "What did life- cleaner mean?" Someone said it indicated that kill others' life or suicide. However, others combined the real life and believed it was cleaning others' memory. So nothing is absolutely one answer and nothing is impossible. It's also a good way to listen. (S3)

Besides the two major types of benefits as mentioned above, some of the students also indicated that by listening to their classmates' certain questions they had realized their own shortcomings or weaknesses in terms of learning:

- There were many questions rising [raised] by my classmates that were showed [shown] in the class. From those questions, I found it interesting to listen to others' questions and learned much from them. I realized that I have ignored many points and I would be more careful next time. (S14)
- I believe that I still need to improve the skills of raising questions. And compared with fellow classmates, I ought to learn more. (S21)
- I benefit from some questions raised by my classmates. One of these is: what is the personality of the old man and Alan? But I only summarize several words to describe their characters.However,in the discussion my classmates thought more words than me.They thought Alan is jealous,immature,narrow-minded and timid.About the old man,they use grave,crafty,sophisticated and insightful. Their answers expand my horizon. (S24)
- Then, Mr Liu came up with a question that the character of the chaser and the old man.My classmates and teachers listed the advanced words I didn't have access to half of the blackboard. I was deeply aware that my vocabulary is small. The classmates used many advanced words to describe individuals, which made me more clearly for the story's deep meaning. (S36)
- From other students' questions, I found that most of them pay more attention to the comprehension of the text but not the words. Next time, I will do that in order to better understand the characters. (S19)

The above feedback was proof that the researcher's involving more students in Q-A interaction, especially interaction initiated by students' questions, had helped strengthen the students' self-awareness or sense of competition in the learning. They were probably more highly motivated as a result of attending to their peer classmates' performance.

Another issue that deserves a mention here is that two students indicated that when they were trying to come up with their own questions while reading the text, they would put themselves in their teacher's position, that is, try to think what kind of questions their teacher would raise about a certain part of the text:

- As far as I am concerned, when I raised questions I would consider how would Mr Liu raise his question here, or how would others think about it. (S23)
- For instance, you had asked us to pay attention to author and title more than once, but in fact, the effectiveness is not equal to your expectation. It is evident that the time when we noticed these details finally is at the class which you introduced them to us. Besides, it's exactly the reason why I raised the question how can we understand the title of unit 7. (S33)

Thus, it can be said that the questions that the researcher designed for the instruction of the previous units played a modelling role for the students. One student acknowledged the value of students' questions in the classroom instruction but added that what is most important is the teacher's questions, for he deemed that the teacher's questions could give them a comprehensive view and stimulate valuable ideas:

- I think our questions can make some benefit, but the teacher's questions are the most important. It give us a whole view about text and some special idea. (S35)

Despite the positive feedback as demonstrated above, two students wrote in plain statements that the researcher had not asked their questions during the instruction:

- Maybe my questions need a lot of thinking, so my teacher did not ask my questions. That was normal because I do not like easy questions, that can not help everyone know themselves better. (S20)
- My questions weren't be displayed in PPT, so I don't know the correctness of my own answers to the question raised by me. (S2)

To the researcher, such statements were neither critical nor negative. Instead, they were evidence of the students' eagerness to get their teacher's feedback or response to their questions.

From the above discussion, it can be understood that the intervention newly introduced in the third cycle of AR, that is, having the students raise their own questions while previewing the text and displaying the selected ones to the whole class, helped to make the classroom interaction more a 'multilogue' (Schwab, 2011; Walsh 2011).

6.4.1.3 Benefits of listening to the teacher's answers

As many of the students' questions were concerned with language problems and it was often hard to elicit a response from the students to that end, the researcher mostly chose to answer such questions by himself. Besides, he would also give his answers to some comprehension and response questions from the students. What the students wrote of the researcher's answering the students' questions was also positive. Quite a few of them explicitly stated that the teacher's answering their questions helped them better understand the text or made them realize certain details they would otherwise have neglected:

- I remembered that several questions of mine had picked up by the teacher. For example, I mentioned before the old man's personality. There is no doubt that we will benefit from this. Connect with the teacher's answers we can hold a better apprehension about the story. In addition, the teacher put forward with another meaning of "Love potions". (S3)
- About teacher's answering question, under the guidance of the teacher's answer, I can understand this article more easily. (S6)
- And when teacher answered our questions, I could comprehend the text better. (S14)
- With regard to the teacher's answering my own or my classmates' questions, I found details I hadn't found before. For example, "Call it glove-cleaner if you like", I didn't know it was "understatement" before you told me. Another example was Alan Austen's emotion change; my focus was not here at that time. (S22)
- As for teacher's answers to my classmates' questions, they also helped me a lot and I learned much. For me, the most impressive question is S33's, because only she asked about the meaning of the title. Frankly speaking, when I saw "the chaser", I just referred to "words and expressions" behind the text. After listening to the teacher's answer, I knew that it also means the people

who try to acquire something. (S30)
- In the process of explaining this unit, teacher mainly pay attention to our questions. First he give a certain praise to our questions, then he explain the knowledge deeply. Teacher made us understand the point we did not catch, especially the story plot. Through these steps, we do understand well. (S38)

Others suggested that the teacher's answers were more helpful in deepening their understanding of the text or broadening their thinking towards certain issues as they thought that the teacher was more professional or richer in life experiences:

- As for the teacher's answers, I hold the view that they are more reasonable but they are also more profound in a way. Sometimes I can't understand it. Yeah, maybe it's time to improve myself. (S4)
- It is nice that teacher answers our questions, because teacher is more professional. (S7)
- As for the teacher's answering my own or my classmate's questions, I think it is necessary. After all, teacher is our guide and we need to get a referential answer which we can say is a revelation to us. (S12)
- Besides, teacher's answer let me understand some points that I didn't care about. Such as the emotions change of Alan. (S17)
- I still remembered that you answer my roommate's question. It was a little hard for me. However, you give me another way of thinking. (S21)
- Furthermore, the teacher's answers and questions are also useful and meaningful. The teacher asked us how people in love treat each other. I believe people in love should respect and understand each other. They need give enough trust to each other. And the teacher supplement that people in love should be independent and give each other freedom to do their own things, give private space. (S24)
- Also you answered our questions. Absolutely you settle them down. But I learnt the open minded when you're solving them and I still studied the text in a simple mind. (S26)

One student, S18, provided an account of the twofold benefit of the teacher's answering students' questions. On the one hand, it satisfied their needs of learning language points; on the other, it served to train their thinking skills:

- Furthermore, it is also conducive to us under the circumstance that the teacher answers our questions when we are in confusion. On the one hand, we can have intense grasp of the point what we want to know clearly. On the other hand, we can exchange our thoughts which can facilitate us to consider in various aspects. What's more, we can learn to think from a more professional perspective which makes us better. Above all, we can benefit from these questions a lot. (S18)

Simply put, as indicated in the students' feedback, it is necessary for the teacher to provide answers, during classroom interaction, not only to his own questions but also to students' questions. To achieve better efficacy, it is advisable to have the students answer the questions prior to the provision of a self-answer as the students suggested that listening to their peer classmates' answers was also enlightening.

6.4.2 Peer observation feedback

Miss Ding, the researcher's colleague who had previously observed his classroom instruction, was invited to observe two sessions of the text instruction of Unit 7. During the post-observation conference, she first gave an overall commentary on the classroom interaction and expressed her amazement at the classroom atmosphere which appeared to be even lighter and more joyous than before. She had the assumption that students would usually get less motivated or less active in participating classroom interaction once they had become adapted to the teaching style of a teacher. Nevertheless, she observed that the researcher's students showed no sign of getting demotivated or deactivated; on the contrary, even the chronically reticent ones were mobilized and seemed eager to take part in the interaction.

When it came to the items of observation given on the field note, Miss Ding also expressed her approval of the researcher's newly devised treatment. She took note of the researcher's attempt to involve more students in classroom interaction as reflected in his allocation of turns to those chronically reticent students. She was impressed that the researcher would at least invite or nominate someone to give a response to a language question before giving his own answer to it. She commented that by so doing the researcher was doing dynamic or diagnostic assessment of the students' knowledge about a certain language feature. She was also impressed with the content orientation of the questions as she observed that the researcher supplemented his list of comprehension questions and response questions with language questions from the students. As for the cognitive demand of the questions addressed in classroom interaction, however, she indicated that most of the questions seemed not to have been enacted in a way to stimulate deep thinking or critical thinking. She proceeded to offer her explanation for this observation, that is, probably the researcher paid more attention to resolving the students' questions than inducing higher-order thinking.

6.4.3 Group discussion notes

Throughout the third cycle of AR, i.e., the instruction of Unit 7 and Unit 10, five groups (Groups #6 to #10) were involved in the after-class group discussions. Group #6 was made up of four girls who all confessed their disappointment in being enrolled into the English undergraduate program for the reason that they had been bad in the English subject in high school. To the researcher's relief, they realized that they had no choice but to finish the courses as required. When the discussion came to the intensive reading course and the researcher's style of teaching, all of them admitted that they had adapted to the new teacher and more than that, as one of them (S14) pointed out and all the others agreed, that they had learned from the researcher's classes that intensive reading is not merely learning new words and expressions but looking into the fine details of the text to figure out what the writer intends to mean and how he conveys his intention. S14 indicated that in the past she would read a text and then forget it, but now she would not only read a text, but also review it and keep thinking about it.

Group #7 consisted of three girls and one boy. The discussion was more like free talk though the researcher requested them to focus on three aspects. One of the girls was weak in spoken English and often switched back to Chinese during the discussion. Nonetheless, the discussion went well as the topics they chose were interesting and the others were not influenced by that girl's code switching. There was someone who complained about the heavy load of work in preparing for the intensive reading lessons. However, the boy, S35, objected to the complaint and stressed that it was the requirement of raising questions before class that made him realize the importance of self-investment in learning the English language. He claimed that he felt fulfilled each time he finished an assignment, be it previewing a text, raising questions, writing a learning log, or writing a summary essay.

Group #8 comprised three of the top students of the class: S5, S20 and S39. At the beginning, they all made some complaints about the heavy coursework of the English undergraduate program because they had a full schedule almost every day. However, when it came to the intensive reading course, they unanimously expressed their preference of the researcher's style of teaching. S39 made it explicit that she had never thought of asking questions on her own while reading a text before the researcher told them to. She found it very beneficial to come up with her own questions and try to resolve them before class and began to realize the importance of taking the initiative to learn any course. S20 suggested that the researcher choose from the students' questions more open ones for discussion. He indicated that the researcher had not displayed to the class any of his open questions and made the wild guess that probably that was because his questions were too open for discussion. The researcher acknowledged to him that there was a good point in making a suggestion like that and explained that questions should be primarily related to the instructional objectives due to the constraint of time and that some less proficient students might be disinterested if too much time had been spent on the discussion of strings of open questions.

The discussions with the other two groups were also like free talk. Though all the participants explicitly expressed their approval of the researcher's style of teaching, they did not give specific comments and suggestions about his interventions.

6.4.4 Stimulated reflection journals

While reviewing the lessons on Unit 7 and Unit 10, the researcher felt satisfied with his organization of Q-A interaction in general. The classroom atmosphere continued to be friendly and joyous as before or even better. To use Allwright's terms, the researcher managed to create "the appropriate socio-emotional atmosphere" or "affective classroom climate" for learning (Allwright, 1984, p. 164). He was in a better position to know the students' needs and wants in learning a text by collecting the students' questions. By integrating the students' questions to the design of questions for the text instruction, he was able to further extend the learning space in the two dimensions of variation, i.e., content focus and cognitive demand. Though the objectives of the course were multi-layered, and the teacher's intended objects of learning were set up correspondingly, the students' level of proficiency and their expectations might not be adaptable to the prescribed objectives and the teacher's intentions. The intervention introduced in this cycle of AR proved effective in helping the teacher to identify the gap between what the students should be able to do and what they were actually able to do.

However, as pointed out by Miss Ding during the post-observation conference, the researcher did not try as hard as before to induce higher-order thinking by some expansion strategies, such as probing. Consequently, it seemed that the intended objects of learning were not successfully enacted through the Q-A interaction. In other words, the questioning sequences were not so successfully carried out in a way to scaffold students' higher-order thinking, as in evaluating the textual messages, appreciating the meta-textual messages, and justifying one's own personal responses to a certain topic. The researcher conceived that there could be two explanations to account for that observation. On the one hand, there might be a tension between the time spent on addressing students' questions and the time spent on the pre-designed questions during classroom instruction. In other words, the researcher should have managed to strike a balance between two types of Q-A interaction, one initiated by the questions designed according to the course objectives and the other initiated by the questions raised by the students. On the other hand, critical thinking not only means the skills of high-order thinking but also the critical thinking disposition (Elder & Paul, 2003; Wen Qiufang, Zhang Lingli, & Sun Min, 2014) and the researcher's organization of Q-A interaction in the third cycle of AR was effective in cultivating the students' critical disposition as they reported in their learning logs that participating in Q-A interaction helped them open up their mind and rethink about their own ideas or thoughts.

6.4.5 Implications

As shown in the evaluating section, the major intervention introduced in the third cycle of AR, i.e., incorporating students' questions into the design of questions for text instruction, was effective in further extending the students' learning space. Firstly, it constituted an effective means for the teacher to look into the students' needs and wants in learning the text. Secondly, as the students were required to raise their own questions, they had to preview the text by encountering or reading it time and again and by so doing they were able to gain a profound comprehension of the text. Thirdly, in order to comprehend the text and to raise their own questions, they had to attack the language problems confronting them, which means, language-focused learning was largely taken care of by the students themselves. In addition, the students' willingness to participate in classroom interaction increased due to their preparation before class and their awareness of peer competition.

In all, the three problems identified in the focusing stage were resolved to a large degree, indicating that questioning sequences supplemented by student questions are conducive to further extending the space for students to experience the objects of learning. Hence, the pedagogical interventions adopted in the three cycles of AR, i.e., trialing questioning sequences, allowing preparation time before class and incorporating student questions, are of rich implications for the design and implementation of teacher questions for classroom instruction. First of all, teachers should identify the key objects of learning and then design questions in accordance with them by varying the acts and contents at the stage of instructional planning. To ensure the effectiveness of Q-A interaction, it would be advisable to have the students prepare to answer teacher questions and raise their own questions before class. As suggested by the students, it is more desirable for the teacher to have the class preview the text in reference to the combination of teacher questions and student questions.

Chapter 7   Further Discussion

This chapter first recapitulates the design and implementation of teacher questions as manifested in the three AR cycles. It then proceeds to discuss the contributions of the pedagogical interventions to student learning before tapping into the major factors that might have contributed to the opening up and closing down of learning space through the use of questioning sequences.

7.1 Design and implementation of teacher questions

A retrospect on the process of the whole AR shows that the design and implementation of teacher questions need to depart with the identification of appropriate instructional objectives of a course, a unit or a lesson. In the meantime, students' needs and wants should be taken into account to ensure that the identified objectives are accessible or achievable to the students, and sufficient preparation time should be given to the students in advance so that they can make full preparation to participate in classroom interaction at ease. Additionally, a friendly teacher-student rapport serves as the lubricant of Q-A interaction and hence the enactment of the instructional objectives through questioning sequences.

7.1.1 Identifying appropriate instructional objectives

As discussed in Chapter Two, EFL teacher questioning is a goal-oriented act which is more than eliciting student response in the target language measured by qualitative and quantitative means in reference to native speakers. Rather, teacher questions should be evaluated primarily in reference to the instructional objectives of a course, a unit or a lesson.

In each of the three cycles of AR, the researcher started his instructional design with identifying the instructional objectives of a unit and relating them to the objectives of the intensive reading course as well as the English major's curriculum. In Marton and colleagues' words, the intended objects of learning should be in correspondence with the educational objectives of a course (Marton & Booth, 1997; Marton & Tsui, 2004). The current research is conducted in an English majors' intensive reading classroom. The overall objectives of the course, according to *the National Curriculum*, focus on the development of text comprehension, language-focused learning, target language production and critical thinking. As critical thinking is embedded in the other three aspects, the course objectives can be reframed into three strands as displayed in Figure 2-3 in Chapter Two. Such a hierarchical framework has been proved to be a valid guide for lesson planning. Once the objectives are set up, lesson planning is a matter of formulating questions by filling in the acts and contents according to the "object = act + content" formula. The key to questioning sequences at this point is the variation in the acts and contents constituting the questions oriented to the instructional objectives.

In the current study, conducted in an intensive reading classroom, the indirect objects of learning are divided into three cognitive levels and the direct objects into three content orientations in view of the course objectives. In teaching each unit, the researcher first set up the instructional objectives by identifying the objects of learning and then designed and implemented sequences of questions accordingly. It has been testified that by varying the cognitive levels required in answering questions directed to a certain focused content orientation, the students can have an enriching experience of the intended object of learning. In the teaching of Unit 3, for example, a sequence of questions was designed and implemented across different phases of instruction to process the title of the text: first to recognize the fact that the title has been adapted by the textbook writers from the original *Why No One Walks* to *Out of Step*, then to differentiate the original and the adapted, and lastly to appreciate whether the adapted title catches the author's purpose of writing. The students' learning logs for Unit 3 demonstrated that they had developed a profound impression of the title due to the researcher's pedagogical treatment. On top of this, many of them had learned to be aware of appreciating the title of a text as they had begun to raise questions to that end while previewing a text.

7.1.2 Sequencing questions by varying acts and contents

In previous research on teacher questioning, as pointed out earlier, individual questions are claimed to be the units of planning and/or analysis. Such an approach has been found to be insufficient as a guide for the design and analysis of teacher questions, at least in China' EFL context. As has been recognized by many, teacher questions are not only goal-directed in the local context of teacher-student communication but also goal-oriented with regard to the instructional objectives. Teacher questions, however effective they might be in terms of their eliciting, interactional and pedagogical functions, should ultimately be evaluated in reference to the instructional objectives. It is thus proposed that questioning sequences rather than individual questions be the units of planning and/or analysis of teacher questioning.

In the current study, as the objects of learning were listed on the basis of the content focus, and the questioning sequences were displayed as if comprised of questions involving different levels of cognitive acts relating to particular contents, it thus seems that a questioning sequence were comprised of questions requiring different levels of cognitive acts in the learning of a particular aspect of content. However, as indicated by the model of questioning sequences in Figure 2-5 in Chapter Two, a questioning sequence can be comprised of questions that vary in both content orientation and cognitive demand. In other words, a sequence of questions can be designed and implemented either to develop a series of hierarchically related acts of learning (i.e., indirect objects of learning) directed towards a single element or content (direct object of learning) or to develop a certain act of learning directed towards a range of different elements. To put it in Nation's words (Nation, 1996), the different strands of a language course need to be balanced in instructional design.

Additionally, though the framework appears linearly hierarchical, a questioning sequence may not be a sequence of questions that go linearly from questions of lower cognitive levels to questions of higher cognitive levels. It may start with a question of high cognitive level and proceed with adjustment in consideration of the students' responses, i.e., in a wavy pattern as demonstrated by Yang Lifang (2015). Furthermore, a questioning sequence can even be a sequence of repeated questions, i.e., the same question repetitively used across different stages of instruction. As can be seen in the questions designed and implemented in the three cycles of AR of the current study, the repetition of certain questions could provoke thinking of different cognitive levels and elicit responses of different degrees of complexity at different stages of instruction, which corroborates Gu Lingyuan's argument that learning by repetition with variation might as well make sense to the learner (Bao Jiansheng, Huang Jinrong, Yi Lingfeng, & Gu Lingyuan, 2003).

7.1.3 Adapting design and implementation based on reflections

A noteworthy point is that the pedagogical interventions adopted in the second and third cycles of AR, though proved to be successful, were a result of reflective practice. The researcher took into account implications derived from his own reflection journals and the students' learning logs and accordingly made adaptations to the design as well as the implementation of teacher questions.

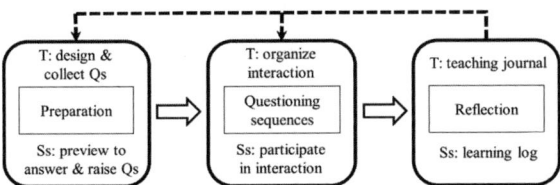

Figure 7-1 A cyclical procedure of reflective practice

Based on the implications discussed in the previous chapters, the action research of the current study could be visualized as a cyclical procedure of reflective practice (See Figure 7-1) consisting of three stages: 1) the stage of preparation where the teacher designs questions in accordance with the objects of learning, hands out his list of questions to the students as a guide for preview, and requires the students to raise their own questions which are to be collected and incorporated into the teacher's questions; 2) the stage of implementation where the teacher organizes classroom interaction by enacting sequences of questions relating to the objects of learning; 3) the stage of reflection where both the teacher and the students reflect on their performance in the two preceding stages and put forth suggestions for further improvement in future classes.

There are problems remaining unresolved with the current study, as demonstrated in the students' learning logs on the third cycle of AR. Nevertheless, solutions can be negotiated and decided through the teacher's and students' reflections. Some students, for instance, pointed out that they were confused about what questions to raise while previewing a text, i.e., whether to include those they could answer on their own or not. This problem could be brought to the class for negotiation, and possible solutions could be gleaned and weighed before putting into trial. Another problem a number of students were concerned about was how to involve some chronically reticent students in classroom interaction. It would also be advisable for the teacher to give an ear to those reticent students for an insider's perception.

In a word, it is necessary and worthwhile for the teacher, and the students as well, to get engaged in reflective practice. The students' learning logs, as utilized in the current AR study, constitute a 'mirror' through which the teacher can reflect on the merits and flaws of his pedagogical practice and then make decisions on adaptation.

7.2 Contributions to student learning

Analysis of the transcripts of focus group interviews and the students' essays reveals that the AR contributed to the students' learning of the intensive reading course in the following respects: 1) the development of autonomous learning, 2) the improvement of text comprehension, 3) the increased willingness to participate in classroom interaction, 4) the cultivation of critical thinking, and 5) the students' renovated perception of the intensive reading course. The first four respects are presented in order of 'thickness' or 'density' as they appeared in the students' verbal and written reports. The

Chapter 7 Further Discussion

fifth respect, however, is by no means less thick than the preceding ones. It is presented lastly because the students' renovated perception of the course resulted from the experience of the other respects.

7.2.1 Development of autonomous learning

Both the focus group interviews and the students' end-of-term reflection essays revealed that the students had become more autonomous than before as a consequence of the pedagogical interventions implemented in the AR.

Focus group interviews

The focus group interviews with the focal students of Groups A, B and C demonstrated that the pedagogical interventions were successful in developing the students autonomous learning.

The students of Group A and Group B indicated that although they had to spend much time in making preparations before class, they found the time spent in doing so was rewarding. S39 of Group A clarified that she had changed from stopping at having a global understanding to going into details while previewing a text, as she had developed the habit of analyzing the structure of the text and that of some key sentences. She added that thanks to the task of raising questions, she had begun to interpret the author's intention of writing the text, to attack such language problems as new words and difficult grammatical points, and to try to imitate some sentence patterns in her own writing.

S14 of Group B replied that she had realized the value of questioning while reading a text:

Interview Extract 7-1, S14, Group B
我觉得，就是带着疑问，就是要提出问题，去研究文章，然后，对文章，会更透彻，了解得。然后，会就从不同的角度，我觉得这样就是有利于开拓我们的思维。……比如说，那个，对文章，一些句子，它的结构，然后言外之意，或者什么，其实我们每个人是有不同的理解的，或者有自己的想法。
I think, that is, if I have questions, or raise questions while scrutinizing a text and then I will have a deeper understanding of the whole text. And then, I will

think about it from different perspectives, which I think is helpful in developing our thinking… . For instance, while reading the text, we may have different understanding of the structure of some sentences, the implied meaning of the sentences and the like. Actually, every one of us has his/her own understanding or thoughts.

S18, another student of Group B, exemplified her autonomy in learning the course with her experience of learning new words:

Interview Extract 7-2, S18, Group B
我觉得就我们对一个单词也会更熟悉啊，因为我们主动去对一个单词进行仔细研究，近义词反义词之类的，然后，我们就容易背单词了，我觉得。……就是有些不认识的单词啊，你就查很多那种同义的、反义的，然后，就更了解一些。
I feel that we can be more familiar with a word because if we explore the details of a word, like synonyms and antonyms, then we will find it easier to recite words. … That is, when you check up the synonyms and antonyms of some unknown words, you will have more knowledge about them.

The students of Group C, though did not explicitly show their attitude towards the time spent on preparing to answer or raise questions, did indicate that they had become more sensitive to some language problems. S35, a boy of Group C, said that if a question listed by the teacher had to do with a language point that was familiar to him, the question would help him recall the relevant knowledge, and if the question concerned a language point that was beyond his range of knowledge, he would be ready to resolve it. S35 was particularly appreciative of the iterated use of questions across different phases of teaching as he said the following when requested to give an overall evaluation of the course:

Interview Extract 7-3, S35, Group C
我首先想的就是，从此，就是因为每一个单元，呃，在课前你要写一篇什么文章，在课后又要总结，还在课堂中间呢，又有很多的问题要，要回答，然后总体下来就是，上完一个单元，你会觉得，就是你感觉什么都做到了……什么都已经，嗯，就是你已经去，尽全力去了解这个单元到底要学什么……就感觉就是很有用，很充实……你就感觉自己，就是感觉这个单元，没有，没有就像，就是只是单纯地过了一遍而已，你就觉得自己已经深入了这个单元，就是这个，大概就是这个含义。
First of all, I think that, ever since (the beginning of the semester), in the teaching of each unit, uh, we have been told before class to write an article of what type, and to summarize the teaching by the completion of the unit, and during the classroom instruction, we are required to answer a lot of questions, and so generally, after learning a unit, you will feel that you have done whatever you should ... uh, that is, you have tried to learn what you need to ... and that is very useful and fulfilling. That is, you feel that after learning a unit you are not just done with it but have gone deep into it. That is what I mean.

S29, a girl of Group C, agreed with S35 and added that questions regarding language points within her command of language knowledge had helped to improve her sensitivity to those language points, just like the function of doing grammar exercises. S29 further clarified the teacher's having the class preview the text with a given list of questions or raise their own questions while previewing the text had helped to promote her agency in learning the course because she had the feeling of getting involved in meaningful communication in the process of asking and answering questions and receiving the teacher's feedback:

Interview Extract 7-4, S29, Group C
因为以前上课嘛，就是跟以前高中好像，老师讲，你记好就行了，没有那种，就是，就是其实很喜欢，就是那种——问题嘛，有问题的时候，就是练习了人跟人的交流……就是以前高中，老师给我们什么，你接着就行了，消化好就行了……然后现在就是，我有反馈，你也有反馈，就有那种，能动性。……就是说实话，我跟我们寝室的同学说，老师其实是把我们当做研究生教，因为你以前说你做研究生的时候，说什么老师给你们书，你自己看，然后来问问题什么的，就是自己交流嘛，上课的时候也是那种提问式的交流。
Because in the past we were taught much the same way as high school students, that is, the teacher lectures, and all you have to do is to take notes and you don't have to ask questions, but I like asking questions very much. If you have questions, you are practising communicating with one another. ... That is to say,

in high school, you just accept and digest whatever the teacher teaches, but now I have my response, and you give us yours, then I have developed the kind of agency. ... To be honest, I once told my roommates that our teacher teaches us as post-graduates because you once mentioned how you had been assigned by your professor to read on your own and raise your own questions, and then bring them to the classroom to communicate with others.

S17, another girl of Group C, commented how she had come to know about her own weaknesses by asking and answering questions as well as attending to her classmates' asking and answering questions in classroom interaction:

Interview Extract 7-5, S17, Group C
我觉得提问吧，我觉得我还好，因为我其实很少提那种我自己不知道答案的问题……就是我们以前老师讲的，就是你只知道自己会了什么，你并不知道自己不会什么，就是那种感觉，就是我不会，我不知道，所以我完全也没有想到具体哪种问题。……通过上课看别人的提问……就是能看到自己，不会哪些东西……然后还有就是自己在意思上理解有一些偏差的东西。As for raising questions, I feel I am OK with it, because as a matter of fact I seldom ask questions that I can't answer by myself ... it's like what one of my previous teachers said, that is, you only know what you can but you don't know what you can't. That is it. I can't, but I don't know that I can't. So I haven't thought of questions as specific as those (raised by my classmates). ... And by attending to questions raised by others ... I can see myself, what I can't ... and on top of this some points that I have misunderstood.

In all, the focal students all agreed that engaging themselves in the pedagogical interventions had helped to promote their autonomy in learning the course. The students of higher and middle proficiency levels explicitly acknowledged that the time spent on previewing as required by the teacher had been rewarding as they had been propelled to read more carefully and think critically. The students with lower proficiency, however, admitted that they found it rewarding to learn from the questions raised by their peer classmates, which had broadened their horizon or enriched their learning experience.

Reflection essays

Besides the focal students involved in the focus group interviews, many a student reported in their reflection essays that they had become more self-dependent or autonomous than before owing to the researcher's teaching of the intensive reading course. One student wrote that the researcher, unlike many other teachers, taught by "inspiring" instead of "enforcing", which could be regarded as the consequence of the intervention:

Essay Extract 7-1, S16
这个学期更多的得到的是来自您给的启发性的教学，感觉您同其他很多老师不一样吧，更重视我们的自主积极式的学习，更多的是启发我们去学习，而不是一味的督促。
What has benefited me most in this semester is your inspiring teaching. I feel that you are not like other teachers. You put more emphasis on our own initiatives in dealing with learning. What you have done is more inspiring than imposing.

Another student illustrated how she would go about previewing the text of each unit, especially after being required to raise questions:

Essay Extract 7-2, S22
我不敢说所有的单元我都预习得特别好，但是有几个单元我的课文上笔记很多，就是从你刚开始说要提问题的时候，有些我自己提出来的问题然后在书上有写，给自己解答，还有一些是你提的问题，我思考了，全都写在书上，有好几次上课你以为没有人之前去思考你的问题，但肯定有啊，我就是一个啊。
I dare not to say that I have previewed all units especially well. But for some units, I made a lot of notes on my textbook, that is, since you first asked us to raise questions. I wrote on the book some of the questions raised and answered by myself, and some of the questions raised by you that I had thought about. Several times in class you thought that no one had ever thought about your questions. There sure were students who had and I was one of them.

Such approval of the interventions introduced in the cycles of AR was echoed by another student who mentioned about her appreciation of the classroom Q-A interaction as implemented in the semester's intensive reading classes:

> **Essay Extract 7-3, S5**
> Some students may complain that we should learn more about words and grammar in this course. There is no denying the fact that they are the foundation of English learning. But we can't be trapped in the language itself. We shall go beyond the language to seek what is behind. It's good to talk more about the author, the passage and do some extension. To raise questions and get them solved in class is helpful. In this way we think actively instead of receiving from teacher passively. And the questions raised by others expose us to the points or details we may miss. Like I said, I wouldn't even go through the text if it were not for this task.

Some students contrasted their way of learning the course before and after attending the researcher's classes. S23, for example, after contrasting how she dealt with learning the course before and after attending this semester's classes, implicitly indicated that the change of her way of learning was the consequence of the researcher's requiring the students to answer the teacher's questions or raise their own questions while previewing the texts:

> **Essay Extract 7-4, S23**
> 就是课文上，以前我学习真的可以说很被动了。非常惭愧的说，是不预习，然后考前复习，听写前就背单词。这个学期的话，至少都有预习，而且会自己下意识去提问题，然后想的也就不只是局限于课本上的东西了。
> In respect of text learning, I used to be rather passive, honestly speaking. What I feel ashamed of mentioning is that I had never previewed any texts, and I would never review until right before the test, neither would I try to memorize new words right before the dictation. This semester, however, I have at least previewed the texts. More than that, I would consciously raise questions, and in doing so I thought much more than what is in the textbook.

The aforementioned comment was confirmed by another student, S29, who also contrasted her way of learning the texts before and after this semester to show how she had changed from following the teacher closely to taking initiatives:

Chapter 7 Further Discussion

Essay Extract 7-5, S29

课文学习，对比之前，我可以肯定是更用心，对课文了解也更透彻，有了自己的看法，而不是追随老师的脚步，老师停在哪里就走到哪里。现在我感觉是更喜欢提问的方式来学习，虽然有时候会不耐其烦，甚至有点讨厌，但是对我来说确实是有帮助的。既然是有帮助的，我就想坚持下去。还有就是在这一串的单元学习中，我逐渐知道对一篇英文文章该如何分析和赏析。

In terms of text learning, in contrast with before, I can say with certainty that I am much more careful, I have a more profound understanding of the texts, and I have more thoughts of my own. In the past, I would simply follow the teacher's steps, stop where the teacher stopped. Now I find I like better the way of learning through questioning. Though sometimes I feel impatient, or even a bit disgusting, I have to confess that it is helpful for me. As it is helpful, I want to follow it through. Moreover, during the process of learning a string of units, I gradually come to know how to analyze and appreciate an English text.

It can be inferred from the above discussion that the students reportedly became more autonomous in learning the intensive reading course. The pedagogical interventions introduced in the second and third cycles of AR were especially noteworthy in that they played a positive role in driving the students to take initiatives in reading the texts carefully to answer the lists of questions given to them ahead of classroom instruction in the second cycle and to raise their own questions to supplement teacher questions in the third cycle. The students of middle and higher proficiency levels all deemed it worthwhile to make such preparations before class, for they were more engaged in 'reading between the lines' and/or 'reading beyond the lines' and hence were better prepared for attending the following classroom instruction. The students with lower language proficiency also benefited from making such preparations for the main reason that they were more sensitive to or aware of some language problems while participating in the teacher-led classroom interaction. Autonomy, as a precondition for effective learning, is one of the prominent themes of language teaching research in the new century (Benson, 2013). While recent research has focused on explicit strategies to train learners to be autonomous, the current study shows that learner autonomy can be developed implicitly through appropriate pedagogical interventions in questioning.

7.2.2 Improvement of text comprehension

Another issue that emerged in the focus group interviews and the students' reflection essays is the deepening of text comprehension, i.e., a more profound understanding of the intensive reading texts covered in the instruction. Such can be regarded as the improvement of the students' reading comprehension as reflected in their performance in the reading comprehension tests before and after AR (Section 7.2.6.2).

Focus group interviews

The focus group interviews revealed that the interventions carried out throughout the AR had helped to deepen the students' understanding of the texts discussed over the semester. The students seemed rather at a loss at the beginning, i.e., when the researcher first attempted to organize his text instruction based on the three types of questions he had designed in advance. However, as the AR proceeded with adaptions made in view of the students' feedback, their comprehension of the texts was promoted with regard to comprehensiveness and profundity.

All the three groups made some comparative remarks on the effects of the major interventions in the second and third stage of AR. Though they found raising questions by themselves more effective and preferred previewing to raise their own questions to previewing to answer teacher questions, they acknowledged that the teacher's giving them questions to prepare in advance was also conducive to a deeper understanding of the text, and played a "modelling" role for them to raise questions on their own.

The students of Group A remarked that they took the researcher's use of questions in text instruction as a means of heuristic teaching when they were first required to preview the text with a list of questions. They added that the teacher's lists of questions handed out to them during the second cycle of AR had played a guiding role for them to raise their own questions in the third cycle of AR. They unanimously showed their approval of previewing to raise their own questions and demonstrated how doing so had strengthened their impression of the message conveyed in a text and hence deepened their understanding of the text as testified by the words of S39 and S1:

Interview Extract 7-6, S39, Group A
我觉得【自己提问】有很大的收获，就是会逐字逐句去看一下这篇文章，然后自己会去思考一遍。但是，如果像以前那种预习方式，可能最多就是分一下段落，看大致讲了什么。这种就是，特别是首先自己对字词进行理解。
I found it very beneficial to raise my own questions because while I am reading the text word by word I will have to think about it carefully. But if I preview the text like before, I would at most stop at dividing the texts into parts and get a global understanding of them. And now, I will start with understanding the words and sentences.

Interview Extract 7-7, S1, Group A
就是深入地理解到底讲了些什么东西。像原来的话，可能就是更偏重于那些单词啊，句子啊，还有语法之类的。像现在的话，我就觉得对整篇文章有了更深入的理解……它要表达一个什么样的主题，作者他的用意，他的感情是怎么样的。……
By raising our own questions, I can have a profound understanding of what is conveyed in the texts. In our classes in the preceding semesters, the teachers put more emphasis on the words, sentences and grammar points, and the like. But this semester, I think I have learned to develop a profound understanding of the whole text … including the theme of the text, the author's intention of writing, and the author's feeling.

The students of Group B confirmed that the teacher's questions delivered to them in the second cycle had served as templates or guides for raising their own questions in the third cycle as demonstrated by their words in the interview:

Interview Extract 7-8, S9, Group B
就感觉【老师发给我们预习用的问题】像模板一样。……就是【带着老师的问题预习】会比之前一二单元理解课文的话会更深入一点，但是相对于七八单元【自己提问】的话，就是七八单元理解又更深了。……一步一步的，上升的，那种。

I feel that the questions you gave us for previewing the text are like templates. ... That is to say, with the questions in hand we can have a deeper understanding of the texts than Unit 1 and Unit 2, and then in Unit 7 and Unit 8, we were required to raise our own questions and by so doing we had a more profound understanding of the texts. ... It's like step by step we understand the texts incrementally.

Another issue is that the students agreed that they had become more capable of catching up with the teacher's instruction and less afraid of getting distracted or sidetracked, for they had been familiar with the texts. In particular, S30 of Group A, who had missed several class the instruction of Unit 7, said that even though she had been absent from the classes, she had no difficulty in catching up with the teacher when she came back:

Interview Extract 7-9, S30, Group A
【这星期】我回家了……但是，我回来的时候，还是能跟上你的，因为我提了一遍问题之后，我基本上都看懂了。……然后，我回来的时候，感觉你才刚开始上。
[This week] I went back home ... but when I returned, I still was able to catch up with you, because after raising my own questions I basically have understood the text. ... And then when I came back I felt that you had just begun the text instruction.

Such a feeling was confirmed by S29 of Group C with elaboration:

Interview Extract 7-10, S29, Group C
以前，以前，自己，就是你提问的时候，你听写的时候，我其实不是很明白你听的是哪一个段落，有时候因为，你看了课文，没有听过录音的话，你突然之间读给我们听写……但是你让我们提了问题，在听写的时候，一下就知道【是哪个部分】。
In the past, when you asked us questions and had us do dictations, actually I wasn't clear about which paragraph you were dictating, because sometimes you just read the text without listening to the tape and suddenly we were asked to do a dictation ... but now you have had us raise our own questions, and then

when we do the dictation, I can immediately know which part it is from.

The students of Group C, though agreed to a large degree with the other two groups about the effectiveness of the pedagogical interventions, provided some different perceptions. They all indicated that their being provided with a list of questions to make preparations ahead of classroom instruction had relieved them of the pressure or stress when they were nominated to answer questions, and the list of questions had guided them in seeking for a deeper understanding of the text. However, S35 added that he had the feeling of being less motivated in class after previewing the texts in reference to the list of questions because he would no longer be curious about what unexpected questions the teacher would ask, as demonstrated by the following quote of his remarks:

Interview Extract 7-11, S35, Group C
我现在觉得，提前提出问题，发给同学的话，可以是可以，但是，就是有的时候，就缺少那种，嗯，灵感，感觉。我以前是觉得这样更好，现在我觉得，就是，课堂上突然提出一个问题，你更有那种创新性爆发性的那种想法。
Now I think handing out the questions to us is OK, but sometimes, I feel that there is something missing in doing so, that is, a lack of inspiration. I used to think that doing so was better, but now I think, if the teacher suddenly asks a question in class, you would have some innovative or explosive idea.

To summarize, the focal students all acknowledged that the pedagogical interventions introduced in the questioning practice had been helpful in deepening their understanding of the texts and signposting or bookmarking their learning of the texts. The students with intermediate and lower proficiency were particularly impressed by the personal response questions, for they found that such questions could help prolong their impression of the texts. Such perceptions were also detected in the students' reflection essays, as presented below.

Reflection essays

Many of the students reported in their essays how taking this semester's intensive reading course had helped to deepen their understanding of the texts, and they attributed this to the teacher's requiring the students to preview a text with reference to the hand-out of questions and then to raise their own questions while previewing a text:

Essay Extract 7-6, S16
这个学期的精读课文确实要比前两个学期更熟悉更透彻一些了，能够读懂一篇课文的感觉很棒，谢谢您让我们有机会自己读懂更多的东西，这不仅仅局限在我们的课本上的课文，还有更多的道理。（S16）
This semester, I am more familiar with and have a more profound understanding of the intensive reading texts. It feels great to comprehend a text fully. Thank you for giving us the opportunity to read and comprehend more, not only the texts in our textbook, but also what is beyond. (S16)

Essay Extract 7-7, S19
在文章的理解方面，以前就是只做到知道文章讲了什么，而没有细究，只做到对文章表面的理解，现在学会了更深刻的去理解和体会作者的意图和写作的目的，对一些问题会引申出来，不能理解的知识点也会花时间去了解。（S19）
In regard of text comprehension, I used to content myself with knowing what is in the text and would not go further into the details, which means I could only have a superficial understanding of the text. Now I have learned to take further step to comprehend and grasp the author's intention and purpose of writing. I will derive some questions out of the text, and make time to attack some language problems therein. (S19)

One student, in particular, related her deeper understanding of the texts to critical reading, which changed her cognition of learning the course:

Essay Extract 7-8, S39
我收获首先是重新找到精读这门课的意义，而不是像以前一样以为记记单词，背背语法就是精读学习的全部内容。其次是对文本提问这个环节提高了我的理解和思辨能力，让我对文章有了更深刻的了解。（S39）
First of all, what I have gained is that I have realized the meaning of the intensive

reading course. I used to think that all I need to do with this course is to memorize words and grammar rules. Next, raising questions while reading a text has improved my reading comprehension and critical thinking abilities, which leads to a deeper understanding of the texts. (S39)

S16 added in her essay some words on how her experience with this semester's intensive reading course was different from before and emphasized how the instruction on issues beyond the texts had helped her have a better understanding of the texts:

Essay Extract 7-9, S16
老师的讲课方式与其他老师似乎有所不同……你就是更注重文章的理解这一块，讲语法或者其他知识点的时候会集中在一起，更注重知识的拓展。我个人觉得有些东西（像语法单词）是靠自己平时的积累的（虽然自己在这方面非常欠缺，但是还是会尽全力的提升自己），所以对知识以及文章给我们的信息的理解很重要。
The teacher's way of text instruction is somewhat different from other teachers. … you put more emphasis on text comprehension, integrating grammar and other language points into text comprehension and stressing the extension of knowledge. I personally think that grammar, vocabulary and the like need to be accumulated everyday (though I myself am rather weak in this regard, I will try my best to improve myself). So what matters is our understanding of knowledge and the messages given in the texts.

In all, the students' development of autonomous learning, especially their use of reading strategies in dealing with the intensive reading texts, and their improvement in text comprehension as a result of the classroom interaction, might have contributed to the enhancement of their reading comprehension. The students' involvement in the pedagogical interventions introduced in the intensive reading course also played a role in comprehending the IELTS reading passages despite their slow speed of reading. It would be safe to say that the pedagogical interventions implemented in the AR in view of the notions of questioning sequences and learning space contributed to the students' development of autonomous learning and their improved use of reading strategies, which then led to the improvement of their reading comprehension.

7.2.3 Increased willingness to participate in classroom interaction

It emerged in both the focus group interviews and the reflection essays that the classroom atmosphere had changed for the better in comparison to the previous semesters. The students were consequently more willing to participate in classroom interaction, which could have contributed to the improvement of their speaking.

Focus group interviews

Despite the students' mixed reactions towards the researcher's style of teaching during the first few weeks of the semester, they seemed to have adapted themselves before long and begun to appreciate the researcher's efforts made to change their experience of the intensive reading course and their experience of learning the English language, and one of the consequences of the successful mutual adaptation was the change of the classroom atmosphere for the better.

All the students of Group A explicitly commented that the classroom atmosphere was much better than before and many of their classmates had become more active in participating in classroom interaction. S39 demonstrated the change in this regard with her observation of several of her classmates who used to be silent and sit back in the classroom in all courses but turned to be active in the intensive reading class throughout the semester:

> **Interview Extract 7-12, S39, Group A**
> 我发现很多同学都有变化……比如说，S17、S18和S13她们三个，以前一般不会坐前面的……然后，现在她们总是坐前面的，但是，其他课她们不坐前面。
> I have found that many of my classmates have had some changes … for instance, S17, S18 and S13, the three of them generally would never sit in the front … However, now they are always seated in the front, but in other teachers' classes, they are not.

While conducting the interview with Group B, the researcher checked S39's words on the change of S17, S18 and S13's positioning in different classes with S18:

Interview Extract 7-11, Group B

T: 她说，你们总是坐第一排。噢，我说，我也注意到了【大家笑】，我以为她们所有的课都是坐第一排。

S2: 没有【大家都跟着说没有】

S18: 我们是那种，如果你没课，就是3-4，就是一上午在同一间教室，坐了你的第一排，然后下节课——

S2: 这节课就坐到后边去——

S18: 就赶快换到后边——

S2: 对对对对对【大家笑】你不说我还没注意到——

S9: 这是真的，因为我们就经常坐她们后面。

T: She [S39] said that in this semester the three of you are always seated in the first row. And I said to her that I have noticed this [all the participants laugh], but I thought they are so seated in all classes.

S2: No [all the others denied too]

S18: We are just like that sort of students, that is, if it is not your course, that is if after attending your classes and then the upcoming classes to be held in the same classroom are not yours, then when your class is over and in the next class we will—

S2: move to the back in the next class—

S18: change to the seats in the back very quickly—

S2: Right right right right [all the participants laugh] I won't have noticed this if you didn't tell us—

S9: That is true, because I am always sitting right behind them.

The change of classroom atmosphere was also confirmed by the students of Group C. S17 stressed that what distinguished the researcher's classes was the harmonious or friendly classroom atmosphere which made it possible for the students and the teacher to interact on equal grounds:

Interview Extract 7-13, Group C

S17: 就是我觉得，课堂，课堂氛围嘛，融洽比较，比较重要。

T: 嗯

S17: 对啊，因为有一种很平等，互相在交流的感觉。

T: 噢，你觉得是一种平等互相交流。

S29: 我觉得大学就是应该这样子。

T: 我觉得我还是基本上做到了，我一直觉得老师跟学生，就是应该这样的，像朋友一样，对吧？

S17: 对，因为——

T: 就一个问题可以平等地去交流意见，而且，就是不管你说的哪怕是和我的观点相反也好，是吧，我觉得都是一样的。

S17: 而且，大学老师一般的概念就是，上完课拍拍屁股走人嘛【大家笑】很多老师我走在路上都不认识，然后，很难有就是关系比较亲近对老师，在大学里，所以我觉得融洽还真的很重要的。

T: 那就是说我们的关系还是比较亲近的了，呵呵【笑】

S17: I feel that, the classroom, the classroom atmosphere should be friendly, this is rather important.

T: En

S17: Right. Because that can make you feel that you are communicating equally and interactively.

T: Oh, you think that is equal interaction.

S29: I think college should be like this.

T: I think I have managed to make it like this. I always hold that teachers and students should be like friends. Right?

S17: Right, because—

T: To communicate ideas on a certain issue on equal grounds, and it doesn't matter even if you disagree with me.

S17: and, college teachers are usually like this, they leave right after class. [all participants laugh] Many teachers, even if I hit across them on the road, are unknown to me. And it's a rare thing for students and teachers to be close to each other. So I think a friendly classroom atmosphere is very important.

T: So you mean that we are close to each other [Laugh]

S29, a participant of Group C, took herself as an example to demonstrate how the researcher's pedagogical interventions, especially the employment of "open questions" in text instruction, had helped to build a friendly teacher-student relationship:

> **Interview Extract 7-14, S29, Group C**
> 就是老师给的那些问题或者自己提问，准备了一遍之后，然后就其实课文就大致都了解了，就是，这种感觉就是，我能跟上你的节奏了，感觉就很好……因为你提前去做了那个准备了吧……而且就是，因为我记得有一些开放式的问题嘛……就是觉得蛮开心，然后老师点名啊，或者老师说到了跟你一样的想法的话，很开心的哦……就是那种共鸣啊……就像你得到别人肯定一样。
> What I want to say is that, whether the teacher gives us questions or we raise our own questions, we have to prepare by ourselves, and then we can have a global understanding of the text. I feel that I can follow the beat of your instruction, and that is good … because you have made preparations in advance … in addition, I remember there are some open questions … which make me feel happy, because when you nominate me to give my answer or when your talk about an idea that is the same as mine, I feel very happy … that is like resonance … like you get approved by others.

When asked about their feelings about the researcher's displaying on the slides the source of students' questions, the students of Group C responded that they would not mind whether the researcher displayed the source of a question or not, but added that if their questions were selected to be displayed, they would feel excited or satisfied because they would take it as a sign of "synaesthesia" with their teacher.

On the whole, from the students' perspective, the pedagogical interventions introduced in the three stages of AR were effective in building a harmonious classroom atmosphere and in establishing a friendly teacher-student rapport. What was perceived to be most conducive to that end was the researcher's design of personal response questions and his organization of Q-A interaction initiated by such questions. The students deemed that the open questions, so as they called, put the teacher and the students on equal grounds of classroom interaction, for there were no single correct or standard answers and all kinds of answers were tolerable or should be respected. Such perception of classroom atmosphere was also supported by the students' reflection essays.

Reflection essays

The majority of the students confessed in their reflection essays that they enjoyed the classroom atmosphere of the researcher's class as they were offered more opportunities to engage in classroom interaction than before, and they attributed this to the use of 'open questions'. S37 expressed that he was particularly fond of the open questions the researcher had employed for classroom instruction:

Essay Extract 7-10, S37
感觉谈不上是收获，就单方面觉得老师讲课的方式有趣……真的是开放的答案很多问题，换个角度去解答问题觉得也行。
I felt that it is not a matter of gains. I simply find the teacher's instruction interesting.... you really raised a lot of open questions, which allow alternative answers.

Some students mentioned about how the researcher's way of teaching had reversed their stereotypical perception of the intensive reading course as being boring or dull. S36 acknowledged that she had changed her view of the course because of the researcher's going beyond the text instead of merely focusing on the text, specifically the use of personal response questions:

Essay Extract 7-11, S36
老师上课的方式是我第一次接触的，不那么注重课本上的题目，而是重点分析课文及有所引申。一开始是不太习惯的，因为我一开始觉得学什么东西都是为考试，所以学好会考的就行了，总是抱着一种应付考试的态度，但是听了几节课后……使我一改对英语精读课枯燥无聊的看法。
The teacher's way of teaching was totally new to me. Instead of putting much emphasis on the exercises provided in the textbook, the teacher focused on analyzing the texts and extended them to different degrees. At first, I couldn't adapt myself to it because I had the assumption that all learning should be test-oriented and we should only learn what would be tested. However, after attending several classes, I found that ... I had totally changed my perception of the intensive reading course as dull and boring.

The students seemed to be appreciative of the researcher's management of classroom interaction. S4 expressed her gratitude to the researcher for his management of classroom atmosphere:

Essay Extract 7-12, S4
每一节课都上得感觉是朋友之间在交谈……让课堂课后的气氛都那么活跃……让我们尤其是我，倍感幸运。
Every class looks like a heart-felt conversation between friends… . You have created an active atmosphere both in and after class … and made us, especially me, feel considerably fortunate.

S17, a focal student of Group C, demonstrated in her reflection essay how she reversed her perception of the intensive reading course, from detesting or almost quitting, to getting deeply involved, and attributed her change of attitude to the friendly classroom atmosphere the researcher managed to bring to them:

Essay Extract 7-13, S17
这个学期最大的收获就是，精读对我来说终于不是最麻烦的一门课了！！！…… This term！我！超级认真的上课！也超级认真的复习了！当然，这跟老师融洽的课堂氛围密不可分，不过当我愿意学一门课的时候，以后我对这门课都会很用心（≥ω≤)/ 所以我觉得吧，从老师身上学会了什么知识是其次，最重要的是我学会了如何学习，以及端正了对学习的态度。
The biggest gain of this semester is that the intensive reading course is no longer the most troublesome!!! ... This term! I! have been attending classes very attentively! And I have reviewed extremely carefully! Of course, all is inextricably connected to the friendly classroom atmosphere. Nevertheless, once I am willing to learn a course, I will learn it conscientiously. So, I feel that what counts most is not that I have learned from the teacher whatever knowledge but that I have learned from the teacher how to learn and rectified my attitude towards learning.

As mentioned earlier, Xie (2009) and Li Qingsheng and Sun Zhiyong (2011) respectively attributed Chinese students' reticence in English classes to teachers' topic control and the influence of traditional cultural values. The current study shows, however, that the key lies in the sufficiency of students' preparation and the teacher-student rapport. As the above discussion shows, students' sufficient preparation before class and the teacher's investment outside the classroom would lead to students' active participation and bring about an enlightened classroom atmosphere, which would in turn strengthen a friendly teacher-student rapport and further increase the students' willingness to participate in classroom interaction.

7.2.4 Cultivation of critical thinking

Analysis of the focus group interviews and the reflection essays shows that the pedagogical interventions had positive contributions to the development of the students' dispositions, if not skills, of critical thinking.

Focus group interviews

When it came to the impact of semester's intensive reading course on the cultivation of critical thinking, all the three groups of students responded that they had learned to 1) respect others' opinions, 2) open up their own minds or horizons in viewing the world and/or life, and 3) be critical about what is in the textbook.

S1 of Group A explicitly showed their preference for the use of 'open questions in this regard:

> Interview Extract 7-15, S1, Group A
> 这种问题，就是比较开放，没有那种平时我们接受标准答案的思维。就是我们更能开发出另外一种思维，就是说，不是仅限于只有一个标准答案的那种问题。……我觉得就像 The Transaction 那样的，两个完全不一样的人……为什么要吵？为什么要吵？我觉得很奇怪的就是，有什么好吵的？每个人都不一样的，对吧？
> Such questions, are more open, and they don't restrict us to the mode of thinking of accepting some standard answers, but rather they lead us to develop an alternative mode of thinking. In other words, they are not questions with only one standard answer. ... I think of an example, that is in the text of *The Transaction*, two totally different persons ... why should they be supposed to quarrel with each other? Why should they? What makes me feel strange is why there should be

things for people to quarrel about? Every person is unique, right?

S1 added that such questions were helpful to make one more careful in observing the surroundings in one's daily life, which was echoed by S6:

Interview Extract 7-16, S6, Group A
我就是觉得讨论很多比较开放的问题，这样就不会说，自己只顾自己的，总觉得自己是对的，不能听别人的。……比如说"Why No One Walks"……为什么美国没有人走路那一篇……然后你就会去观察，观察身边有没有这样的事情。
I feel that getting engaged in the discussions over many questions that are relatively more open can help to prevent us from being stubborn or assertive or unwilling to listen to others. ... For example, after learning the text of *Why No One Walks* ... the text about the fact that Americans don't walk ... you will begin to observe whether there are such people around you.

The students of Group B also acknowledged that their teacher's having them preview the texts and prepare their answers to a list of questions or raise their own questions was conducive to developing their awareness of critical thinking. Interestingly, they used some specific words to speak of such pedagogical interventions. S9 commented that raising questions helped to expand one's horizon as one gets involved in "divergent thinking" (发散性思维) and that seeing her classmates' questions generated "a feeling of novelty" (新奇的感觉). S14 confessed that seeing others' questions on the PPT was like a "collision of thoughts" (思想的碰撞) which brought to light something she had missed or provided "an alternative perspective" (不一样的视角). S2 illustrated how she had learned to be more cautious while reading a text, i.e., not ready to take the textual messages for granted, with her understanding of the last words uttered by the old man in the text of Unit 7 (*The Chaser*):

Interview Extract 7-17, S2, Group B
就是我觉得印象最深的就是最后那个 old man 说的那个法语。……就我觉得挺那个的。……一开始，我真的不知道它是法语，后来我看到编者的翻译，我才知道是法语，就是再会的意思。……然后就留下了一个悬念，我就觉得还挺那个的。……一开始，别人跟他说 good bye 的时候，我就想他说的也就是一种礼貌的回应吧，然后后面我去看翻译的时候，我才知道，原来是法语的再会的意思。然后就会去想，为什么要说这一句话？

What impressed me most is the French words said by the old man. … I felt curious about it. … At the very beginning, I didn't know that it was French. It was when I read the translation given by the textbook writers that I got to know that it means see you later. … Thus it leaves a suspense, and I felt curious. … At first sight, I thought it is just a polite response to goodbye. But after reading the translation, I found that the French words means see you later. And then I began to think why the old man should say so.

The students of Group C all agreed that the pedagogical interventions introduced to classroom questioning were conducive to the development of critical thinking. S29 made a special mention of her appreciation of the researcher's having them raise their own questions while previewing the texts:

Interview Extract 7-18, S29, Group C
现在感觉就是会有不一样，而且，而且就是说实话，我跟我们寝室的同学说，老师其实是把我们当做研究生教，因为你以前说你做研究生的时候，说什么老师给你们书，你自己看，然后来问问题什么的，就是自己交流嘛，上课的时候也是那种提问式的交流。

I now have a very different feeling, and, to be honest, I once said to my roommates that our teacher is teaching us as post-graduate students, because you once talked of your studying in the graduate school. Your teacher asked you to read the books on your own and bring to the classroom your questions and communicate with each other. So you are teaching as you were taught, that is, teaching by questioning.

Reflection essays

What emerged in the focus group interviews about critical thinking was corroborated by the students' reflection essays as well. Many of the students mentioned how participating in classroom Q-A interaction benefited their critical thinking and/or divergent thinking, especially their "critical disposition" as demonstrated by the following extracts from their reflection essays:

Chapter 7　Further Discussion

Essay Extract 7-14, S1
个人收获：形成了一种带着问题看世界的批判性思维，发散性思维，更广的视野。
In terms of personal gains, I have developed a critical thinking mode, that is, viewing the world with questions, a divergent thinking mode and a wider horizon.

Essay Extract 7-15, S2
上课的方式可以让我们更能熟悉书本内容，能让我们自己独立思考，可以学习借鉴别的同学的思维方式，很新颖，很有趣。
Your way of teaching can have us be more familiar with what is in the textbook, think independently, learn from other students' thinking, which is novel and interesting.

Essay Extract 7-16, S15
就是听取别人的意见很重要，上课做了这么多次的讨论，以及课文预习时的提问和回答，不是每一个人的思维都是一样的，我们也不能要求别人与我的一样，自己也要学会去接受别人的意见，这是必要的。
It is very important to listen to others' ideas. After so many discussions throughout this course, and raising and answering questions while previewing the texts, I have come to realize that not everyone's thoughts are the same, we cannot impose our thoughts on others, and we need to learn to accept others' ideas, which is necessary.

What they had benefited in terms of thinking was not limited to the attitude towards their peer classmates' ideas or thoughts, but reached into the attitude towards learning, both general learning and language learning, as indicated by S3:

Essay Extract 7-17, S3
对于我个人来说，经历过这个学期的精读学习，我的收获更多的是多了一种思维方式，原来学习并不仅仅是停留在课本，还有更广阔的天地，让我懂得学习并不仅仅是为了应试，更多的应该是培养自己英语学习的思维，这样才能享受学习，培养自己的兴趣。
Personally speaking, after taking this course in this semester, what I have gained is more a mode of thinking. I have found that learning should not be stopped at the textbook, but be extended to the wider world. I have also realized that learning should not be aimed at passing exams, but at cultivating a mode of

thinking that fosters learning English. Only in this way can we enjoy learning and develop an interest in it.

One student, S33, gave a vivid account of how she, after attending the researcher's classes, began to realize the importance of learning with a critical mind and relating the textbook to the real life:

Essay Extract 7-18, S33
老师我觉得你在启发学生思考这一层面上真的做的挺好又循循善诱……这个学期的精读课就让我觉得有很大的不一样了，比如"Fun, Oh boy, you could die from it."这篇，我还很清楚的记得一些词句……我也不知道该怎么形容这种感觉，就是从这些课文上的词句传达的内容，开始有了自己的体会开始会思考这些观点对反映在我自己身上是怎样的，开始形成思辨的眼光去审视自己。
Sir, I think you have done a very good job in inspiring the students to think. … The intensive reading course of this semester brought me a considerably different feeling. For example, I can still remember some words and sentences of the text of *Fun. Oh Boy. You Could Die From It!* … I don't know how to describe this feeling. I just began to have my own thoughts after learning what is conveyed in these words and sentences. I began to think: what if these opinions were reflected onto myself? I began to scrutinize myself with critical eyes.

The above analysis shows that the students self-reportedly confirmed the development of critical thinking due to the pedagogical interventions employed in the design and implementation of teacher questions. It has been noted for long about the importance of 'involvement' or 'investment' in language learning (Allwright, 1984). Recent research, however, converges on the task effect on vocabulary learning, with the body of research testifying the Involvement Load Hypothesis (Hulstijn & Laufer, 2001; Keating, 2008; Laufer, 2013). The current study constitutes a piece of exploratory practice in exploring how teacher questions can be designed and implemented to increase students' involvement in all the strands of language learning.

To sum up, the students were generally approving of the pedagogical interventions, which, as demonstrated in the focus group interviews and the end-of-term reflection essays, had contributed to the friendly classroom atmosphere, cultivating their critical thinking, deepening their understanding of texts, and developing their awareness of autonomous learning. To put it in dialectical terms, it is the pedagogical interventions that involved the students in preparing to answer the teacher's questions or to raise their own questions, and it is the students' involvement in learning as required by the teacher that led to their perceived improvement in their comprehension, production and critical thinking.

7.2.5 Renovated recognition of course objectives

The intensive reading course, or alternatively referred to as Integrated English, is meant to be a course that integrates the development of all these capabilities. The researcher's design and implementation of teacher questions, in light of the notion of learning space, proved to be effective in involving the students in developing their integrated knowledge and skills, and hence renovated the students' recognition of the instructional objectives of the course.

Focus group interviews

In the focus group interviews, the students of all the three groups indicated that they had realized that the intensive reading course is intended to develop their integrated skills, including listening, speaking, reading and writing, rather than the mere amass of discrete language points. S39 of Group A, in particular, mentioned that she had never related the intensive reading course to writing before attending the researcher's classes, for she had been bearing the idea that intensive reading was nothing more than the accumulation of grammatical and lexical knowledge. However, as being pushed to attack the language points of the texts on her own, she began to realize that she could borrow some chunks or patterns of language from the texts for her own writing, which brought her enjoyment in learning the course:

Interview Extract 7-19, S39, Group A
比如，我会自己想办法去搞清楚近义词和反义词。……还有以前预习的时候，就是大概理解课文的意思或结构，现在的话，就要自己仔细地看，也会分析句子的结构……因为我特别喜欢写作这一部分的东西，然后就是，我看见一个好的句子或者词，就是，看见一个就感觉很享受……要是以前，就不会把精读课当做写作课来，感觉就是，上精读课，对我来说，就跟写作课一样。

For example, I myself would try to clarify the synonyms and antonyms… . In addition, in terms of previewing, I used to stop at having a global understanding of the main idea or structure of the texts. But now, I will read carefully as well as analyze the sentence structures … because I am especially fond of writing. So when I see a good sentence or a good word, I will feel a sense of enjoyment… . In the past, however, I would never look upon the intensive reading as a writing course. I feel that attending the intensive reading course is no different from attending the writing course.

The students of Group B all stressed how classroom interaction and discussion around topics beyond the texts changed their perception of the intensive reading course from the mere emphasis on language knowledge to the extension of knowledge external but related to the texts:

Interview Extract 7-20, S2, Group B
我自己的感觉就是……你聊的不仅仅是课文上的，就还会给我们涉及到其他，就比如说上课，讲到这个点，然后就会拓展到其他方面，就会，就会聊的更多。
I feel that the most distinctive feature of yours … is that … you not only talk of what is in the texts, but also what is beyond the texts. For instance, in text instruction, when you come to a certain point, you would extend it to other aspects and by so doing you would talk much more.

Interview Extract 7-21, S9, Group B
我觉得……最主要的……就是……小组讨论，然后，大家的互动多，比之前，感觉比之前的多……我觉得挺好的。
I think what is most distinctive is that you have engaged us in group discussion. And we have a lot more interaction than before, which I think is very good.

In the interview with Group C, S35 reported how the involvement in learning before, in and after class in the process of learning each unit had brought to him a sense of fulfillment and hence served to change his perception of the course:

Interview Extract 7-22, S35, Group C

我首先想的就是，从此，就是因为每一个单元，呃，在课前你要写一篇什么文章，在课后又要总结，还在课堂中间呢，又有很多的问题要，要回答，然后总体下来就是，上完一个单元，你会觉得，就是你感觉什么都做到了……什么都已经，嗯，就是你已经去，尽全力去了解这个单元到底要学什么……就感觉就是很有用，很充实……你就感觉自己，就是感觉这个单元，没有，没有就像，就是只是单纯地过了一遍而已，你就觉得自己已经深入了这个单元，就是这个，大概就是这个含义。

First of all, I think that, ever since (the beginning of the semester), in the teaching of each unit, uh, we have been told before class to write an article of what type, and to summarize the teaching by the completion of the unit, and during the classroom instruction, we are required to answer a lot of questions, and so generally, after learning a unit, you will feel that you have done whatever you should ... uh, that is, you have tried to learn what you need to ... and that is very useful and fulfilling. That is, you feel that after learning a unit you are not just done with it but have gone deep into it. That is what I mean.

Reflection essays

The students' reflection essays also lent support to the argument that a balanced design and implementation of different strands of questioning sequences can help create a comprehensive experience of a course. Many of the students wrote of how they had changed their perception of the intensive reading course after attending the researcher's classes.

S39, who spoke of her realization of the intensive reading course as connected to writing as displayed in the Interview Extract 7-38, commented in her reflection essay that the intensive reading course was superior to all the other skills-oriented courses and it suffices for a program to offer this course alone:

Essay Extract 7-19, S39

老师真正贯彻了精读，把听力、写作、阅读、翻译合为一体，有时候会想干脆就上一门精读好了。

The teacher has put into practice what intensive reading is meant to be, by integrating listening, writing, reading and translation into one course. I sometimes conceive that it suffices to have one course—the intensive reading.

Another student, S26, confessed that she had been in the dark about the purpose and significance of the intensive reading course before this semester, which brought light to her that the course was intended to help one realize the importance of learning and applying new methods, discovering one's own weaknesses and attempting to overcome them, and relating to the wider world:

Essay Extract 7-20, S26
对我而言，本学期的最大的收获是……学习到了我们必需的态度和认识。坦白讲，在这个学期之前，我不懂得精读开设的目的和意义，我也不知道这门科目我自己的收获是什么。可是一个学期下来，我开始明白了。……我想，精读是让我们在学习的过程中不断学习到新的方法并为之运用，精读是让我们不断发现自己知识的欠缺并为之努力，精读是让我们在学习课文的过程中认识到更广阔的世界。

For me, the biggest harvest is that I have learned the right attitude towards and the right cognition of learning. To be frank, before this semester, I was in the dark about the purpose and significance of the intensive reading course, neither did I know what I could gain form learning it. But this semester, I begin to know better... . I think, intensive reading is to have us incessantly learn new methods and put them into use, to have us discover the shortcomings of our knowledge and endeavor to overcome them, and to have us know about the wider world while learning the texts.

S33, whose reflection essay has been cited in Section 7.2.5 about the cultivation of critical thinking, also indicated that she had an extended view of the intensive reading course due to her engagement in preparing for, participating in and reflecting on classroom interaction:

Essay Extract 7-21, S33
单就老师这学期对我们班的教学来说，我觉得我自己收获是还蛮多的……这学期有好多课文，我都还蛮有印象，而且对这些课文产生的一些想法，在另一方面上也算是我的一种成长……让我觉得有很大的不一样了。
In regard of the teacher's instruction in this semester, I think that I have gained a lot. ... I am rather deeply impressed with quite a few texts, and some of the ideas

generated from those texts can be counted as my growth... . The intensive reading course of this semester, however, brought me a considerably different feeling.

In a word, the pedagogical interventions adopted in the different phases of text instruction helped to enrich or expand the students' perception of the intensive reading course. As indicated earlier in the preliminary work, the students once had the impression that the intensive reading course was only meant to enlarge their vocabulary size and strengthen their grammatical knowledge. By the end of the semester where the AR was conducted, however, the students realized that the integrated nature of the intensive reading course, lies not only in the development of their linguistic competence or language proficiency, but also in the development of their critical thinking, the expansion of their world view, the enrichment of their personality traits, etc.

7.2.6 Further evidence

A comparison between the results of the tests and questionnaires conducted before and after the AR lends further evidence for the effectiveness of the pedagogical interventions as presented above.

7.2.6.1 Use of reading strategies

A comparison of the overall averages of the students' use of each set of strategies before and after the AR (See Table 7-1) shows that the students have improved their use of reading strategies for dealing with the intensive reading texts.

Table 7-1 Comparison of the students' use of reading strategies before and after AR

Reading strategies	Before AR		After AR		Improvement
	Mean	SD	Mean	SD	
Text function strategies	2.59	0.83	3.36	0.88	0.77
Text summary strategies	2.76	0.90	3.54	0.85	0.78
Text structure strategies	2.71	0.91	3.38	0.94	0.67
Text meaning strategies	2.84	0.94	3.50	0.90	0.66

The statistics (See Figures 7-2, 7-3 and 7-4) show that there is a high correlation between the student's use of each set of reading strategies before and after the AR and the improvement in their using of each set of strategies is statistically significant. What deserves a particular mention here is that one student told the researcher after delivering the questionnaire that she felt her use of strategies to read the intensive reading texts had improved much due to having been required to preview the texts either to answer a list of questions or to raise their own questions.

Paired Samples Statistics

		Mean	N	Std. Deviation	Std. Error Mean
Pair 1	FunctionPost	3.3553	38	.69982	.11353
	FunctionPre	2.5877	38	.59621	.09672
Pair 2	SummaryPost	3.5368	38	.61531	.09982
	SummaryPre	2.7632	38	.66390	.10770
Pair 3	StructurePost	3.3772	38	.61474	.09972
	StructurePre	2.7061	38	.58822	.09542
Pair 4	MeaningPost	3.5000	38	.61268	.09939
	MeaningPre	2.8421	38	.64369	.10442

Figure 7-2　Paired samples statistics of the reading strategies surveys

Paired Samples Correlations

		N	Correlation	Sig.
Pair 1	Function2 & Function1	38	.801	.000
Pair 2	Summary2 & Summary1	38	.714	.000
Pair 3	Structure2 & Structure1	38	.695	.000
Pair 4	Meaning2 & Meaning1	38	.760	.000

Figure 7-3　Paired samples correlations of the reading strategies surveys

Paired Samples Test

		Paired Differences					t	df	Sig. (2-taited)
		Mean	Std. Deviation	Std. Error Mean	95% Confidence interval of the Difference				
					Lower	Upper			
Pair 1	Function2-Function1	.76754	.42010	.06815	.62946	.90563	11.263	37	.000
Pair 2	Summary2-Summary1	.77368	.48585	.07881	.61399	.93338	9.817	37	.000
Pair 3	Structure2-Structure1	.67105	.47059	.07634	.51637	.82573	8.790	37	.000
Pair 4	Meaning2-Meaning1	.65789	.43659	.07082	.51439	.80140	9.289	37	.000

Figure 7-4　Paired samples test of the reading strategies surveys

7.2.6.2 Reading comprehension

Statistics in Figures 7-5, 7-6 and 7-7 show that the students' scores in the reading comprehension tests are highly correlated and demonstrate a statistically significant increase. What is noteworthy is that the average scores in the two tests are both lower than half of the total. A closer look at the students' performances reveals that the problem could be accounted for their slow speed of reading. Most of them failed to complete all the items and even some of them was half done in either test. Hence, it might be safe to infer that the students' text comprehension had improved in respect of accuracy despite their slow speed of reading.

7.2.6.3 Speaking

As can be seen in Figures 7-8, 7-9, and 7-10, the students' scores in the speaking tests are highly correlated and demonstrate a statistically significant increase in all the four dimensions. Among the four dimensions, the improvement in the dimension of fluency is the greatest, which could partially be the result of the students' getting used to talking to the researcher while taking his course for throughout the semester.

7.2.6.4 Summary writing

As can be seen in the statistics of the summary writing tests (Figures 7-11, 7-12, and 7-13), the average score increased in each dimension and the difference between the two tests is statistically significant in all the dimensions except the first (exactitude of summary) and the sixth (grammatical range and accuracy). However, as there is no statistically significant correlation between the pre- and post-test scores in each dimension, it is only safe to infer that from an overall perspective the students' summary writing skills show signs of improvement. As stated earlier in Chapter 3, the first four indicators, i.e., 1) exactitude of summary, 2) explicitness of thesis statement, 3) clarity of argumentation, 4) coherence, point to critical thinking. The students' statistically significant improvement in these aspects, as discussed earlier, could be ascribed to the use of questioning sequences in the text instruction as well as in the writing assignment.

Paired Samples Statistics

		Mean	N	Std. Deviation	Std. Error Mean
Pair 1	Reading2	18.05	38	4.274	.693
	Reading1	14.92	38	4.750	.771

Figure 7-5   Paired samples statistics of reading tests

Paired Samples Correlations

		N	Correlation	Sig.
Pair 1	Reading2 & Reading1	38	.623	.000

Figure 7-6   Paired samples correlations of reading tests

Paired Samples Test

	Paired Differences					t	df	Sig. (2-tailed)
	Mean	Std. Deviation	Std. Error Mean	95% Confidence Interval of the Difference				
				Lower	Upper			
Pair 1 Reading2-Reading1	3.132	3.940	.639	1.837	4.427	4.900	37	.000

Figure 7-7   Paired samples test of reading tests

Paired Samples Statistics

		Mean	N	Std. Deviation	Std. Error Mean
Pair 1	FC2	4.692	39	.8986	.1439
	FC1	3.782	39	.8074	.1293
Pair 2	LR2	4.545	39	.8309	.1330
	LR1	3.763	39	.7694	.1232
Pair 3	GRA2	4.494	39	.7641	.1224
	GRA1	3.776	39	.7604	.1218
Pair 4	Pron2	4.897	39	.6456	.1034
	Pron1	4.365	39	.8108	.1298

Figure 7-8   Paired samples statistics of speaking tests

Paired Samples Correlations

		N	Correlation	Sig.
Pair 1	FC2 & FC1	39	.796	.000
Pair 2	LR2 & LR1	39	.794	.000
Pair 3	GRA2 & GRA1	39	.770	.000
Pair 4	Pron2 & Pron1	39	.721	.000

Figure 7-9   Paired samples correlations of speaking tests

Paired Samples Test

		Paired Differences					t	df	Sig. (2-tailed)
		Mean	Std. Deviation	Std. Error Mean	95% Confidence Interval of the Difference				
					Lower	Upper			
Pair 1	FC2-FC1	.9103	.5516	.0883	.7315	1.0891	10.306	38	.000
Pair 2	LR2-LR1	.7821	.5168	.0827	.6145	.9496	9.451	38	.000
Pair 3	GRA2-GRA1	.7179	.5168	.0827	.5504	.8855	8.676	38	.000
Pair 4	Pron2-Pron1	.5321	.5654	.0905	.3488	.7153	5.877	38	.000

Figure 7-10 Paired samples T-test of speaking tests

Paired Samples Statistics

		Mean	N	Std. Deviation	Std. Error Mean
Pair 1	Summary2	3.50	33	.392	.068
	Summary1	3.45	33	.409	.071
Pair 2	Thesis2	3.61	33	.300	.052
	Thesis1	3.02	33	.532	.093
Pair 3	Argument2	3.55	33	.303	.053
	Argument1	2.95	33	.533	.093
Pair 4	Coherence2	3.44	33	.370	.064
	Coherence1	3.13	33	.391	.068
Pair 5	Lexlcal2	3.42	33	.356	.062
	Lexlcal1	3.17	33	.383	.067
Pair 6	Grammar2	3.39	33	.390	.068
	Grammar1	3.37	33	.381	.066
Pair 7	Syntactic2	3.65	33	.405	.070
	Syntactic1	3.25	33	.380	.066

Figure 7-11 Descriptive statistics of writing tests

Paired Samples Correlations

		N	Correlation	Sig.
Pair 1	Summary2 & Summary1	33	.231	.196
Pair 2	Thesis2 & Thesis1	33	.021	.907
Pair 3	Argument2 & Argument1	33	-.081	.652
Pair 4	Coherence2 & Coherence1	33	.123	.495
Pair 5	Lexical2 & Lexical1	33	-.029	.872
Pair 6	Grammar2 & Grammar1	33	.102	.571
Pair 7	Syntactic2 & Syntactic1	33	.076	.674

Figure 7-12 Paired samples correlations of writing tests

Paired Samples Test

		Paired Differences					t	df	Sig. (2-tailed)
		Mean	Std. Deviation	Std. Error Mean	95% Confidence interval of the Difference				
					Lower	Upper			
Pair 1	Summary2-Summary1	.055	.497	.086	-.121	.231	.639	32	.528
Pair 2	Thesis2-Thesis1	.583	.605	.105	.369	.798	5.540	32	.000
Pair 3	Argument2-Argument1	.598	.634	.110	.374	.823	5.422	32	.000
Pair 4	Coherence2-Coherence1	.311	.504	.088	.132	.489	3.540	32	.001
Pair 5	Lexical2-Lexical1	.250	.530	.092	.062	.438	2.708	32	.011
Pair 6	Grammar2-Grammar1	.023	.517	.090	-.161	.206	.253	32	.802
Pair 7	Syntactic2-Syntactic1	.402	.534	.093	.212	.591	4.321	32	.000

Figure 7-13 Paired samples test of writing tests

7.3 Major factors affecting instructional effectiveness

In the focus group interviews and the reflection essays, the students were invited to point out problems concerning the design and implementation of teacher questions and make suggestions on future improvement. Despite the positive evaluation given by the majority of the students as discussed above, some of them did bring forth some problems remaining to be resolved and correspondingly suggested possible solutions. While most of the problems and suggestions pointed to their own learning, such as the need of a sizeable vocabulary, the poverty of grammatical knowledge, the lack of confidence in speaking, the shortage of self-discipline, etc., some problems drew attention to some factors that might account for the effectiveness of classroom Q-A interaction. As the focus of the research is on the interaction initiated by the sequences of questions designed and implemented for the fulfillment of specifically identified instructional objectives, the following discussion is meant to be an exploration to that end.

It emerged in the qualitative data collected by the end of the AR and in the process of the three cycles of AR that the effectiveness of the design and implementation of teacher questions was affected by such factors as 1) the difficulty of questions, 2) the students' varied needs, 3) the sufficiency of preparation, and 4) the teacher-student rapport.

7.3.1 Difficulty of questions

It has been found that the quality of student responses to teacher questions are affected by the difficultly of the questions, specifically, the cognitive challenge, the topic familiarity and the complexity of language to be used in answering the questions (Walsh & Sattes, 2005).

As demonstrated in Chapters Four to Six, a questioning sequence in the current study consists of a series of questions of different cognitive levels relating to a common content focus. Observing at the preliminary phase of the AR that students of different proficiency levels showed preferences to questions of different cognitive levels, the researcher would allocate questions requiring different levels of cognitive processing in accordance with the students' proficiency levels as answering higher-order questions usually involves using more complex language.

Whereas the teacher can adjust the cognitive challenge of questions and can assist the students' responses with scaffolding during the Q-A interaction around a certain content focus or topic, the issue of topic familiarity is not so easy to deal with if a question or a sequence of questions concerns a topic that is unfamiliar to the students. That is probably the reason why the students of all the three levels of proficiency explicitly showed their preference of 'open questions' related to their own life over questions focusing on the textual and/or meta-texual messages.

S18, one of the focal students of Group B, for example, told the researcher in the focus group interview that though she chose to sit in the front she remained silent most of the time in class, but when the teacher asked questions about some topics familiar to her, she would be active to respond:

Interview Extract 7-23, S18, Group B
有时候有些问题就会比较——比如说老师你就问过,是喜欢到大城市还是小城镇生活,就是这种小问题,也跟我们实际生活相关嘛,然后我就会思考。每个人当然会有自己不同的看法,然后我们会有自己的看法,然后我们又会表达,我就觉得小城镇比较好嘛,我现在是说实话。那我们就会发现一个观点表达出来嘛,就是跟实际生活挺密切的那种,就是。
Sometimes some questions are relatively—for instance, you once asked such

a question, whether we like to live in a big city or in a small town. Such small questions are closely connected to our life and would set me thinking. Certainly, every one may have different views and we may have our own and can express them. I hold the view that living in a small town is better, and I am telling the truth. Then we will find that one view is shared that is closely related to our life. That's it.

Personal response questions are welcomed by students in that there are no preset standard answers to them and the students are especially willing to communicate if such questions are closely related to their own lives, i.e., familiar to them. However, as advocated by Nation (1996, 2007, 2010), the strands of a language course should be balanced and accordingly the questions of different content focus should be balanced as well. In other words, the teacher should take into account the students' life experiences and design questions related to their lives, but should never accommodate their preferences by keeping them in their 'comfort zone' at the cost of comprehending the textual messages or learning the relevant meta-textual messages.

7.3.2 Students' varied needs

As can be noted in the previous discussion and the description of the three cycles of AR, students of different language proficiency levels voiced different requests in the learning logs, group discussions, focus group interviews and reflection essays. Though the researcher had endeavored to take full account of their needs and wants during the AR, it was hard for him to come up with a 'one-size-fits-all' approach especially when their needs and wants were conflicting.

In the focus group interviews, there were students in both Groups A and B who suggested that questions be asked at the beginning of each class to review what had been discussed previously. In the meantime, others counter-argued that they should depend on themselves in respect of reviewing instead of on the teacher. Such a conflict is demonstrated by the following extracts of interview:

Interview Extract 7-24, Group A

S6: 老师，好像上课少了一个环节——课后的复习的环节。

T: 嗯。

S1: 问题是，精读的内容很多，老师怎么复习？

T: 要复习什么呢？比如说？

S6: 词汇，语法，或者课文的那个概意什么的。

S1: 复习应该是自己的事。

S6: Sir, it seems to me that there is something missing in our class, that is reviewing.

T: En.

S1: The problem is, the intensive reading course concerns such a wide range of contents and how our teacher can go about reviewing.

T: What should we review? Can you give us an example?

S6: Vocabulary, grammar, or the main ideas of the texts, and the like.

S1: Reviewing should be taken care of by ourselves.

Interview Extract 7-25, Group B

S9: 单从课本上，就是课本上的知识来说，我觉得可以，就是上课前加——个小 Quiz，就是小测试——

T: 噢

S9: 就是 Review 之前我们的知识点

T: 嗯，看你有没有 Review，对不对？

S9: 哎

S2: 嗯对……

S9: 有时候我觉得就是有必要监督，就是督促他们，就是有些人可能不会看，但是［这样］

S14: ［这样］

S2: ［但是］，你课前的话，我觉得，有些同学还没来呢——

S9: 对，就是我说，课前是什么呢，应该是上课后的前几分钟。

T: 嗯

S14: 但是，大学生不是要靠自觉嘛

S2: 对，对，我觉得要靠自觉，也是

S14: 大家都是成年人啦

S2: 该懂事就懂事了【大家笑】

S14: 该对自己负责了，不应该叫别人来——

S2: 对对

S9: As far as the knowledge from the textbook, I think it is OK. But I think we can have a quiz before starting the class—

T: Oh

S9: to review the knowledge points we have discussed before

T: En, to see whether you have reviewed, right?

S9: Eh

S2: En right

S9: Sometimes I think it necessary to supervise and urge them to do so, otherwise some of them would never review. But [so]

S14: [so]

S2: [but], if you review before class, I think, some students are not there yet—

S9: Right, that is, before class, it should be the first few minutes of class time.

T: En

S14: But college students should depend on themselves.

S2: Yeah, yeah, I think we should depend on ourselves, too.

S14: We are all adults.

S2: We have reached the age to know better [all laughing]

S14: We should be responsible for ourselves rather than depend on others—

S2: Right right.

A few higher proficiency-level students indicated that the time spent on dealing with language points or answering language questions resulted in less time on open questions which they thought valuable in training their critical thinking and practising their language skills, as S1 wrote in his reflection essay:

Essay Extract 7-22, S1
1. 效率低。课程可以压缩到两节课结束（一节课讲文章，一节课讲问题）（虽说不好统筹也是一回事，但是课堂效率的确需要提高）。
2. 课外话题需要增加。因为我们的课程与社会有些脱节，所以与社会相关的需要探讨的话题需要增加。
1. Low efficiency. The time for text instruction could be reduced to two class hours (one devoted to the text, the other to questions) (though it is not easy to find a solution that satisfies every one, classroom efficiency is really in need of improvement)
2. Extracurricular topics should be augmented, for the course is disconnected

with the society. Thus we need to have more topics that are related to the society and in need of exploration.

However, it seems that there was a conflicting view from students of lower proficiency, who indicated that they felt uncomfortable with the researcher's insufficient attention to language points and his fast pace of teaching, as S6 and S29 wrote in their reflection essays:

Essay Extract 7-23, S6
如果非要说提一点小小的建议的话，那就是希望老师在以后的授课中，多把时间花费在知识讲解上，并放慢讲课的速度，让我们更易于吸收、接受。因为，现在的我们正面临专四大考，需要存储一定的专业知识。
If there is any minor suggestion that I have to make, it is my hope that the teacher can, in his future classes, spend more time on explicating knowledge, and slow down the pace of instruction, so that we can absorb and accept more easily. The reason for doing so is that we are faced with the TEM4 and need to store a certain amount of specialized knowledge.

Essay Extract 7-24, S29
我希望老师能够规范一下提问方向，以文字形式，有时甚至不会想到语言问题，大多是文章内容的思考。没有这个意识的话，会下意识忽略。我觉得在仅仅能够读懂的情况下，我是没有办法像读中文那样感受到语言之美。
I hope that the teacher can regulate his direction of questions. When we read the words of a text, there are times we cannot think of language problems because most of the time we contemplate on the content. Without this awareness of language points, we would subconsciously neglect them. I feel that I can by no means appreciate an English text as I do a Chinese if I stop at a literal understanding of a text.

Interestingly enough, there was one student of lower proficiency who took side with S6 regarding the pace of instruction but agreed with S1 about the employment of open questions, and suggested a practical solution to the dilemma:

Essay Extract 7-25, S2

问题就是会让课堂时间过的很快，书本进度有点紧凑，但是我觉得还挺好的。如果老师在以后上课前都让我们做到事先已经熟悉课文了，这样上课的时候效率就会很高，因为如果在我们课前熟悉书本内容的基础上拓展一些其它的东西就不仅不会浪费课堂时间，还能让我们拓展其它方面的知识，是不是挺好的。

The problem is that time passes very fast in classroom instruction and the schedule of text instruction is a bit tight. But I feel that is good. If in the future, the teacher could make us familiar with the text before class, then the efficiency of classroom instruction would be very high, for if we are familiar with what is in the text before class, then talking about topics other than the text would not be a waste of time but rather a contribution to the extension of our knowledge. That must be good.

While there exists a body of research on conducting needs analysis of language program or curriculum design (e.g., Hutchinson & Waters, 1987; West, 1994; Benesch, 1996; Long, 2005), little has been done to examine learners' needs for the learning of a lesson or a unit of a course. The above discussion indicates that students of different proficiency levels may have different needs and wants in learning and that students with different interests may have different preferable questions. It seems to be a dilemma for the teacher how he/she can strike a proportional balance betweenquestions of different types. It is maintained that the teacher should first of all attempt to know what the students' needs, wants and interests are before making decisions about the design and implementation of questions. It is found in the current study that collecting students' questions is an effective way to that end and incorporating their questions into teacher questions can not only meet their needs but also plunge the students into reflecting what they are exactly in need of.

7.3.3 Sufficiency of preparation before class

As discussed earlier in Section 7.2, the students' being required to preview the texts either to answer a list of questions or to come up with their own questions played a role in engaging the students in autonomous learning and hence was conducive to the improvement of their awareness of autonomy, text comprehension, and critical thinking as well. What is to be reiterated here is that the degree to which the students make preparation before class in correspondence with the pedagogical interventions can have an impact on the efficiency of the Q-A classroom interaction and ultimately on the effectiveness of the sequences of questions designed and implemented for the instructional objectives.

Both the focus group interviews and the reflection essays indicated that sufficient preparation before class was conducive to their involvement in classroom interaction and learning. S29 confessed in the interview that she found previewing the texts as guided by a list of teacher questions helped her keep abreast with the researcher's instruction and otherwise she would have had an incoherent experience:

> **Interview Extract 7-26, S26, Group C**
> 那些问题就是准备了一遍之后，然后就其实课文就大致都了解了，就是，这种感觉就是，我能跟上你的节奏了，感觉就很好，就是有时候就会，可能自己会走神啊，一不小心开小差啊什么的，然后就会跟不上，然后就……感觉没有那种一整堂课下来，就没有那种连贯性。
> Those questions to which I had prepared my answers provided me with a global understanding of the whole text. Such a feeling is like I can catch up with your rhythm of instruction and it is good. That is, sometimes I may get lost or shift my attention to something else, and then I will fail to keep up with you, and ... I will have the feeling that there is a lack of coherence after attending a class.

In her reflection essay, however, S29 wrote in English about how raising her own questions had helped her catch the key points in the process of classroom instruction:

> **Essay Extract 7-26, S29**
> Before, I felt <u>tried</u> [tired] after having <u>a</u> [the] intensive class. But this term, I know that intensive class also can be <u>relax</u> [relaxing]. The key aspect is that we <u>are</u> [have] learnt to raise questions during study. It is a good way to learn English well. Then I can catch the key points accurately, which <u>is</u> [can] improve my study

efficiently. And I know my problem better.

Such a view was confirmed by another student, S33, who wrote in her reflection essay on the importance of making full preparations in advance, which made it possible for her to keep track of the instruction with ease:

Essay Extract 7-27, S33
感觉上老师的课，课堂上不用怎么花心思，人在那坐着不带书去都可以，但是要投入，课下就要下功夫，无论课前课后准备工作都要做足，这里面哪个环节出了纰漏，就很容易从老师的教学步伐里掉队。
It seems that while attending your classes I don't have to give too much thought. I can just sit there even without taking my book. But if I want to get engaged in it, I need to do a lot of work outside the classroom, either before or after class. If I fail to do the work accordingly, it is very easy to lag behind the teacher's steps.

Despite the students' positive comments on the advantage of making full preparation before class, some of them told the researcher their being perplexed or confused about what to do and how to do in respect of raising their own questions. The students of Group A in the focus group interview talked of whether they should stop at merely delivering their own questions to their teacher or move on to preview the text once again in reference to the teacher's questions, or invert the order of the aforementioned steps in previewing. The students of Group C, however, pointed to the problem of what questions to raise, only those they could not answer on their own or whatever questions that came to their mind.

The above discussion boils down to two sub-issues concerning before-class preparation. One is the extent to which the students are involved in making the expected preparations. It appears that the deeper their involvement is with the text, the better they are in a position to follow the researcher's thread of text instruction, i.e., the steps he takes to reach the instructional objectives, or more specifically, to participate in the 'multilogic' Q-A interaction (Schwab, 2011). The other sub-issue relates to the design features of the previewing task devised by the researcher. It is suggested that the combination of teacher questions and student questions in making preparations before class can help promote the effectiveness of classroom interaction.

Wait time has been one of the key concerns in existing research on teacher questioning. Both educational and applied linguistic researchers have examined the influence of extending wait time on student learning (e.g., Rowe, 1986; Walsh & Sattes, 2005; Ellis, 2012; Lightbown & Spada, 2013). However, the current study indicates that it is advisable to have the students prepare in advance to answer the teacher's questions or raise their own questions concerning the text.

7.3.4 Management of classroom interaction

One issue that emerged in the students' reflection essays and deserved due attention was the allocation of turns during classroom Q-A interaction. A few students illustrated the advantages of nominating individuals over inviting volunteers or eliciting chorus responses with their own feelings of being nominated to answer questions. S29, for example, suggested that the researcher nominate students to answer questions, for she had the belief that being nominated to answer questions could stimulate or drive the students to make due preparations before class:

> **Essay Extract 7-28, S29**
> 课文后面的作业，建议老师叫人起来回答问题。每当我没做的时候，特别怕老师叫我回答问题。如果老师叫我起来回答问题，而我没有做，为了防止下一次的尴尬和忐忑，我会做完下一个单元。
> I have a suggestion for dealing with the textbook exercises, that is, to nominate students to answer them. Every time when I failed to finish the exercises before class, I would be especially afraid of being nominated to give my answer. If I were nominated by the teacher to give my answer to an exercise that I did not finish, then to avoid embarrassment and anxiety in the next time, I would finish the exercises of the next unit.

Another student, S30, expressed her hope that the researcher would pay more attention to those reticent students, implying that if they were allocated more turns to answer questions, they would be mobilized in participating in classroom interaction and motivated in learning the course:

> **Essay Extract 7-29, S30**
> 希望你能多关注上课比较安静的同学，调动他们的学习积极性，毕竟曾经我也是上精读课时的低头族。
> I hope that you can pay more attention to the students who are more reticent in class, and encourage them to take initiatives in learning. After all, I used to be one of those who would always lower their heads in the intensive reading class.

Both S29 and S30 admitted that they had belonged to those who would sit back in the classroom and remain reticent during classroom interaction and that their experience of being nominated and encouraged to answer questions had resulted in an increased motivation to participate in and make their due contributions to classroom interaction.

It has been maintained that teacher questions can be employed to improve students' motivation and participation (Chuska, 1995; Qin, 2007; Oliveira & Oliveira, 2013). Some empirical studies on classroom discourse departing from a sociocultural perspective (e.g., Schmidt, Lyutykh, & Shumow, 2012; Adams & March, 2015) have demonstrated how well-designed teacher questions can help improve students' 'perezhivanie' (emotional experience) of science teachers' classroom instruction. The current study, however, shows that there is a reciprocal relationship between students' participation in classroom interaction and their motivation for learning a course. Some of the previously reticent students, having been invited to participate in meaningful communication, realized how they could benefit from participating in classroom interaction and hence were ready to take initiatives in making due preparations, which in turn contributed to their performance in later classes.

7.3.5 Teacher-student rapport

It seems to the researcher that the success of the AR can be partly attributed to the well-established teacher-student rapport, or the friendly and egalitarian teacher-student relationship. It has been argued that the teacher is not only responsible for the management of classroom interaction but also for planning and establishing a positive 'affective climate' or 'socio-emotional atmosphere' (Allwright, 1984, p. 164; Allwright & Bailey, 1991, pp. 21-28; Crabbe, 2003, 2007). It is found in the current study that the teacher's investment both inside and outside the classroom is conducive to the researcher's winning the students' trust and building a 'receptive' rather than 'defensive' teacher-student relationship, which in turn increases the students' willingness to accept the researcher's invitation to participate in and contribute to classroom interaction.

As demonstrated in Sections 7.2, the focal students indicated in the focus group interviews that the researcher's efforts in building up an equal teacher-student relationship and a light classroom atmosphere had contributed to relieving the students' anxiety, increasing their motivation and participation, and enhancing their autonomous learning. Particularly, a number of students indicated that the researcher's use of 'open questions' or 'personal response questions' during classroom interaction was conducive to creating an atmosphere where the teacher and the students could communicate on equal grounds. Some students also indicated that the researcher's 'off-topic talk' on matters beyond the text, such as films, novels, anecdotes of historical figures, his own stories, and the like, had helped to shorten the teacher-student psychological distance and hence establish a friendly teacher-student rapport.

Besides his efforts inside the classroom, the researcher's investment outside the classroom was appreciated by the students as well, which could be viewed as a sign of winning the students' trust. Such inference is demonstrated by some of the students' reflection essays. For instance, S36 commended the researcher's doing everything he could to give the students timely feedback on their learning, including their participation in classroom interaction, their involvement in the group discussions, their performances in doing the dictation, writing their learning logs, etc. She understood that all of these were aimed at making precise judgments about their learning and providing them with appropriate guidance:

Essay Extract 7-30, S36

老师每次带着录像机来上课，把上课的全程拍下来，把课堂听写分数等级整理分类，要求我们在一个学期做了三次 talk，每个星期有 GPS Learning log 的作业，对于懒惰又口语不好的我来说简直是要命，但是每次完成了又是满满的成就感。老师总是花大量的时间来整理这些数据，为了给我们的努力的方向做一个最准确的判断。

Sir, each class you would bring a camera to the classroom, and videotape the whole process of classroom instruction. You would also grade our dictation work, require us to talk with you three times throughout the semester, assign us to write GPS learning logs. It is really tough for me to do all these because of my laziness and poor spoken English, but every time I finish all these I will be filled with a sense of achievement. You've always spent a lot of time sorting out these data to make right judgments as to the direction in which we should work.

Chinese EFL scholars (e.g., Wang Baoshun, 2012) have illustrated the key to learning and teaching English by citing Lu You's poetic words "If you really desire to learn poetry, your efforts should be directed elsewhere"(汝果欲学诗,功夫在诗外). The quote applies to the management of classroom interaction as well. The teacher's efforts towards classroom interaction inside the classroom, including the initiation of interaction, the provision of feedback, the elicitation of post-expansion responses, etc., could be reinforced by his/her efforts outside the classroom, such as getting to know the students' needs and interests, giving timely feedback and encouragement on their learning, and the forth.

7.5 Summary

This chapter provides further discussion on the three research questions of the current study. It is maintained that teacher questions should be designed in correspondence with the instructional objectives. To extend the learning space, the questions should be sequenced according to two dimensions of variation, one in the cognitive act, and the other in the content of learning. Students should be allowed sufficient time before class to prepare for participating in classroom Q-A interaction, to familiarize themselves with teacher questions and to raise their own questions. Additionally, students' needs and wants in learning should be taken into account to ensure maximal student involvement.

The employment of questioning sequences as described above in classroom Q-A interaction has had manifold contributions to student learning. Though it may be assertive to attribute the students' improvements to the pedagogical interventions, analysis of the focus group interviews and the reflection essays reveals that the AR did have an impact on autonomous learning, text comprehension, classroom atmosphere, critical thinking and perception of the course in general.

The efficiency of questioning sequences can be influenced by such factors as the difficulty of a question, the students' varied needs, the sufficiency of students' preparation before class, the teacher's management of classroom interaction, and the teacher-student rapport. It is suggested that teachers need to take these factors into account while designing and implementing questions for classroom instruction.

Chapter 8   Conclusion

This chapter is a wrap-up of the whole study. It first gives a summary of the major findings of the research, and then proceeds to derive implications for research and pedagogy. After pointing out limitations inherent in the current study, it provides suggestions for future research on L2 teacher questions.

8.1 Major findings

As revealed by the three cycles of AR, the model of questioning sequences in the light of learning space can be exploited as a guiding framework for the design and implementation of teacher questions. Teacher questions oriented towards the two dimensions of variation can improve students' learning experience in multiple aspects.

First, teacher questions thus designed and implemented can improve students' reading comprehension, including their understanding of the texts and their use of reading strategies. The main reason is that the students can be involved in processing the texts more profoundly and comprehensively due to the opportunities to experience variation afforded by the questions.

Second, teacher questions thus designed and implemented can help create and maintain a receptive classroom atmosphere. Sequences of questions that vary in content focus and cognitive demand can not only meet the needs of students of different proficiency levels but also cater to their varied interests or inclinations. The students involved in the current study were in favor of personal response questions, i.e., questions that relate to their real life and allows different answers. Such questions were found to be especially effective in stimulating the students' willingness to communicate during classroom interaction.

Third, teacher questions thus designed and implemented can play a crucial role in cultivating students' critical thinking. While the variation in the dimension of cognitive demand engages the students in different levels of cognitive processing and hence can strengthen their critical thinking skills, the variation in the dimension content focus invites the students to expand their views or perspectives and hence can enhance their critical thinking disposition.

Additionally, getting students involved in preparing to answer teacher questions as well as to raise their own questions is helpful in promoting autonomous learning. As demonstrated in the second AR cycle, having the students preview the texts to prepare their answers to teacher questions, not only familiarized them with the texts but also invited them to negotiate with the teacher on the learning of the texts. Having them preview the text to come up with their own questions, incorporating their questions to the teacher's questions and displaying the source of each question incorporated, as proved in the third AR cycle, were especially effective in enhancing the students' awareness of peer competition, which in turn stimulated them to shift their perspectives and sharpen their views.

What is most important of all, probably, is that the variation built in the teacher questions is helpful in enriching students' experience of a course. The pedagogical interventions adopted in the current piece of AR, significantly renovated the students' perception of the course, from a course focusing on the learning of grammar and vocabulary to a course encapsulating all the objectives as stated in the *National Curriculum*.

Nevertheless, to maximally open up the space for learning, it is advisable for the teacher to take into account a host of factors that may impact the effectiveness of teacher questions. The proficiency levels of different students, their varied needs and wants, their learning styles (e.g., some chronically reticent students are reported to have learned much from listening to others during classroom interaction), the degree of teacher-student rapport, etc., can all have an effect on the progression of teacher-student Q-A interaction. To involve students of different proficiency levels in classroom interaction, questions of different cognitive levels should be designed and allocated accordingly. To maintain students' engagement in interaction, questions relating to different topics or content orientations should be incorporated to cater to their varied needs, wants and/or interests. Reticence in classroom interaction should be tolerated, though it can be relieved at times through nomination. An "affective classroom climate" (Allwright, 1984, p. 164) or a friendly classroom atmosphere could be created naturally if there were a good teacher-student rapport which could result from the teacher's investments.

8.2 Implications

The current research, though exploratory, can offer implications for both action research and pedagogical practice.

The current study, despite its being a preliminary attempt with a narrow focus on L2 teacher questions, might afford implications for classroom-based AR concerning such issues as the building of mutual trust, the role of student participants and the tool for reflection.

The current piece of AR indicates that to gain understanding of "how things work for the purpose of making practical decisions about how to proceed" (Allwright, 2001, p. 116) what the teacher-researcher needs to do primarily is to establish mutual trust with the student participants otherwise the data collected through either verbal or written reports would be invalid or irrelevant. And to establish and strengthen the mutual trust necessitated for the AR, the teacher-researcher should invest efforts both inside and outside the classroom.

Student participants, as indicated in the current study, once mobilized or actively involved, can offer valuable insights regarding the ongoing procedure of AR. As noted earlier, the pedagogical interventions introduced in the second and third cycles were informed by the students' verbal and written reports on the problems they had encountered and the suggestions provided for resolving them. In the meantime, the students' engagement in monitoring and evaluating the AR by doing GPS reflections rendered them to be more autonomous learners with critical eyes. It is through their autonomous learning and critical thinking that they renovated their perception of the intensive reading course as well as their English major identity. The insiders' views provided by the students enriched the researcher's knowledge about classroom interaction and language pedagogy. Thus, the role of student participants in navigating AR should never be belittled. Rather, they should be regarded as co-researchers.

Reflection is "one of the most basic and essential aspects" of teacher development (Burns, 2010, p. 142). For action researchers, it is a dynamically ongoing process that permeates the whole experience of action research. While reflecting on the efficiency of Q-A interaction, the researcher focused on the four aspects of interaction in relation to the realization of the instructional objectives. The reflection journals, classroom observation notes, and peer conference memos were all formulated around them. It is demonstrated that the four types of interactional organization constitute an accessible tool for teachers to reflect on teacher talk. Undoubtedly, researchers can develop their own tools for reflection as well. A caveat is that whatever tool is established for such purposes, it should be used systematically and consistently.

The current study also has some implications to offer on the design and implementation of teacher questions for classroom instruction as well as the design of questions in textbooks. It is maintained that both teacher questions and textbook questions afford learners the space for the experience of variation oriented towards the objects of learning.

As mentioned previously, research on the effectiveness of teacher questions should be evaluated in reference to the instructional objectives. Such should be the primary concern when teachers design and implement classroom questions as well. The lack of explicitly specified objectives in teacher questions has been criticized by many and is claimed to be one of the major signs of inefficient teaching (e.g., Qin Xiubai, 2012; Qu Weiguo, 2016;

Shu Dingfang, 2013).

The preliminary research of the current study reveals that due to the students' habitual narrow experience of classroom Q-A instruction, their perception of the intensive reading course was confined to the learning of vocabulary and grammar. Nevertheless, as stated in the course description in *the National Curriculum*, the intensive reading course is one expected to provide a comprehensive experience with the English language, including the learning of language knowledge, the training of language skills and the development of critical thinking. Instructional objectives or objects of learning of a unit or a lesson should be identified in accordance with the objectives of the course. For integrated courses such as intensive reading, the objectives should be set up in consideration of the balance of the different strands of a language course (cf. Nation, 1996, 2007), and teacher questions should be designed and implemented accordingly.

As having been reiterated previously, variation in content focus and cognitive demand is the key to the effectiveness of teacher questions. The three cycles of AR demonstrated how teacher questions can be designed and sequenced across different phases of instruction to afford the space for students to experience the variation. Though the study was conducted in an intensive reading classroom, the findings can be well extended to the teaching of other courses. Taking the extensive reading course as an example, the instructional objectives may center around text comprehension or the understanding of messages conveyed in the texts, and hence it is not requisite to vary the content focus of teacher questions at a certain phase of instruction. Nevertheless, varying the cognitive demand, or asking questions that meet the requirement of hierarchical variation would bring about a profound understanding of the content under discussion. By so doing, critical thinking can be extended as well.

In addition, preparation time should be offered and student needs should be taken into account. It is suggested that students' preparation for answering teacher questions be made before class so that wait time can be saved and that students can be put in a better position to keep abreast of the instruction.

Questions designed solely by the teacher may not cater to the students' needs and/or wants. It is found that having students raise their own questions while previewing the text can bring to light what the students are in need of or interested in. More than that, incorporating their questions to teacher questions and displaying them to the whole class can not only increase the students' motivation for participation but also promote their awareness of autonomous learning.

One issue that remains to be examined is whether teacher questions should be handed out before having the students raise their own questions or otherwise. The students seemed to prefer that they raise questions before exposure to the teacher's questions. It might be worthwhile to conduct another cycle of AR to decide on the sequence of the two. Another unresolved issue is about the type of questions to be raised by the students while previewing. In the focus group interviews, several students expressed that they were confused about whether they should write down questions they could not answer or whatever questions they could think of. Though some students indicated that it would be sufficient to write down those questions they could not answer by themselves, it is maintained that listing all questions that come to their mind is valuable as they can inform the teacher of the students' preview work.

Textbook questions are an important resource to be exploited for classroom instruction. While some well-designed textbook questions can be directly used for Q-A interaction without any adaptation or revision, others can serve as references or reminders of what questions to be raised or complemented. During the course of the current study, the questions given in the textbook were largely incorporated into the teacher's classroom questions. However, as the textbook questions are mainly concerned with text comprehension, i.e., dominated by questions requiring inference or interpretation, the researcher was obliged to design questions of other types on his own. That is to say, the sole use of textbook questions is not sufficient to afford the space for students to experience variation in the objects of learning.

It is felt necessary that varieties of questions that vary in content focus and cognitive demand be provided in the teacher's manuals to help relieve the pains of generating a bulk of questions. One textbook series that provides varieties of questions for teachers to choose is *Zooming In: An Integrated English Coursebook* edited by Professor Qin Xiubai and published in 2007 (first edition) and 2014 (second edition) by Shanghai Foreign Language Education Press. In the teacher's manual, a series of content questions and extended questions are listed for each paragraph of a text, and reference answers are provided as well. The content questions mainly deal with comprehension of the text and the extended questions go beyond the text. Though the questions may not be clearly connected to particular instructional objectives identified by the teacher, they can serve as models or references for the teacher to come up with appropriate questions on his/her own.

It is yet a question to be resolved as for what questions to provide in a textbook, including the student's book and teacher's manuals. Like teacher questions, textbook questions are supposed to serve the instructional objectives and create the space for the experience of variation. There have appeared studies abroad on textbook questions in some global ESL textbooks, such as Freeman (2014) and Lee (2015), whereas textbook questions in China's EFL textbooks remain yet to be investigated.

8.3 Limitations

Though it has been widely agreed that AR is not to be judged in terms of generalizability and reliability but in terms of trustworthiness and meaningfulness (Burns, 1999, 2010; Ellis, 2010; Nunan & Bailey, 2007), there are voices calling for transferable conclusions in this type of research. However, as acknowledged earlier, the findings of the current study on teacher questions are rather tentative than conclusive due to limitations in the research design.

First and foremost, as a case study conducted in a single class of English majors, though the number of student participants is as many as 39, the samples are largely homogeneous regarding gender, age and, most important of all, language proficiency. As shown in the test results, a majority of the students belong to intermediate or lower-than-intermediate English learners despite their being English majors. In particular, the pedagogical interventions were implemented in the teaching of one single class and no control group was involved. Thus, what proves effective in the local context may not be fully applicable in another.

Secondly, learning logs, group discussions, focus group interviews and reflection essays were the means to collect data from the student participants. The students knew very well that their teacher was the only reader of their written reports and the only audience of their verbal reports. That means, the students might have been unavoidably or unconsciously induced to report in favor of their teacher's expectations. The potentially biased qualitative data could have affected the internal validity of the research.

Thirdly, throughout the AR, altogether 8 units were instructed and three cycles AR conducted but surveys on the students' attitude towards teacher questions and tests on the instructional effects were administered neither in correspondence with the progress of the instruction nor with the stages of the AR. Consequently, it was implausible to examine with rigor the effects of the pedagogical interventions on the students' learning. In other words, it appears assertive to attribute the changes in the students' perception of the course and the improvements in their performances to the treatments of the AR.

The fourth limitation relates to the rigidity of the phenomenographic analysis in the three cycles of AR. Due to the difficulty in closely tracing the students' learning, especially in catching the instant outcomes of their learning as a result of the pedagogical interventions, it was thus not feasible to do rigid phenomenographic analysis of the objects of learning, i.e., to draw comparisons and contrasts between the intended, enacted and lived objects of learning. It is maintained by Marton and associates that the space of learning, i.e., what is possible to learn, can only be measured in terms of what is intended to be learned and what is actually learned. For want of effective means of measuring what is actually learned on the part of the students, it is hard to infer whether the teacher's instruction has afforded the space of learning what is intended to be learned and resulted in what is actually learned.

The fifth limitation concerns the lack of an instrument tracking the students' affective or emotional experience of the instruction, especially the Q-A interaction initiated by questions sequentially implemented across the different stages of instruction. As revealed in the discussion, the students had different emotional responses towards different types of questions which partly determined their willingness to participate in classroom interaction. Affective engagement is of no less importance than cognitive engagement in classroom interaction (Schmidt, Lyutykh, & Shumow, 2012). It was not anticipated at the onset of the research that affective engagement would have a significant impact on student learning and hence no instruments were designed to collect the relevant data.

Lastly, collaboration was not sufficient in the AR. Though colleagues were invited to observe classroom teaching in all the three cycles of AR, they were different individuals sitting in the classroom at different points of time. That means, the observation might not be consistent and the feedback provided afterward might not be strictly relevant to the purposes of the research. Consistently involving more peer observers throughout the whole process of the research would have rendered data of higher validity data and informed the researcher of pedagogical interventions more appropriate to the students.

8.4 Suggestions for future research

Drawing on the implications and reflections presented above, the researcher suggests that the following issues be attended to in future research on L2 teacher questions.

The research focus can be narrowed down to the impacts of the employment of questioning sequences on such specific topics of critical thinking, learner autonomy, emotional experience or affective engagement, etc. As revealed in the analysis of the students' verbal and written reports, the students expressed that the researcher's use of questions of different cognitive levels and content focuses had helped broaden their horizon or mind, strengthen their critical thinking skills, realize the importance of autonomous learning, and promote their willingness to participate in classroom interaction. Nonetheless, the current study is only exploratory in those regards and it remains unknown as how sequences of questions contribute to the development of students' critical thinking, learning autonomy, and emotional experience and what factors may affect the development.

All of the above-mentioned topics deserve further investigation While researching these issues in the classroom context, as indicated in the previous section, more participants can be engaged to ensure higher degrees of transferability and more peer observers to be involved to guarantee consistency.

To research questioning sequences and critical thinking, more rigorous instruments need to be used, particularly well-established critical thinking tests, reflection journals and stimulated recall interviews, to trace the changes of the students' critical thinking abilities and relate the changes to the use of questioning sequences. Microgenetic analysis (Wen Qiufang, 2003; Zhou Dandan, 2012) could be adopted to analyze how the teacher's sequencing of questions leads to subtle changes in the students' critical thinking.

As discussed in the previous chapter, having students preview the text in reference to a list of questions and having them raise their own questions while previewing the text are especially conducive to the development of autonomous learning. However, it remains yet to be resolved as to how autonomous learning is enhanced and why it is so. What is especially interesting is how the teacher's incorporating the students' questions and displaying them to the whole class during instruction contribute to the improvement of students' awareness of peer competition and their learning autonomy. To find answers to these questions, well-designed questionnaires and interviews may be needed to examine how the students' learning autonomy develops as the course progresses.

The emotional experience of teacher questions sequentially implemented for the realization of certain object of learning is worthy of researching in that, as indicated above, it is one of the crucial factors that determine the students' willingness to participate in classroom interaction. Whereas Schmidt, Lyutykh and Shumow (2012) found that teacher questions are more effective than other types of teacher talk in promoting students' affective engagement in classroom interaction. To catch the students' emotional experience at particular points of time, think-aloud protocols and/or stimulated recall interviews can be utilized in combination with mutimodal text analysis as suggested by Gu Yueguo (2012).

Besides practitioner research, theoretically-motivated 'formal research' (Ellis, 2012, p. 23) can also be designed to investigate these issues. Experiments involving treatment and control groups can be designed to look into the effect of particular interventions of questioning sequences on critical thinking, learning autonomy and emotional experience. Surveys or questionnaires can also be developed to examine the correlations between certain types of questions on those aspects of learning.

The taxonomy of teacher questions established as an alternative for the current study can be employed to describe the proportion or distribution and evaluate the effectiveness of the different types of questions used by teachers in classroom teaching. It can also be applied to the evaluation of textbook questions in China's EFL textbooks as Freeman (2014) did with global ESL textbooks.

Bibliography

[1] Adams, M., & March, S. (2015). Perezhivanie and classroom discourse: A cultural-historical perspective on "Discourse of design based science classroom activities." *Cultural Studies of Science Education, 10*(2), 317-327.

[2] Advisory Board [高等学校外语专业教学指导委员会英语组],（2000），The National Curriculum for English as a Specialty in Chinese Tertiary Institutions [高等学校英语专业英语教学大纲], 北京：外语教学与研究出版社。

[3] Advisory Board [教育部高等学校教学指导委员会],（2018），普通高等学校本科专业类教学质量国家标准, 北京：高等教育出版社。

[4] Allwright, D. (2001). Three major process of teacher development and the appropriate design criteria for developing and using them. In B. Johnston & S. Irujo (Eds.), *Research and Practice in Language Teacher Education: Voices from the Field. CARLA Working Paper 19* (pp. 115-133). Minneapolis.

[5] Allwright, D., & Bailey, K. (1991). Focus on the language classroom: An introduction to classroom research for language teachers. NY: Cambridge University Press.

[6] Allwright, R. L. (1984). The importance of interaction in classroom language learning. *Applied Linguistics, 5*(2), 156-171.

[7] Banbrook, L., & Skehan, P. (1990). Classrooms and display questions. In C. Brumfit & R. Mitchell (Eds.), *Research in the language classroom (ELT Documents 133)* (pp. 141-152). Modern English Publications in association with The British Council.

[8] Bao, J. S., Huang, J. R., Yi, L. F., & Gu, L. Y. [鲍建生、黄荣金、易凌峰、顾泠沅],（2003），变式教学研究,《数学教学》,（01）: 11-12。

[9] Barnes, D. (1969). Language in the secondary classroom. In D. Barnes, J. Britton, & H. Rosen (Eds.), *Language, the Learner, and the School* (pp. 11-77).

Harmondsworth: Penguin.

[10] Basturkmen, H. (2001). Descriptions of spoken language for higher level learners: The example of questioning. *ELT Journal, 55*(1), 4-13.

[11] Bellack, A. A., Kliebard, H. M., Hyman, R. T., & Smith, F. L. (1966). *The language of the classroom*. New York: Teachers College Press, Columbia University.

[12] Benesch, S. (1996). Needs analysis and curriculum development in EAP: An example of a critical approach. *TESOL Quarterly, 30*(4), 723-738.

[13] Benson, P. (2013). *Teaching and researching autonomy* (2nd ed.). New York: Routledge.

[14] Bloom, B. S., Englehart, M. D., Furst, E. J., Hill, W. H., & Drathwohl, D. R. (1956). *Taxonomy of educational objectives: The classification of educational goals*. London: Longmans.

[15] Brock, C. A. (1986). The effects of referential questions on ESL classroom discourse. *TESOL Quarterly, 20*(1), 47.

[16] Brown, H. D. (2001). Teaching by principles: An interactive approach to language pedagogy. London: Longman.

[17] Bruce, C. D., Shosh, J. M., & Riel, M. M. (2017). *The Palgrave international handbook of action research*. New York: Palgrave Macmillan.

[18] Burns, A. (1999). Collaborative action research for English language teachers. Cambridge: Cambridge University Press.

[19] Burns, A. (2010). *Doing action research in English language teaching: A guide for practitioners*. New York, NY: Routledge.

[20] Carlsen, W. S. (1991). Questioning in classrooms: A sociolinguistic perspective. *Review of Educational Research, 61*(2), 157-178.

[21] Cazden, C. B. (2001). *Classroom discourse: The language of teaching and learning*. Portsmouth, NH: Heinemann.

[22] Chang, F. (2009). *How teacher questioning behaviours assist and affect language teaching and learning in EFL classrooms in Taiwan*. The University of Warwick.

[23] Chaudron, C. (1988). *Second language classrooms: Research on teaching and learning*. Cambridge: Cambridge University Press.

[24] Chen, R. N. [陈蕊娜],(2013),近十年国外概要写作过程研究评介,《贵州民族

大学学报（哲学社会科学版）》, 137（1）: 112-116。

[25] Chen, Z. H. [陈则航], (2016), 英语阅读教学与研究 [Teaching and researching English reading], 北京: 外语教学与研究出版社。

[26] Chin, C. (2007). Teacher questioning in science classrooms: Approaches that stimulate productive thinking. *Journal of Research in Science Teaching, 44*(6), 815-843.

[27] Chuska, K. R. (1995). *Improving Classroom Questions: A Teacher's Guide to Increasing Student Motivation, Participation, and Higher-Level Thinking.* Phi Delta Kappa Educational Foundation.

[28] Coghlan, D., & Brydon-Miller, M. (Eds.). (2014). *The SAGE encyclopedia of action research.* Los Angeles: SAGE Publications, Ltd.

[29] Collins COBUILD. (1990). *Collins Cobuild English Grammar.* Harper Collins.

[30] Crabbe, D. (2003). The quality of learning opportunities. *TESOL Quarterly, 37*(1), 9-34.

[31] Crabbe, D. (2007). Learning opportunities: Adding learning value to tasks. *ELT Journal, 61*(2), 117-125.

[32] Creswell, J. W. (2012). *Educational research: Planning, conducting, and evaluating quantitative and qualitative research* (4th ed.). Boston: Pearson.

[33] Dahlgren, L. O. (1979). Children's conception of price as a function of questions asked. *Reports from the Institute of Education,* 81, University of Gothenburg, Sweden: University of Gothenburg.

[34] Dantonio, M., & Beisenherz, P. C. (2001). *Learning to question, questioning to learn: Developing effective teacher questioning practice.* Allyn & Bacon.

[35] Dewey, J. (1933). *How we think: A restatement of the relation of reflective thinking to the educative process* (2nd ed.). Chicago: Henry Regnery.

[36] Dillon, J. T. (1982). Cognitive correspondence between question statement and response. *American Educational Research Journal, 19*(4), 540-551.

[37] Elder, L., & Paul, R. (1998). The role of Socratic questioning in thinking, teaching, and learning. *Clearing House: A Journal of Educational Strategies Issues & Ideas, 71*(5), 297-301.

[38] Ellis, R. (2012). *Language teaching research and language pedagogy.* West Sussex: Wiley-Blackwell.

[39] Farrel, T. S. C. (2007). Action research in language teaching. *Reflective Language Teaching: From Research to Practice*, (2001), 94-106.

[40] Farrell, T. S. C., & Mom, V. (2015). Exploring teacher questions through reflective practice. *Reflective Practice*, *16*(6), 849-865.

[41] Fereday, J., & Muir-Cochrane, E. (2006). Demonstrating rigor using thematic analysis: A hybrid approach of inductive and deductive coding and theme development. *International Journal of Qualitative Methods*, *5*(1), 80-92.

[42] Freeman, D. (2014). Reading comprehension questions: The distribution of different types in global EFL textbooks. In N. Harwood (Ed.), *English language teaching textbooks: Content, consumption, production* (pp. 72-110). London: Palgrave Macmillan.

[43] Fulcher, G., & Davidson, F. (2007). *Language testing and assessment: An advanced resource book*. New York, NY: Routledge.

[44] Gall, M. D. (1970). The use of questions in teaching. *Review of Educational Research*, *40*(5), 707-721.

[45] Good, T. L., & Brophy, J. E. (2007). *Looking in classrooms* (10th ed.). Boston: Pearson Education, Inc. Boston: Pearson Education, Inc.

[46] He, A. P. [何安平]，（2003），基于语料库的英语教师话语分析，《现代外语》，（2）：55-64。

[47] Ho, D. G. E. (2005). Why do teachers ask the questions they ask? *RELC Journal*, *36*(3), 297-310.

[48] Hosoda, Y., & Aline, D. (2013). Two preferences in question-answer sequences in language classroom context. *Classroom Discourse*, *4*(February 2015), 63-88.

[49] Howard, A. (2010). Is there such a thing as a typical language lesson? *Classroom Discourse*, *1*(1), 82-100.

[50] Hu, Q. Q. [胡青球]，（2007a），优秀英语教师课堂话语特征分析，《山东外语教学》，（1）：54-58。

[51] Hu, Q. Q. [胡青球]，（2007b），中外教师英语课堂话语对比分析—个案研究《国外外语教学》，（1）：32-37。

[52] Huang, Y. S. [黄源深]，（1998），思辨缺席，《外语与外语教学》，（7）：2+18。

[53] Huang, Y. S. [黄源深]，（2010），英语专业课程必须彻底改革—再谈"思辨缺席"，《外语界》，（1）：11-16。

[54] Hulstijn, J. H., & Laufer, B. (2001). Some empirical evidence for the involvement load hypothesis in vocabulary acquisition. *Language Learning, 51*(3), 539-558.

[55] Hutchinson, T., & Waters, A. (1987). *English for specific purposes*. Cambridge: Cambridge University Press.

[56] Kayi-Aydar, H. (2013). Scaffolding language learning in an academic ESL classroom. *ELT Journal, 67*(3), 324-335.

[57] Kearsley, G. P. (1976). Questions and question-asking in verbal discourse: A cross-disciplinary review. *Journal of Psycholinguistic Research, 5*(4), 355-375.

[58] Keating, G. D. (2008). Task effectiveness and word learning in a second language: The involvement load hypothesis on trial. *Language Teaching Research, 12*(3), 365-386.

[59] Kemmis, S., McTaggart, R., & Nixon, R. (2014). *The action research planner: Doing critical participatory action research*. Singapore: Springer.

[60] Kirchhoff, P., & Klippel, F. (2014). On the role of teacher questions in EFL classrooms: analysing lesson videos. In M. Pawlak, B. Jakub, & A. Mystkowska-Wiertelak (Eds.), *Classroom-oriented Research: Achievements and Challenges*. Springer International Publishing Switerland.

[61] Ko, P. Y., & Marton, F. (2004). Variation and the secret of the virtuoso. In F. Marton & A. B. S. Tsui (Eds.), *Classroom discourse and the space of learning* (pp. 43-62). Mahwah, NJ: Lawrence Earlbaum Associates, Inc.

[62] Ko, S. (2014). The nature of multiple responses to teachers' questions. *Applied Linguistics, 35*(1), 48-62.

[63] Koole, T., & Elbers, E. (2014). Responsiveness in teacher explanations: A conversation analytical perspective on scaffolding. *Linguistics and Education, 26*(1), 57-69.

[64] Koshik, I. (2002a). Designedly incomplete utterances: A pedagogical practice for eliciting knowledge displays in error correction sequences. *Research on Language and Social Interaction, 35*(3), 207-309.

[65] Koshik, I. (2002b). A conversation analytic study of yes/no questions which convey reversed polarity assertions. *Journal of Pragmatics, 34*(12), 1851-1877.

[66] Koshik, I. (2003). Wh-questions used as challenges. *Discourse Studies, 5*(28), 51-77.

[67] Koshik, I. (2005). Alternative questions used in conversational repair. *Discourse Studies, 7*(2), 193-211.

[68] Lam, H. C. (2013). On generalization and variation theory. *Scandinavian Journal of Educational Research, 57*(4), 343-356.

[69] Lam, H. C. (2017). Using phenomenography to investigate the enacted object of learning in teaching activities: the case of teaching Chinese characters in Hong Kong preschools. *Scandinavian Journal of Educational Research, 61*(2), 169-186.

[70] Lam, H. C., & Tsui, B. M. A. (2013). Drawing on the variation theory to enhance students' learning of Chinese characters. *Instructional Science, 41*(5), 955-974.

[71] Laufer, B. (2013). Involvement load hypothesis. In P. J. Robinson (Ed.), *The Routledge encyclopedia of second language acquisition* (pp. 344-346). London: Routledge.

[72] Lee, H. A. (2015). Thinking levels of questions in Christian reading textbooks. *Journal of Research on Christian Education, 24*(2), 89-100.

[73] Lee, Y.A. (2006). Respecifying Display Questions: Interactional Resources for Language Teaching. *TESOL Quarterly, 40*(4), 691-713.

[74] Lefstein, A., Snell, J., & Israeli, M. (2015). From moves to sequences: Expanding the unit of analysis in the study of classroom discourse. *British Educational Research Journal, 41*(5), 866-885.

[75] Li, L., & Walsh, S. (2011). 'Seeing is believing': looking at EFL teachers' beliefs through classroom interaction. *Classroom Discourse, 2*(1), 39-57.

[76] Li, Q. S., & Sun, Z. Y. [李庆生、孙志勇],（2011），课堂提问：是获取信息还是挑战？—对大学英语课堂中教师提问功能的会话分析,《中国外语》, 8（1）：58-64。

[77] Lightbown, P. M., & Spada, N. (2013). *How languages are learned* (4th ed.). Oxford: Oxford University Press.

[78] Lin, H. H. [林慧华],（2012），乐学始于善诱—大学英语课堂有效提问叙事探究,《外语教学理论与实践》,（2）：23-29。

[79] Lo, M. L., Marton, F., Pang, M. F., & Pong, W. Y. (2004). Towards a pedagogy of learning. In F. Marton & A. B. S. Tsui (Eds.), *Classroom discourse and the space of learning* (pp. 189-226). Mahwah, NJ: Lawrence Earlbaum Associates, Inc.

[80] Long, M. H. (2005). *Second language needs analysis*. Cambridge: Cambridge University Press.

[81] Long, M. H., & Crookes, G. (1986). *Intervention points in second language classroom processes. RELC Regional Seminar, Singapore, 21-25 April 1986.*

[82] Long, M. H., & Sato, C. J. (1983). Classroom foreigner talk discourse: Forms and functions of teachers' questions. In H. W. Seliger & M. H. Long (Eds.), *Classroom-oriented research in second language acquisition* (pp. 268-285). Rowley, MA: Newbury House Publishers, Inc.

[83] Lu, Y. F., & Lv, D. L. [鲁艳芳、吕道利],（2011），英语精读课上的有效提问对比研究,《外语研究》,（4）: 75-80。

[84] Macalister, J. (2016). Applying language learning principles to coursebooks. In W. A. Renandya & H. P. Widodo (Eds.), *English Language Teaching Today* (pp. 41-51). Springer International Publishing.

[85] MacMillan, C. J. B., & Garrison, J. W. (1988). *A logical theory of teaching: erotetics and intentionality*. Dordrecht: Kluwer Academic Pubishers.

[86] Manzo, A. V., & Manzo, U. C. (1993). *Literacy disorder: Holistic diagnosis and remediation*. Fort Worth: Harcourt Brace Jovanovich College Publisher.

[87] Marton, F. (2015). *Necessary conditions of learning*. New York: Routledge.

[88] Marton, F., & Booth, S. (1997). *Learning and awareness*. Hillstdale: Lawrence Earlbaum.

[89] Marton, F., & Pang, M. F. (2006). On some necessary conditions of learning. *Journal of Learning Sciences, 15*(2), 193-220.

[90] Marton, F., & Tsui, A. B. S. (2004). *Classroom discourse and the space of learning*. Mahwah, NJ: Lawrence Earlbaum Associates, Inc.

[91] Marton, F., Runesson, U., & Tsui, A. B. S. (2004). The space of learning. In F. Marton & A. B. S. Tsui (Eds.), *Classroom discourse and the space of learning* (pp. 3-42). Mahwah, NJ: Lawrence Earlbaum Associates, Inc.

[92] Marzano, R. J., & Simms, J. A. (2014). *Questioning sequences in the classroom*. Bloomington, IN: Solution Tree Press.

[93] Maybee, C., Bruce, C. S., Lupton, M., & Rebmann, K. (2017). Designing rich information experiences to shape learning outcomes. *Studies in Higher Education, 42*(12), 2373-2388.

[94] McCormick, D. E. (1997). *Using questions to scaffold language learning in an ESL classroom- A sociocultural case study.pdf*. University of Pittsburgh.

[95] Mccormick, D. E., & Donato, R. (2000). Teacher questions as scaffolded assistance in an ESL classroom. In J. K. Hall & L. S. Verplaetse (Eds.), *Second and Foreign Language Learning Through Classroom Interaction* (pp. 183-202). Lawrence Erlbaum Associates, Inc.

[96] McNeil, L. (2012). Using talk to scaffold referential questions for English language learners. *Teaching and Teacher Education, 28*(3), 396-404.

[97] Mills, G. E. (2011). *Action research: A guide for the teacher researcher (with MyEducationLab)* (4th ed.). Upper Saddle River, NJ: Pearson/Allyn & Bacon.

[98] Nation, I. S. P., & Macalister, J. (2010). *Language curriculum design*. New York: Routledge.

[99] Nation, P. (1996). The four strands of a language Course. *TESOL in Context, 6*(2), 7-12.

[100] Nation, P. (2007). The Four Strands. *Innovation in Language Learning and Teaching, 1*(1), 2-13.

[101] Nowell, L. S., Norris, J. M., White, D. E., & Moules, N. J. (2017). Thematic analysis: Striving to meet the trustworthiness criteria. *International Journal of Qualitative Methods, 16*(1), 1-13.

[102] Nunan, D. (1987). Communicative language teaching: Making it work. *ELT Journal, 41*(April), 136-145.

[103] Nunan, D. (1990). The questions teachers ask. *JALT Journal, 12*(2), 187-202.

[104] Nunn, R. (1999). The purposes of language teachers' questions. *IRAL—International Review of Applied Linguistics in Language Teaching, 37*(1), 23-42.

[105] Oliveira, P. C., & Oliveira, C. G. (2013). Using conceptual questions to promote motivation and learning in physics lectures. *European Journal of Engineering Education, 38*(4), 417-424.

[106] Pang, M. F., & Ki, W. W. (2016). Revisiting the idea of "critical aspects." *Scandinavian Journal of Educational Research, 60*(3), 323-336.

[107] Park, Y. (2014). The roles of third-turn repeats in two l2 classroom interactional contexts. *Applied Linguistics, 35*(2).

[108] Paul, R., & Elder, L. (2008). Critical thinking: The art of Socratic questioning, Part III. *Journal of Developmental Education, 31*(3), 34-35.

[109] Peters, M., & Robinson, V. (1984). The origins and status of action research. *The Journal of Applied Behavioral Science, 20*(2), 113-124.

[110] Qin, X. B. [秦秀白],（2012），警惕课堂教学娱乐化,《当代外语研究》,（7）：1-2+79。

[111] Qin, X. B., et al. [秦秀白、蒋静仪、肖锦银、崔岭],(2010),加强评判性阅读,提高学生的思辨能力——"新世纪大学英语系列教材"《综合教程》第五、六册简介,《外语界》,（2）：83-86。

[112] Qu, S. M. [屈社明],（2006），大学英语课堂提问主体转换的实验研究,《外语教学》,（5）：66-68。

[113] Qu, W. G. [曲卫国],（2015），缺乏的到底是思辨能力还是系统知识？——也谈外语专业学生的思辨问题,《中国外语》,12（1）：60-66。

[114] Qu, W. G. [曲卫国],（2016），课文在英语综合课上作用的探讨,《外语电化教学》,（3）：3-8。

[115] Quirk, R., Greenbaum, S., Leech, G., & Svartvik, J. (1972). *A Grammar of contemporary English*. Longman.

[116] Reason, P., & Bradbury, H. (2007). Introduction. In P. Reason & H. Bradbury (Eds.), *The SAGE handbook of action research: participative inquiry and practice* (2nd ed.). Los Angeles: SAGE Publications.

[117] Redfield, D. L., & Rousseau, E. W. (1981). A meta-analysis of experimental research on teacher questioning behavior. *Review of Educational Research, 51*(2), 237-245.

[118] Richards, J. C., & Lockhart, C. (1996). *Reflective teaching in second language classrooms*. Cambridge: Cambridge University Press.

[119] Sacks, H., Schegloff, E., & Jefferson, G. (1974). A simplest systematics for the organization of turn-taking for conversation. *Language, 50*(4), 693-735.

[120] Sadker, D., Sadker, M., & Zittleman, K. R. (2010). Questioning Skills. In J. M. Cooper (Ed.), *Classroom teaching skills* (9th ed., pp. 107-152). Wadsworth: Cengage Learning.

[121] Sagor, R. (2005). *The action research guidebook: A four-step process for educators and school teams*. Thousand Oaks, CA: Corwin Press.

[122] Schegloff, E. A., Koshik, I., Jacoby, S., & Olsher, D. (2002). Conversation analysis and applied linguistics. *Annual Review of Applied Linguistics, 22*, 3-31.

[123] Schmidt, J. A., Lyutykh, E., & Shumow, L. (2012). A study of teachers' speech and students' perezhivanie in high school physics classrooms. In *Annual Meetings of the American Educational Research Association*. Vancouver, BC.

[124] Schmuch, R. A. (2006). *Practical action research for change*. California: Corwin Press.

[125] Schmuch, R. A. (2008). Lewinian lesson for action researchers: Traveling the second path. *Polskie Forum Psychologiczne, 13*(2), 141-156.

[126] Schwab, G. (2011). From dialogue to multilogue a different view on participation in the English foreign language classroom. *Classroom Discourse, 2*(1), 3-19.

[127] Seedhouse, P. (2005). Conversation analysis and language learning. *Language Teaching, 38*(4), 165-187.

[128] Seedhouse, P., & Walsh, S. (2010). Learning a second language through classroom interaction. In *Conceptualising 'learning' in applied linguistics* (pp. 127-146). New York, NY: Palgrave Macmillan.

[129] Sert, O., & Walsh, S. (2013). The interactional management of claims of insufficient knowledge in English language classrooms. *Language and Education, 27*(6), 542-565.

[130] Shu, D. F. [束定芳],（2013），英语专业综合课目标与教师素质——第三届"外教社杯"全国高校外语教学大赛授课比赛述评,《外语界》,（2）：43-49。

[131] Shu, D. F. [束定芳],（2014），外语课堂教学中的问题与若干研究课题,《外语教学与研究》,46（3）：446-455。

[132] Sinclair, J., & Coulthard, M. (1975). *Towards an analysis of discourse: the English used by teachers and pupils*. London: Oxford University Press.

[133] Thompson, G. (1997). Training teachers to ask questions. *ELT Journal, 51*(April), 99-105.

[134] Todd, R. W., Srimavin, W., & Boonyuen, T. (2007). Problems Analysing Discourse and Teacher Questions from a Researcher's Perspective. *REFLections*, (10), 1-9.

[135] Truscott, D. M. (1994). Reviewed work: Literacy disorders: Holistic diagnosis

and remediation by Anthony V. Manzo, Ula C. Manzo. *Journal of Reading*, *37*(8), 707-709.

[136] Tsui Bik-may, A. (1992). A functional description of questions. In M. Coulthard (Ed.), *Advances in spoken discourse analysis* (pp. 102-110). London: Routledge.

[137] Tsui, A. B. S. (2004). The semantic enrichment of the space of learning. In F. Marton & A. B. S. Tsui (Eds.), *Classroom discourse and the space of learning* (pp. 139-164). Mahwah, NJ: Lawrence Earlbaum Associates, Inc.

[138] Tsui, A. B. S., Marton, F., Mok, I. A. C., & Ng, D. F. P. (2004). Questions and the space of learning. In F. Marton & A. B. S. Tsui (Eds.), *Classroom discourse and the space of learning* (pp. 113-138). Mahwah, NJ: Lawrence Earlbaum Associates, Inc.

[139] Turnbull, N. (2004). What is the status of questioning in John Dewey's philosophy? In *Australasian Political Studies Association Conference*. University of Queensland.

[140] Van Lier, L. (1988). *The classroom and the language learner*. London: Longman.

[141] Verplaetse, L. S. (2014). Using big questions to apprentice students into language-rich classroom practices. *TESOL Quarterly*, *48*(3), 632-641.

[142] Wallace, C. (2003). *Critical reading in language education*. New York: Palgrave Macmillan.

[143] Walsh, J., & Sattes, B. (2005). *Quality questioning: Research-based practice to engage every learner*. London: A Joint Publication.

[144] Walsh, S. (2003). Developing Interactional Awareness in the Second Language Classroom Through Teacher Self-evaluation. *Language Awareness*, *12*(2), 124-142.

[145] Walsh, S. (2006). *Investigating classroom discourse*. London: Routledge.

[146] Walsh, S. (2011). *Exploring classroom discourse*. London: Routledge.

[147] Wang, B. S. [王保顺]，（2012），汝果欲工诗，功夫在诗外—浅谈英语学习七大误区,《英语世界》,（1）：4-5。

[148] Wang, J., & Zhang, J. [王健、张静]，（2008），大学英语课堂沉默现象的解析与对策,《中国大学教学》，第 1 期。

[149] Wang, Q. [王蔷]，（2002），英语教师行动研究：从理论到实践，北京：外语

教学与研究出版社。

[150] Wang, Q., & Zhang, H. [王蔷、张虹],（2012），英语教师行动研究（修订版），北京：外语教学与研究出版社。

[151] Wang, X. Y. [王晓妍],（2013），大学英语口语课堂中的教师话语研究,《外语学刊》,（3）：119-122。

[152] Waring, H. Z. (2009). Moving out of IRF (initiation-response-feedback), A single case analysis. *Language Learning, 59*(4), 796-824.

[153] Waring, H. Z. (2012a). Yes-no questions that convey a critical stance in the language classroom. *Language and Education, 26*(5), 451-469.

[154] Waring, H. Z. (2012b). "Any questions?": Investigating the nature of understanding-checks in the language classroom. *TESOL Quarterly, 46*(4), 722-752.

[155] Weir, C. J. (2005). *Language testing and validation: An evidence-based approach*. New York: Palgrave Macmillan.

[156] Wells, G. (1993). Reevaluating the IRF sequence: A proposal for the articulation of theories of activity and discourse for the analysis of teaching and learning in the classroom. *Linguistics and Education, 5*(1), 1-37.

[157] Wen, Q. F., & Liu, R. Q. [文秋芳、刘润清],（2006），从英语议论文分析大学生抽象思维特点,《外国语》, 162（2）：49-58。

[158] Wen, Q. F. [文秋芳],（2003），微变化研究法与二语习得研究,《现代外语》,（03）：312-317+311。

[159] Wen, Q. F. [文秋芳],（2011）,《英语教学中的行动研究方法》评介,中国外语教育（季刊）, 4（3）：59-63。

[160] West, R. (1994). Needs analysis in language teaching. *Language Teaching, 27*(1), 1-19.

[161] Wood, D., Bruner, J. S., & Ross, G. (1976). The role of tutoring in problem solving. *Journal of Child Psychology and Psychiatry, 17*(2), 89-100.

[162] Wu, K. (1993). Classroom interaction and teacher questions revisited. *RELC Journal, 24*(2), 49-68.

[163] Xia, Ganlin. [夏甘霖],（2008）普通工科高校新生英语阅读策略使用状况因素分析,《外语教学理论与实践》,（1）：64-69。

[164] Xie, X. (2009). Why are students quiet? Looking at the Chinese context and

beyond. *ELT Journal, 64*(1), 10-20.

[165] Xie, X. (2011). Turn allocation patterns and learning opportunities. *ELT Journal, 65*(3), 240-250.

[166] Xu., F. [许峰]，（2003），大学英语课堂提问的调查与分析，《国外外语教学》，（3）：30-34。

[167] Yang, L. F. [杨莉芳]，（2015），阅读课堂提问的认知特征与思辨能力培养，《中国外语》，12（2）：68-79。

[168] Yang, X. Y. [杨雪燕]，（2007），外语教师课堂提问策略的话语分析，《中国外语》，（1）：50-56。

[169] Yang, X. Y., & Xie, M. [杨雪燕、解敏]，（2012），外语教师课堂提问的互动性分析，《当代外语研究》，（3）：142-148, 162。

[170] Zeng, B. H. [曾炳辉]，（1989），《英语概要写作与智力训练》，外语与外语教学，41（1）：31-34。

[171] Zhang, W. J. [张文娟]，（2017），"产出导向法"应用于大学英语教学之行动研究，北京外国语大学。

[172] Zhao, N. S. [赵妮莎]，（2012），基于"支架"视角的英语专业课堂中教师提问的探讨，《外国语文》，28（5）：133-139。

[173] Zhao, X. H. [赵晓红]，（1998），大学英语阅读课教师话语的调查与分析，《外语界》，（2）：18-23。

[174] Zhou, D. D. [周丹丹]，（2012），应用语言学中的微变化研究方法，北京：外语教学与研究出版社。

[175] Zhou, X., & Zhou, Y. [周星、周韵]，（2002），大学英语课堂教师话语的调查与分析，《外语教学与研究》，（1）：59-68。

Appendices

Appendix A: Questionnaire on students' attitude towards teacher questioning and the intensive reading course
学生对教师提问和精读教学的态度问卷

A. Demographic information

1. Gender: □ Male; □ Female　　性别：□男；□女
2. My student ID is _____ (Optional) 我的学号是：_____ (可不填)
3. Self-perceived proficiency level: □ lower; □ middle; □ higher 英语水平的自我感觉：□较低；□中等；□较高

B. Factors related to learners' attitudes

□1 (strongly disagree), □2 (disagree), □3 (agree) and □4 (strongly agree)
□1 非常不符合，□2 不符合，□3 符合 and □4 非常符合

4. I like to major in English. 我喜欢英语专业。
5. The intensive reading course is important. 精读这门课很重要。
6. Speaking English fluently is a symbol of qualified English majors. 口语流利是合格英语专业毕业生的标志。
7. I think that enthusiastic participation will contribute to my own English language learning. 我认为积极参与课堂互动有助于学好英语。
8. I am more willing to respond in class if I prepare in advance. 如果事先有所准备，我比较愿意回答老师的问题。
9. I am more willing to speak in class if I am not the only person

answering a question. 如果不是单独回答老师的问题，我比较愿意在课堂上发言。

10. I feel more comfortable answering the teacher's questions when I do not have to do it in front of the whole class. 如果不用当着全班同学发言，我会比较自在地回答老师的问题。

11. I would not want to answer a question because I may not be correct. 我不想回答老师的问题，是因为我的答案可能是错的。

12. I prefer being called upon by the teacher rather than volunteering an answer. 我喜欢老师点名回答问题，而不是学生自愿回答。

13. I feel less comfortable about answering teacher questions in front of my classmates whom I know very well. 在熟悉的同学面前回答老师的问题，我觉得比较不自在。

14. When the teacher asks a question in class, I prefer not to respond to it even if I know the answer. 当老师在课堂上提问时，即使我知道答案，我也倾向于不回答。

15. Usually, I do not respond to questioning during whole-class discussion unless I am called upon. 通常我不在全班同学面前主动回答老师的问题，除非老师点名要求我回答。

16. If I often volunteer to answer questions, my classmates may think I am showing off. 如果我经常主动回答老师的问题，我的同学会认为我在出风头。

17. If I answer questions in English, my classmates may think I am showing off. 如果我用英文回答老师的问题，我的同学会认为我在出风头。

C. Factors related to dynamic classroom interaction

18. Our teacher often encourages us to speak in class. 我们的老师经常鼓励我们在课堂上发言。

19. My classmates in this class do not respect each other's views. 我们班的同学不尊重他人的观点。

20. I feel *uncomfortable* if I do not respond to the teacher's questions in class. 如果我在课堂上不回答老师的问题，我会觉得不自在。

21. Our English teacher is supportive *when we are answering his/her*

questions. 当我们回答老师的问题时，老师会提供支持。

22. My classmates are supportive *when their peers are answering the teacher's questions.* 同学们在回答老师的问题时会互相支持。

23. Our English teacher has a good sense of humor. 我们的老师很幽默。

24. When responding to the teacher's questions, my classmates depend on a few students to do it. 我们班仅靠少数几位同学回答老师的问题。

25. Our teacher does not interrupt students when they are speaking. 同学们发言时，老师不会打断他们。

26. My classmates discourage others from appearing too confident. 同学们会打消那些太过自信的同学的积极性。

27. My classmates do not pay attention when others are speaking. 同学们不会认真听别的同学发言。

28. Our teacher respects what we say. 老师尊重我们的发言。

29. This class has helped to strengthen my friendships with others.

30. 在这门课上，我增进了和同学之间的友谊。

31. Our teacher praises students very often. 老师经常表扬学生。

32. Generally speaking, I feel confident to speak in this class. 一般来说，在这门课上发言，我觉得自在。

D. Attitudes towards language use

33. I think that responding to questions in English can help me learn English better. 我认为用英语回答老师的提问，有助于学好英语。

34. I do not want to answer in English because I think my English is not good enough. 我不想用英语回答老师的提问，因为我觉得我的英语不够好。

35. I feel more comfortable when answering teacher's questions in Chinese. 当我用汉语回答老师的提问时，我觉得比较自在。

36. When the teacher asks questions in English, I would prefer answering in English. 当老师用英语问我问题时，我倾向用英语回答。

37. When the teacher asks questions in Chinese, I would prefer answering in Chinese. 当老师用汉语提问时，我倾向用汉语回答。

38. When I feel that the teacher's question is difficult, I would prefer

answering in Chinese. 当我觉得老师的问题很难时，我倾向用汉语回答。

E. Puzzlement and suggestions

39. What makes me most puzzled about the intensive reading course? 关于精读课的教学，最让我觉得困惑的是 _____.

40. What are my suggestions for next semester's teaching of the course? 我对下学期精读课的教学建议 _____.

[Based on Chang (2009)]

Appendix B: Questionnaire on reading strategies

姓名 /Name：_____   学号 /Stu ID：_____

请认真回想你在过去一个学期阅读精读课文的过程中使用的阅读策略，然后根据以下叙述选择：1 非常不符合，2 不符合，3 不确定，4 符合，和 5 非常符合。

Please recall the reading strategies you used to read the intensive reading text in the past semester. Mark each of the following statements by choosing: 1 strongly disagree, 2 disagree, 3) half agree and half disagree, 4 agree, and 5 strongly agree.

B1	迅速浏览全文，确定文章主题和阅读目的。 Scan the text quickly to identify the theme of the text and the purpose of reading.
B2	迅速浏览寻找与自己的阅读目的相关的信息。 Scan the text quickly to find information related to the purpose of reading.
B3	根据快速浏览所获信息，预测文章内容和领域。 Predict the content and domain of the text according to what has been scanned.
B4	提出关于文章内容的问题，预期在文中寻找答案。 Raise questions concerning the content of the text and expect to find answers to them from within the text.
B5	根据快速浏览所获信息，推测作者写作前对读者知识领域或观点的假设。 Scan the text and make inferences about the author's hypotheses about the reader's knowledge domains or ideas.
B6	根据阅读目的和所获信息初步判断文章组织方式。 Make preliminary judgments about the textual organization according to the purpose of reading and information acquired.
B7	辨别理解标志语篇结构关系的词和短语（如标志事件顺序的、篇章组织结构的和作者观点的）。 Identify and understand words and phrases indicating textual structural relationships (such as those indicating the chronological order, the textual organization or the writer's opinion).

Continued

B8	边读边根据已经掌握的内容预测接下来将要出现的内容。 Predict what is to occur in the coming part on the basis of what has been grasped while reading.
B9	边读边根据已经掌握的内容进行合理的推断，推理出作者暗示的内容或结论。 Infer the author's implied ideas or conclusions on the basis of what has been grasped while reading.
B10	划分文章组织结构，分析各部分之间的关系（采用编写大纲，画结构图等方式）。
B11	分析较为复杂的段落内部结构和句子之间的组织关系。 Analyze the internal structure of complex paragraphs and the relationship between sentences.
B12	概括文章的主要内容。 Summarize the main idea of the text.
B13	总结概括各个部分或段落的主要内容。 Generalize and summarize the main idea of each part or paragraph.
B14	边读边对已经读过的内容进行概括总结。 Summarize what has been read while reading.
B15	区分直接叙述的主题句和暗示的主题。 Distinguish between explicit and implicit thesis statements.
B16	区分事实和观点，概括性的叙述和支持性细节表述。 Distinguish facts from opinion, and general statements from supporting details.
B17	区分主要信息和次要信息，与主题相关和不相关的信息。 Distinguish between the major and minor information as well as the relevant and irrelevant information.
B18	分析复杂句、难句的句法结构，使之简化而易懂。 Analyze the structure of complex and difficult sentences to make them easy to understand.
B19	注意识别和解释句子内部和句子之间的衔接手段，从而理解句子的真正意义。 Identify and explain the cohesive devices within and between sentences to understand the true meaning of sentences.
B20	根据句子意义推断句子的语篇功能（如定义、描写等）。 Infer the textual functions (for example, defining, describing, etc) of certain sentences based on their meaning.
B21	遇到生词时，根据上下文的线索推断词义。 Infer the meaning of new words according to the clues in the text.

Continued

B22	遇到生词时，根据词汇的语法功能推断词义（主谓宾等）。 Infer the meaning of new words according their grammatical functions (subject, predicate or object, etc.)
B23	遇到生词时，根据词汇的内部结构，即构词法，来推断词义。 Infer the meaning of words according the internal structure of them, i.e., word-formation.
B24	综合推断作者的写作目的、语气、观点、态度和结论。 Generalize and infer the author's purpose, tone, opinion, attitude and conclusion.
B25	综合归纳文章的主要内容。 Integrate and generalize the main idea of the text.
B26	对文章内容、观点及写作手法和特色等进行评述。 Evaluate the content and ideas conveyed by the text as well as the writing techniques and features.
B27	评估自己对文章内容的理解和记忆。 Evaluate what you have understood and memorized about the text.
B28	归纳总结需要掌握和记忆的内容。 Summarize and generalize what needs to be grasped and memorized.
B29	归纳挑选需要掌握的词汇和短语。 Summarize and select words and phrases worth mastering.

[Based on Xia Ganlin (2008)]

Appendix C: Summary writing rating scale

[Based on Wen Qiufang & Liu Run Qing (2006) and the current TEM-4 rating scale for summary writing]

等级	概括准确性	论点明确性	说理透彻性	篇章连贯性	词汇	语法	句型
5	用自己的语言，准确表述材料主题，准确表述材料中心内容，全面抓住材料要点	讨论部分中心论点清楚、恰当，分论点清楚、恰当	讨论部分各分论点论述逻辑性强，论据恰当，具体	缩写和讨论部分顺序安排合理，过渡自然；缩写和讨论部分内部结构完整；讨论部分各分论点之间的关系符合逻辑，且清楚、明确	词汇运用准确，词汇丰富，词汇运用自然	语法正确	句式丰富多样，句式自然
4	用自己的语言，准确表述材料主题，较准确表述材料中心内容，材料要点有少量遗漏	讨论部分中心论点清楚、恰当，大部分分论点清楚、恰当，个别分论点不清楚	讨论部分各分论点论述逻辑性强，但不具体：分论点较恰当，逻辑性较强，部分分论点论据不具体，部分分论点论据无论据	缩写和讨论部分顺序安排合理，有过渡；缩写和讨论部分内部结构基本完整；讨论部分各分论点之间的关系符合逻辑且清楚、明确，但不十分明确	词汇运用较准确，有少量错误，但不影响理解，词汇量较丰富，词汇运用较自然	少量语法错误，但不影响理解	句式较丰富多样，句式较自然
3	用自己的语言，基本准确表述材料主题，表述材料中心内容有一些偏差，材料要点部分遗漏	讨论部分中心论点主题清楚、恰当，有些分论点比较清楚，分论点有些不清楚	讨论部分各分论点论述清楚，论点结构有部分遗漏，太少或论据不具体或不恰当	缩写和讨论部分顺序安排基本合理，没有过渡；缩写内部结构有部分遗漏；讨论部分各分论点之间的关系清楚、明确，但逻辑性不够	词汇运用有错误，且对理解有一定影响，词汇量较有限，词汇运用不够自然	有一些语法错误，对理解有一定影响	句式不够丰富多样，仅能使用少数种类句式，或者句子错误较多，句式不够自然

325

Continued

等级	概括准确性	论点明确性	说理透彻性	篇章连贯性	词汇	语法	句型
2	材料主题和中心内容与原文相关，但分论点不太清楚，有较大偏差。	讨论部分中心论点比较清楚，大部分分论点清楚，但分论点不太清楚或与中心论点不相关。	讨论部分分论点讨论述比较清楚，无论据或论据不恰当，具体或不恰当。	缩写和讨论部分顺序安排合理，没有过渡，部分内部结构有较多遗漏，部分论据各分论点之间的关系不清楚，需要读者花力气才能读懂。	词汇运用有较多错误，较严重影响理解，词汇量极其有限，词汇运用很不自然。	有较多语法错误，对理解产生较严重影响。	句式不够丰富，仅能使用少数种类句式，或者句子错误较多。
1	材料主题和中心内容与原文相关，但有较大偏差；不能总结要点，仅是罗列部分细节。	讨论部分中心论点不清楚，分论点也不太清楚。	讨论部分说理大不清楚，无论据或论据不恰当。	缩写和讨论部分顺序安排不合理，没有过渡，部分内部结构有较多遗漏，论据部分各分论点之间的关系不清楚或无必然联系。	词汇严重贫乏，基本不能运用词汇表达意义。	语法知识贫乏。	基本不能写出完整的句子。

Appendix D: Peer classroom observation sheet

同行听课记录 /Peer Classroom Observation Sheet

课程 /Course:	班级 /Class:	教师 /Teacher:
时间 /Time:	地点 /Venue:	观察人 /Observer:
观察点 /Items	观 察 记 录 [Field Notes]	
提问内容 [Content focus]	[教师提问的内容是否与教学目标相关？] [Are the teacher questions related to the instructional objectives?]	
提问层次 [Cognitive level]	[教师提问的层次是否学习者的认知能力相符？] [Are the cognitive levels of teacher questions in correspondence with the students' cognitive abilities?]	
叫答方式 [Turn allocation]	[教师提问后是否给学生足够的准备时间？话轮分配是否合理？] [Are the students given sufficient preparation time? Are the turns appropriately allocated?]	
教师反馈 [Teacher feedback]	[教师在学生回答问题后是否给予有效的反馈？] [Does the teacher give effective feedback to the students' responses?]	
课堂气氛 [Classroom atmosphere]	[学生是否积极参与课堂互动？课堂气氛是否活跃？] [Do the students take active part in classroom interaction? Is the classroom atmosphere active?]	
改进意见 [Suggestions]	[您对该教师的课堂提问行为有何改进意见？] [Do you have any suggestions on how the teacher can improve his/her questions?]	

Appendix E: Questions for the after-class group discussions

Welcome to this group discussion. We are to discuss for about half and one hour about 1) your campus life, 2) your English major studies, and 3) our intensive reading course.

- Let's come to the first topic. What do you think of your campus life?

- Now let's come to the second topic. What do you think of your English major studies, or more specifically being an English major at this university?

- Lastly, let's come to our intensive reading course. What do you think of the intensive reading course? Please give your comments on its status in the English major program, the teachers' teaching the course, and the way you deal with it.

Appendix F: Questions for the focus group interviews

(These questions serve as an outline for the interview. They will be revised and additional questions will be asked spontaneously during the interview.)

Now that we are approaching the end of the semester and our intensive reading course is finished, I would like to know your evaluation of the course, especially of classroom questions or classroom Q-A interaction.

1. First stage of AR

After teaching the first two units of the textbook, we got adapted to each other and then I taught the next two units—Unit 3 and Unit 4—mainly by asking varieties of questions.

1.1 Do you think that those questions helped you understand the texts? Why or why not?

1.2 Do you think that participating in classroom Q-A interaction helped improve your oral English? Why or why not?

1.3 Do you think those questions were helpful in learning language knowledge? Why or why not?

1.4 Do you think participating in classroom Q-A interaction helped improve your critical thinking?

2. Second stage of AR

In teaching Unit 5 and Unit 6, I handed out to you the questions I had designed for the instruction of each unit and asked you to prepare answering those questions while previewing the texts.

2.1 Do you think that by doing so you had a better understanding the texts? Why or why not?

2.2 Do you think that by doing so you were better prepared for participating in classroom Q-A interaction? Why or why not?

2.3 Do you think that doing so was more helpful in learning language knowledge? Why or why not?

2.4 Do you think that doing so was more helpful in training your critical thinking? Why or why not?

3. Third stage of AR

In teaching the last two units—Unit 7 and Unit 10, I did not hand out my questions to you. Instead, I had you raise your own questions while previewing the texts. After collecting your questions, I selected those that were beyond mine and incorporated them into my courseware and then displayed them and the sources to the whole class.

3.1 Do you think that by doing so you had a better understanding of the texts? Why or why not?

3.2 Do you think that by doing so you were better prepared to participate in classroom Q-A interaction? Why or why not?

3.3 Do you think that doing so was more helpful in learning language knowledge?

3.4 Do you think that doing so was more helpful in training your critical thinking?

4. Overall evaluation

What's your general impression of this semester's intensive reading course and do you have any suggestions for further improvement?

Appendix G: Transcription system

T:	Teacher
S1:	Student (numbered in order of their student ID)
Sx	Student (not identified)
Ss	Students (more than one student speaking)
Yes/yes/yes	Simultaneous utterances by more than one speaker
.	Falling tone in normal speech
?	Rising tone in normal speech
[What do you mean?] [I want to]	Overlap between teacher and student, or several students
=	One turn follows another without clearly identifiable pause
…	Ellipsis of unrelated talk
(.)	Pause less than half a second
(0.8)	Pause longer than a half second
@hehe@; @haha@	Laughter
((Students laugh 12))	Notes on what happens, with the number indicating the duration of time
↑	An obviously rising tone
↓	An obviously falling tone
-	Halted speech
<>	Speaker speaks lower than normal
><	Speaker speaks faster than normal
I <u>like</u> it very much	Underlined words (speaker's emphasis)

[Based on Walsh (2011)]

Acknowledgments

I am so much indebted to the people who have offered me generous assistance and constant support in accomplishing my dissertation that I am afraid I cannot find the proper English words to acknowledge them.

First and foremost, I would like to express my heartfelt gratitude to my supervisor, Prof. Zhang Xuemei, for her encouragements, inspirations, insistence, and patience in navigating me throughout my doctoral studies. It was Prof. Zhang who ushered me into the colorful and practical field of second language acquisition. Her lectures and seminars helped me narrow down my focus on the role of teacher questions in classroom instruction. Without her meticulous supervision and constant guidance, the action research could not have progressed smoothly; neither could the dissertation have been accomplished successfully. The journals that I have written after the lectures, seminars, and discussions are filled with Prof. Zhang's comments and suggestions on how to do applied linguistic research with validity, reliability, consistency and rigidity, which is the biggest fortune that I have ever made in my SISU years.

I am also extremely grateful to a host of other SISU professors, Prof. Dai Weidong, Prof. Zou Shen, Prof. Zheng Xinmin, Prof. Wang Xuemei, and Prof. Zhang Jidong, for their wonderful lectures and sparkling ideas on research in their specialized fields as well as applied linguistics in general; Prof. Wang Miao, Prof. Cai Junmei, Prof. Zhang Xinbin, and Prof. Yang Yingying, for their generosity in

Acknowledgments

helping me out with a research project on teacher talk which rendered rich implications for the current study; and Prof. Peng Mei, Prof. Qin Yue, for their advice on weighing up the data and writing up the thesis.

I would also like to extend my acknowledgments to my SISU friends and fellow PhD students, Dr. Ke Yuguo, Dr. Chen Zhongyi, Dr. Wang Baolong, Dr. Jing Feilong, Dr. Xu Bin, Dr. Zhang Junmin, Miss Yu Hanjing, Mr Du Lei, Mr Li Feng, Mr He Zhongbao, and Mr Song Zhenjun for their kindness in listening to my groans and moans, cheering me up with jokes and comforts, and sharing with me their ideas when I got stuck with the study; and Dr. Chen Fu, Miss Liu Ping, Miss Li Siyuan, Mr Zheng Hongbo, Miss Lu Yanfang, and Miss Yang Shun'e, for offering me valuable feedback and critical remarks concerning my dissertation.

I am very appreciative of my GMU super-ordinates, Vice President Prof. Liu Min for his keen concern about my studies, Prof. Jiao Peihui for her never-ending encouragement and support, and Prof. Zhong Meizhu for her generous assistance. I also owe a lot to my GMU colleagues, Miss Zhu Xiufang, Miss Luo Jiangxia, Miss Zhou Rong, Mr Huang Xiaojun, Miss Xia Haijuan, Miss Li Ping, Miss He Chen, Miss Wang Shuxian, Miss Ding Yihua, and Miss Yang Jing, for their unfailing collaboration. I am also much obliged to my committed student participants, without whose participation and cooperation the action research wouldn't have taken place.

Last but not least, I am more than indebted to my beloved family. My parents, who had received little formal education and spent their lifetime farming in the remote countryside, have struggled every means to afford my schooling and support my post-graduate studies. My wife and my daughter have been extremely understanding and supportive when I couldn't be with them in the past years.